RECOLLECTIONS OF A HAPPY LIFE • VO NORTH

Publisher's Note

The book descriptions we ask book-sellers to display prominently warn that this is an historic book with numerous typos or missing text; it is not indexed or illustrated.

The book was created using optical character recognition software. The software is 99 percent accurate if the book is in good condition. However, we do understand that even one percent can be an annoying number of typos! And sometimes all or part of a page may be missing from our copy of the book. Or the paper may be so discolored from age that it is difficult to read. We apologize and gratefully acknowledge Google's assistance.

After we re-typeset and design a book, the page numbers change so the old index and table of contents no longer work. Therefore, we often re-move them; otherwise, please ignore them.

Our books sell so few copies that you would have to pay hundreds of dollars to cover the cost of our proof reading and fixing the typos, missing text and index. Instead we let most customers download a free copy of the original ty-po-free scanned book. Simply enter the barcode number from the back cover of the paperback in the Free Book form at www.RareBooksClub.com. You may also qualify for a free trial membership in our book club to download up to four books for free. Simply enter the barcode number from the back cover onto the membership form on our home page. The book club entitles you to select from more than a million books at no additional charge. Simply enter the title or subject onto the search form to find the books.

If you have any questions, could you please be so kind as to consult our Fre-quently Asked Questions page at www. RareBooksClub.com/faqs.cfm? You are also welcome to contact us there.

General Books LLC™, Memphis, USA, 2012. ISBN: 9781154125870.

❧ ❧ ❧ ❧ ❧ ❧ ❧

RECOLLECTIONS OF A HAPPY l Vol. n OF
A HAPPY LIFE
BEING THE AUTOBIOGRAPHY OF
MARIANNE NOETH
EDITED BY HER SISTER
MRS. JOHN ALDINGTON SYMONDS
IN TWO VOLUMES
VOL. II
SOCIETY
JLontion
MACMILLAN AND CO.
AND NEW YORK
1892

UNIVERSITY LIBRARY CONTENTS

CHAPTER X HILL PLACES IN INDIA

Masuri is a long scattered place, cov-ering an uneven ridge for about three miles, looking over the wide Dun valley on one side, and into the rolling sea of mountains on the other. The ever-changing lights and shadows over the great mountains were a continual won-der to me to watch. I wondered others did not care to watch them too. The nearer mountains were topped with pines, terraced with burnt-up corn and grass crops. All the rest was bare, ex-cept some narrow strips of green fol-lowing the watercourses. Over all was

26,000 e peak idea of seeing them over so many ranges of moun-tains, themselves so very high and close, they would certainly have hidden any European line of snow-peaks (such as that which one sees from Berne for instance). After my arrival we had tremendous storms of rain and hail; the air became cold again, and every one had to go to the dining-room in doolies, or to be halfdrowned in crossing the garden. Colonel and Mrs. W. came to see me, and insisted on my leaving the hotel and going to stay with them; and I spent a most delightful fortnight in their pretty house. The hotel, in its way, amused me. There were twenty ladies and two men, owing to the war; but how those men did flap their wings and crow, and how the young VOL. II B ladies cackled! The whole day long there were parties of ladies sitting under the verandah and never going beyond it,— much the same life they led on board ship.

Mrs. W. took the greatest pains to show me all the most beautiful points in the country. We went everywhere in dandies, like the rest of the Masuri world, with our carrying men dressed in a sort of livery of black native flan-nel, knickerbockers, and jackets edged with scarlet, scarlet turbans and sashes. She had five and I had five. Two men at a time balanced the small canoe in which we sat, or rather reclined. They liked to go at a fast trot through the streets, and it was rather nervous work when the bazaars were crowded, for no one would slacken pace or give way to others. They were wonderfully strong, those Masuri men, with nice frank faces; and after carrying us all day up and down the most breakneck precipices, would trot along the Mall laughing and singing, tossing us over from shoulder to shoulder, without changing step, as if we were feathers. One day we went up the hills and saw a tribe of black-faced monkeys, with long tails and gray whiskers, jumping from tree to tree and shaking the very trunks with their weight and sudden springs. Those hills were full of wild nooks, great overhanging rocks, and scraggy twisted oaks, with the gay leaves of the Virginian creeper looped about them. They must have been quite dazzling in autumn. There were also masses of white dogrose, with a much larger flower than ours, and two primulas and an androsace were creeping over all the dry banks. The hills were all very steep at Masuri, and our heels often went higher than our heads when the dandy-men forgot to turn us and carry us backwards up the steep hills. The climate was delicious between the showers, which were as frequent as in England, and I doubt whether England itself could have shown finer roses than grew in the gardens about that place. At last I turned away. Both my friend and myself spent two days at Dehra, with Dr. and Mrs. J. Once the old gentleman was showing me some of his flower-paintings in the garden behind the house, when a violent dust-storm came on all in a moment. It became quite dark, and the paintings were blown all about the garden in every direction. There was a grand scramble to gather them together, and to get everything safely inside the house before the rain came, which soon followed in torrents.

I went on to Amritsar, where the hotel was not bad. At breakfast one of the officers told me he had been there some months, and never yet had had the curiosity to see the Golden Temple! I went at once, having picked up a garry-driver at the station, who talked some English. It was a real gem, half white marble lace-work, and half gilt copper, with rich dark hangings and carpets, built out in the middle of a clear lake, smooth as glass, in which every line was accurately reflected; a long causeway of marble leading to it was always crowded with finely-dressed people. The lake was surrounded by trees and picturesque buildings. The holy book of the Sikhs was

kept in the temple, and no shoes were admitted all round the sacred tank. I set to work at once on a sketch, and no one interfered with me the first day, but on the second they said, "No orders give chair," and would not let me sit, even on my own, anywhere. However, I had done most of my work, and did not care.

Plenty of cashmere embroidery is done in Amritsar, in the open shop-fronts; in others, people are carving ivory, stringing flowers into necklaces, or winding coloured silks with the help of their great toes, making shoes with curly tips and every shade of colour; pots, pans, and jewellery. It is a very busy place, and the houses are all gaily painted and ornamented. Sheep with huge fan-tails also painted magenta and blue were tied to the house-doors, with goats, birds in cages, and parrots hung over them. They had even hawks chained to their perches, and the people had sharp good-humoured faces, very different from any in Southern India, and might some day give us trouble if they became too independent and overeducated. They have abundant energy, which the Southerners have not. There is a beautiful garden belonging to the old Palace, with fine old ruined gates covered with creepers, bougainvillea, blue thunbergia, scarlet and orange bignonias, etc.; one of these I sketched, and longed to restore and live in, but probably the white ant would have already loosened all the nails, and the roof was more likely than not to come tumbling in before long.

I soon went on to Lahore, where I stayed with the Judge and Mrs. E. in a most delightful garden. The flowers at Lahore were in their most gorgeous state. The Amaltas or Indian laburnum was a perfect mass of yellow, with flowers and pods more than a foot long, and the tanks were full of tall pink lotus. The native women dress gorgeously, wearing necklaces and ear-rings made of jasmine and other sweet white waxy flowers strung together and tied up in bunches, as well as their gold and silver ornaments. Deep red trousers and a light green veil edged with gold is a favourite mixture. The swells among the men

have a great liking for spotted muslin, through which their dark limbs show curiously, and they wear as many bangles as the women.

The drives round the old city are most charming, with noble trees shading the road, and beautiful peeps through them of the old walls, gates, mosques, and minarets. The principal group surrounding the old Fort, with Runjeet Singh's white marble tomb, and the great red mosque with its marble bulbs, is one of the finest collections of buildings I know in the world, backed as it is by the richly wooded and cultivated plain, and a grand river winding through it. A concert had been arranged for me at Runjeet Singh's tomb one day. The musicians were all blind men. They played curious instruments, made out of gourds and bamboos. One of them had a still more elaborate instrument with a double set of strings,— three metal strings raised by means of bridges high above the thin gut strings. The former he played with a bow, the latter with his fingers like a guitar. These blind men sang songs, with a terrible number of verses, and most monotonous howling.

Dr. L., who arranged this concert for me, also showed me the different treasures in the museum, where he had collected together remarkable specimens of the Greek and Buddhist carvings from the neighbourhood of Peshawar and elsewhere, —some of them really beautiful. He had some small bits of terra cotta with such subjects as Hector and Andromache, and coins which were probably brought over by the Greek artists themselves.

All the country round Lahore abounds in fine tombs, and many of the European houses are made out of them—even the Governor's own house and the English church, the grand domes making fine central halls. At the Governor's one was used as a dining-room. Tombs and gates are covered with beautiful encaustic tiles, and one mosque outside the city was quite a botanical study. All the best-known country plants, as well as the iris of Persia, were represented in a kind of tile mosaic, up to the very tops of the minarets,—beautiful turquoise and lapis lazuli,—blue, green, and yellow being the prevailing tints. The streets are full of colour, and the houses of the Sikhs high and square-topped, so that I found incessant ready-made pictures, if I had but had time to paint them.

But, after the two first hours of the morning, it got too hot for working out of doors. Mrs. E. seldom went out till after six. Then came the sunset, and the day was over. The English have done much towards beautifying Lahore, making roads and a beautiful garden all round the outside of the walls.

The night journey to Ambala was hot, though I had a big carriage all to myself, and all the windows open. At daylight I got into a garry, which took me to breakfast at Kalka, after which I had eight hours shaking up the hill in a tonga—a kind of low dog-cart. I sat next the driver in front, and nearly knocked off his blue turban in my dreams, occasionally varying the entertainment by cracking my own skull against the woodwork of the cart-frame. But to keep awake was impossible after such a night, so I rolled my head and face up in muslin to keep the small gravel from getting into my eyes, as it often blinds unwary visitors to the Hill Capital of India. We went full gallop all the way, up and down very steep inclines, but over an excellent road, changing horses every three miles. They were capital beasts, and the driver managed them cleverly. We met strings of camels going and coming with provisions, looking as if they hated it and all the world besides. The little baby-camels trotting beside their mothers were very pretty. The hills are bare (with ugly euphorbias, something like the candelabra of Teneriffe); all are dusty, and there is no water in the gullies. Nearer Simla, the fir-trees begin; then come the deodaras and enormous masses of clustered white roses over the trees, even finer than they were at Masuri; and those, with St. John's wort, and the green snakelike arums, were the only flowers I saw.

At last we came to the end of the dawk road, and I found men in royal red coats and a jampany waiting to carry me up to the Deputy Governor of the Panjab, where I was most heartily welcomed by Philip Egerton's brother, the great man himself: one of those who work hard and like it. He showed me into my room, sent me some tea, and took pains to make me feel at home (Mrs. Egerton and her daughter were in England). My window looked over endless hills, with great deodara branches, their stems and cones for foreground. Two ayahs followed me in, and fought for the possession of me, though I wanted neither. It seemed to be expected of me that I should have one while I stayed there, and as I found out that the elder one was in some way connected with the head butler, I chose her. She used to watch me about, and sleep on my floor, and to get perpetually in my way most good-naturedly. She was not a costly impediment, and understood no English, so did not bore me by relating scandal.

I went out in the jampany (an arm-chair with bearers) up to the top of the hill before breakfast, and saw three separate sets of snow-mountains, with craggy hills in front, having large pines and oaks perched on them; nearer still, native houses and bazaars, all most picturesque, with wonderful pinetops and deodaras to fill up awkward places. I wondered what people had meant when they told me Simla was not beautiful. I found endless subjects to paint close to the Governor's house, and used to slip out before the live bundles in the hall had done sleeping, and shaken themselves up into a sitting posture for the day (which was all the toilet they ever performed). Simla was lovely in the early morning, but I met few people out then except natives. The English made the cooler climate an excuse for returning to their late home-hours. Lord Lytton set them a bad example, keeping up very late at night, and of course not appearing early in the morning. The visiting hours were from twelve till two, the hottest hours of the whole day. I used as usual to work indoors during the heat, and generally the Governor called me out for a stroll with him in the evening.

He knew more about the plants and trees than any one I met in India.

One afternoon he proposed going in to the Simla Monday Popular Concert close by, and before I knew where I was, I found myself sitting in a great arm-chair next the gorgeous and lovely Lady Lytton in front of everybody, in my old looped-up serge gown and shabby old hat; the Governor being on the other side! I consoled myself by thinking it was quite distinguished to be shabby in Simla; and the Queen of Simla made everybody believe she was entirely devoted to them and interested in their particular hobbies while she talked to them. I was bad enough, but not quite so bad as the Governor's faithful bulldog Flora, who always wanted to keep her master in sight, and came and sat down opposite to her ladyship, staring into her face, with great teeth grinning ferociously. The very sight of her frightened ladies into fits sometimes. The concert was chiefly an amateur one, and because one of the ladies was nervous, Lady Lytton made the Governor encore her song to encourage her. It was impossible not to love that beautiful lady. I took my paintings one day, and had luncheon with them, in the middle of which entertainment the Viceroy lit his cigarette (like Salvatore Politi). He was interested in my work, and spent an hour or more looking at it. One night I went to a tremendous dinner there. About fifty sat down in the great dining-room, and a band played all the while. The table was quite covered with green ferns and ivy laid flat upon it, with masses of different coloured flowers also laid on, in set patterns. The yellow bracts of the benthamia, with bougainvillea, hibiscus, etc., formed separate masses of colour. The ladies' dresses were magnificent, Lady L. herself so hung with artificial flowers that she made quite a crushing noise whenever she sat down. Lord and Lady L. came in arm in arm, just as dinner was announced. I seemed to know nearly every one there in some way or other. After dinner an A.D.C. carried a small chair for Lady L., who went about talking to every one in turn. The Viceroy also did his best to be civil to people. Our journey home was very amusing,—about three miles of road along the ridge in the bright moonlight, the ladies all in jampanys, the men on horseback. I had a continual gossip all the way with different people, and did not wonder at Anglo-Indians raving about the delights of Simla and its society, for there of course one met the very best people in India, in the very easiest and pleasantest way.

Our house was on the southern side of a mountain-top called Jako. On that side the deodara had it all its own way. On the north the oaks turn it out; and under them there was more variety of vegetation. The benthamia was the most striking thing, with its four primrose-coloured bracts, shaped like the bougainvillea. There was a delicate white-flowered spinea, which Anglo-Indians called the white thorn, pale pink, wild indigo, many varieties of dog-roses, columbines, delphiniums, primulas, a tiny white lily, orchids, and cypripediums. I walked all over Jako with the Governor, and had a nice walk one day with General and Mrs. S., at the other end of the place. The General was another walking botanical dictionary. Then I went to stay with Sir Andrew and Lady C., at that same end, and saw quite a different set of people in their house. Lady C. delighted in society, and had constant dinner and luncheon parties. She was very lively and goodnatured, kept her house in perfect order and comfort, and was devoted to two twin Japanese Chin-chins, most absurd little atoms with silky hair and goggle eyes, who had a native in scarlet livery to carry them when they went out for a walk. Sir Andrew was a practical, clever man, who told me about Australia (where he had begun life), and a thousand other interesting places and things. He was head of all the civil engineers in India; also of the Famine Commission, when I was at Simla.

One evening I dined at the Lyells', and met Colonel Colley, who said I ought to go and make some sketches at Nahl Dehrah, and arranged it all for me; and I went off there round Jako, through a tunnel, and on to the viceregal

camp, under the splendid old deodaras, which surround the quaint little wooden temple of Nahl Dehrah. Below that was the deep valley of the Sutlej, and noble mountains beyond it, leading up to the perpetual snows. The place was like a hive of bees when I arrived. All the grand people were doing "kef" after breakfast under the trees. They had a tray brought back for me. Then I painted all day in a very dusty, dirty state, for there was no tent to be had till they had all departed in the afternoon, when Lady Lytton was to leave me in sole possession of her own. But her manners were as kind and sweet as if I had been as well dressed as herself. It was a pretty sight to see all the party depart, and reminded me of a hunting-field at home, so many red coats among the green meadows and trees. After that it became quite quiet; only a few tent-men and servants were left to wait on me. Lady C. had lent me her mate or head road-man, and young C. his "boy," so I was well guarded, and the Viceroy's last words as he rode off were, "Not to be frightened if I heard noises in the night. There were no robbers—only leopards and bears." But they did not think me worth eating, and all was peace.

I can never forget that sunset and sunrise. The flat-topped old deodaras draped with Virginian creeper made delicious foregrounds; the young green cones looking almost white against the dark foliage and boughs. Great golden eagles came rushing across the deep valley, looking really golden in the slanting sun's rays, against the blue misty mountains. I had to hasten back to dine with Sir John and Lady S., or I could have lingered longer at Nahl Dehrah.

The C.s also took me an expedition for three days, sending on a perfect cavalcade of servants and luggage, and taking five A.D.C.S and two Chin-chins. It was much ado about nothing, but amusing in its way. At last the much-longed-for rain had begun. We started in the dust which preceded it, and which hid all views like a London fog. We passed from Mashooba into the property of a native Rajah, who liked making money,

and was cutting and burning down the most noble smithiana and webbiana pines to sell for firewood to the English at Simla, leaving the poor hillsides bare, or covered with untidy blackened stumps. We met a continual string of poor coolies, male and female, with great boards fastened on their backs, who had to go sideways like crabs when they met us in the narrow paths. When not absolutely ruined by overwork, they were a fine, strong, handsome race, wearing pretty silver ornaments, with blue and green enamel. When we arrived at the rest-house at Fargoo, we found it filled by other guests, and only one room free, in which Sir Andrew C.'s servants had laid out all his and his wife's dressing things, as if they were going to a ball. We dined there, and then the room was left for me. The next day we had the place to ourselves, and a red man arrived with the mail, no end of newspapers and home letters, over which we dawdled till past noon, when we set off in the full heat down the hill to visit a grand forest of old deodaras, drawn up as tall as Californian pines. They were just like cedars of Lebanon, but more slender than those I had seen at the original old grove in Syria. Soon after we returned to Simla I went a couple of hundred yards down the hill to Mr. A. C. L.'s, the Foreign Secretary, quite the cleverest man I had seen in India. His talk was full of odd original ideas; but he was much overworked, and often did not talk at all. I liked Mrs. L. very much, too. She at once understood my wish to get to Markunda before the rains rendered it impossible; and that every day was of consequence,—a fact no one else in Simla had believed, they were so accustomed to feminine helplessness.

Mrs. L. at once arranged that I should have a chaprasi from Captain N. and a man of her own to cook, and sent me off. The first day was over bare hills, steep, with some terrace-cultivation on the lower slopes, with yellow burnt-up crops. The road was a grand one, nearly level, over the tops of the hills. One could trace it for miles, though it was only wide enough for riding on jampanys. There was constant traffic going and coming, and it would have taken me on to Thibet in time if I had gone far enough. We met a party coming from that country driving a flock of goats with white and brown hair and low horns. Little packs were tied on their backs, carrying tea and borax from those far regions. They were perfectly composed in manner, with an air of responsibility about them, and did not scramble over the rocks, but walked straight along the paths. The women in charge wore light blue cotton trousers and red jackets, and were loaded with ornaments, half a dozen rings in each ear, and a jingling thing over their foreheads, beside huge nose and ankle rings, and long lank locks. Men and women looked alike.

There were pretty potentilla flowers, of many tints of pink, crimson, scarlet, and chocolate, and a little lilac orchid peeping through the grass like a gem; white jasmine, which was as common as honeysuckle in England, and a white anemone with a blue eye, some quite blue; but the cobra arum, with its long black tongue, was the commonest thing, poking its nasty venomous-looking head through all the surrounding weeds. It rained and thundered at intervals, and when we left Fargoo one of the coolies tried to escape. They hated getting wet, like cats, having like them only one set of clothes. It was always a work of trouble to collect and start these men, and the chaprasi did that. We went through the edges of several storms, but my men carried me like a feather, and my waterproof sheet kept me dry. Once we came to a place where the road was washed clean away, and without any notice the men went up the bank with my feet high above my head, and scrambled over with me, and down again beyond the bad place, only laughing when I feebly asked to be allowed to walk. At last we came to the summit of the pass,—a rude cairn or temple, stuck all over with bits of red cloth and rags,— and descended on the other side fifty feet to the resthouse of Markunda. A perfect sea of cotton-wool clouds surrounded it, and it was very cold; but at sunset they all cleared off, and I had the full view of the great snow range, one of the finest in the world, with some of the highest peaks quite crimson, and the rest in shade.

The ascent was nearly perpendicular in some places, and the eight coolies were quite disappointed that I did not submit to be carried all the way. They put on tandem pulleys with ropes, and at one place a man got under the jampany on all fours and let it rest on his back. It was not an agreeable process, and I walked all the way down. The ground was blue with forget-me-nots and blue anemones, just like our white wood-anemones. The maidenhair fern covered the ground between the flowers, as grass does in England. The road beyond Markunda wound along through the grandest forests of pines 200 feet high, often draped to the very tops with Virginian creeper, and the peeps of snow-mountains and blue sky seen through these were enough to drive one wild. Then the grand figures one met: women with enormous loads on their heads, and splendid folds of hanging drapery, in every shade of fadiness and dirt; the children in one garment of the same, which had often begun by being red; the men lazily carrying their own queerly shaped pipes and nothing else, always followed by goats or sheep as in England they would be by dogs. They were merry and strong as mountaineers are all the world over. They picked me a huge bouquet of pink roses of different shades, and large-flowered jasmine, which was deliciously sweet

Our return journey was made through torrents of rain. It was as much as I could do to keep emptying the pools of water which collected on my mackintosh cover, and every flower which could shut itself up, did. My men carried me splendidly, though it was so slippery they could scarcely keep on their feet. The path went for miles on a mere hanging shelf over a precipice nearly perpendicular above and below, 2000 feet sheer down in places. We were all in thick clouds, and sometimes when they cleared off I could see the rice and other crops and the groups of huts in the depths below.

I went down the hill and back to Dr. and Mrs. J.'s at Saharanpur for a couple of nights, and there I heard, "Oh, you will have to stay here, for the road to Darjeeling has been washed away, and has been impassable for four days." They showed me the paragraph in the paper, and telegraphed to the Calcutta dawk-contractor for the truth, and the answer was, "Both the roads interrupted." It was hot at Saharanpur in July. Poor Mrs. J. looked washed-out and limp. We were both inclined to sit in rocking-chairs and read novels, and little else, but had a stroll in the beautiful gardens before breakfast.

As I could not get to Darjeeling, I determined to return to Kamaun for a month. I reached Bareilly at ten at night, got into a dawk-garry which was waiting, spread my bed on its boards, and jolted on it to Kalydongi with its large mangotrees, and after breakfast started up the hills in a dandy. This way up to Naini Tal is far more beautiful than the other road, but also much longer. Half-way up the men rested and fed, and were very lazy about moving again, and I had to get into a rage to make them go, which did not help to make the day cooler; but we had grand views over the plain, and passed fine specimens of the excelsa pine, as well as oaks, rocks, and two small lakes, and at last we looked down into the lovely lake of the goddess again. It felt almost like coming home. Sitting there in perfect solitude and hot sunshine was great enjoyment, listening to wild birds singing and watching the moving clouds and gay butterflies. What a contrast to my last visit as a wretched invalid, hardly able to crawl! I could scarcely make up my mind to come down. Then I went to see Mr. G., the Head of all the Forests, and his wife. He lent me his map, and sent me with a note to the magistrate to beg the loan of a chaprasi, an official who wore a band which gave him a certain authority over the natives everywhere. All travellers have a right to the services of such a man. He was better than any other servant, and only cost six rupees a month. He found me ten coolies to carry myself and all my goods, and the landlord lent me an old dandy.

My first day's road was lovely, under the great oaks with their branches covered with ferns, greenness everywhere. We turned the shoulder of the mountain and passed the great barrack and fort to the south of Naini Tal, then plunged into lovely oak-woods and valleys full of cultivation, with abundant streams and waterfalls, and narrow deep lanes like those of Devonshire, along one rich bed of a dried-up lake, then down to Bhime Tal, where the nice little bungalow looked like a Swiss farmhouse in the midst of its green meadows and grazing cattle; but some bananas told one where it was. There was a small old Hindu temple of gray stone close to the edge of the green lake, and an island. I crossed the end of the lake and up to pretty tea-plantations, and, after rounding them, came on lovely oak groves, with meadows between them, where strange cattle were feeding. The shepherds who guard them wear thatched roofs over their heads made of bauhinia leaves cleverly sewn together and stretched on a cane frame. The leaves were of a deep red colour. One of the buffaloes had his horns curled downwards and meeting under his chin; he was a most evil-looking beast.

Salti Tal is a deep blue lake in a hole, some hundred feet below, and very hot, with great rank anthurium and caladium plants about it. The next day we mounted 6000 feet higher, and got among rhododendron trees, with pink twisted stems, quite as big as the oaks the colour of their trunks gave a peculiar character to the woods. The ferns were in enormous luxuriance and variety, and the alpinias and a small-flowering scarlet lily were very beautiful. I was quite sorry to descend to the bungalow of Ramgarh. The next day we went up a very steep road, a hard nine miles, to Bhurnia, where we ought to have had a grand snow view. The storm-clouds were glorious, and a beautiful statuesque figure of a girl was at work on the roof of a cottage, spreading her peas to dry, with a kid following her about. The country people use their roof a great deal, and it seemed a favourite place for resting and taking their siestas. They were much gayer figures than the people about Simla, and wore many colours, but their ornaments were mere bent bars of silver, while the Simla ornaments were very fine. The Anglo-Indians often bribe the poor women to sell them, causing them to get beaten on their return home, as those ornaments are wedding presents, and only parted from in conjunction with loss of character and respectability. From Bhurnia we mounted, then descended over 2000 feet, down to the suspension-bridge at the junction of two mountain rivers, and came into a bare stony set of hills, quite treeless—excepting their summits—round Almora.

I wrote to ask Captain K., the treasurer, to change me a £2 note; for one of the difficulties a traveller has in India is to get change. He very kindly came and paid me a long visit in the afternoon. He said the people there were great thieves, and I ought not to go without a second chaprasi. He said also that the natives had quite a fancy for pictures, so that telling them what was in the heavy box would not save it, and he promised me coolies to take me up to the Governor's, Sir Henry Ramsay, at Binsur, about fourteen miles off.

After two days' incessant rain, I had a tolerable morning for my start, and a lovely road all the way up to Binsur, 8000 feet above the sea. The house was most comfortable and unpretentious, with a verandah from whence one could see mountain above mountain, and two of the grandest snowmasses in the world (when visible). The morning after my arrival, which was glorious, I saw all the giants perfectly clear against the blue sky, and had time to sketch them. They all came upon me at once,—five separate mountains, not a long chain as at Simla or Masuri. The oak-trees had their branches hung with lichens and mosses, while the rhododendrons were almost as big, with pink bark. There were endless studies everywhere. Lady Ramsey was a charming hostess; she had a garden round the house full of sweet English flowers—roses, sweet verbena, heliotrope, and flowering myrtle in abundance. Her husband, who was generally called the King of Kumaun, a grand man, was most proud of his garden, in which he had grown and ripened the first gooseberry ever produced in India, and his Ribston Pippins might have taken prizes in any show in Europe. But, as in Europe, he had been forced to build a wall round his garden to keep out "the boys," whose ways are the same all over the world. The clouds were always rolling about and playing fantastic games in the sky, sending down wonderful purple shadows on the hills below. There were strange views on every side. Almora, with its scattered white houses, shone on a ridge in the middle distance on one side; on another there was an emerald-green valley, glittering among the blue hills. There were snow-peaks poking their heads through the black clouds above, and close below the house was a damp little valley with clear stream, and a Hindu temple covered with ferns and saxifrage. General Ramsey was a huge man, with great bodily strength. He rode forty miles home the day after I arrived, and played at backgammon with his little wife all the evening. He used to dig and slave in his garden like an English labourer. He planned out an expedition for me (as it was too wet to go nearer the snows), and he lent me his travelling cook and canteen.

The second chaprasi had orders to hunt up coolies for me. Poor things, they did not go away from their farms willingly, and were a poor weak set from working so constantly in the feverish valleys. I cannot say that travelling on their heads and shoulders was all enjoyment, and they preferred balancing the dandy on two heads to carrying it on their shoulders, folding up their plaids and putting them on the tops of their turbans first, which raised one to a great height above the ground. When going along narrow paths at the tops of precipices I occasionally found it best not to look too much over the side, but never met with any accident. I came down to Almora from Binsur with a regular gang of young ragamuffins, all howling and screaming at once, one of them playing a reed pipe, more classical than VOL. 11 C agreeable. I had sent on my old chaprasi early to deposit my trunks with Dr. Pearson, so there was nobody to keep order, and the young savages nearly jolted me to death.

It was very enjoyable (in spite of clouds and occasional showers) going six or seven hours a day through that fine country, and living in clean rest-house rooms the rest of the time, or wandering about alone in search of flowers. I was fed most abundantly by the General's cook, who walked off before me in the morning, with his attendant boy carrying a lantern, and always had tea ready for me when I arrived. He and the chaprasis slept in the verandah in front of my door, rolled up in brown woollen shawls or blankets, and lived on a little rice or beans, which were white, but otherwise like the *Fejao* of Brazil. Sensible Anglo-Indians often breakfast off it regularly.

Deber Dhoora Dee was the object of my pilgrimage. It was a very singular place—a nest of poor little temples and great granite boulders. There were six noble deodaras with flat tops like cedars, but they were not finer than those of Nahl Dehrah and many of the large ones near Simla. A fair was still going on, chiefly of Manchester cottons, and the pavement near the chief shrine was still covered with the blood of buffaloes sacrificed to Shiva. Goats were also killed and eaten, after being roasted whole, the head and feet being given to the priests. All those ceremonies are very like the old Jewish ones. I saw a very primitive temple on my way back—a mere square wall of stones, roofed with stones laid over one another pyramid fashion; no support inside, no cement, and an earthenware chatty on the top as an ornament, with the entrance so low one had to go on hands and knees to get in. A rude lion was carved in stone, sitting like a sphinx at the entrance to guard it.

The Kumaun country-women were far more graceful than any other hill-women I had seen. They wore a very short embroidered jacket with short sleeves, a veil on their heads hanging down behind, and they covered the lower half of their faces when looked at by strangers in a pretty modest way. They worked quite as hard as the men, poor things. My dandy-bearers were nice obliging fellows, and very careful of me. They jogged me far less than the regular dandy-bearers of fashionable places, but they used occasionally to come down from sheer weakness; and when one happened to be on the top of two of their heads, the sudden descent was startling, not to say dangerous, with a precipice on each side! One morning I had a specimen of how natives treat natives. I was going to give the bungalow-keeper the usual shilling for backshish, when the cook snatched it away, and began boxing his ears instead. There was a grand row, and he explained, "That boy very bad; no fire, no hot water, no milk, no nothing." The man fell on his knees and worshipped the man who cuffed him, and no one took his part. My ugliest coolie, a giant with a most wicked expression, crept into my room one afternoon and gave me a bunch of scarlet potentilla and buttercup flowers tied up with grass. He left them with a grin and disappeared. Sometimes, as we went on, he would stoop down, pick up a few tiny flowers by their heads, and fling them on my lap with a Caliban grin. My old chaprasi did a deal more for me than John ever did,—cleaned shoes, brushed my clothes, lit my fire, etc.

I admired Almora more and more, with its rich gardens of pomegranates, bananas, apples, and apricots; then its rocky bare hill, leading to terraces of corn, quite golden in the sun's rays; gray mountains and clouds, with the silvery river far below winding away for miles. The old town, too, had a most curious long bazaar, with houses much carved and painted, running all along the top of the Hogsback hill, fully a mile long. From Almora I descended to Ramshat, then on through a smiling country all ups and downs, passing rivers, villages, and miles of corn, three sorts of millet, rice, buckwheat, and a kind of gray foxglove, grown for the sake of the oil from its seeds. At last we reached Duara, a most holy place of the Hindus, with numbers of small temples spread over its rich valley. A mad fakir came up, in more paint than drapery, presented me with a bassia leaf, filled with jasmine and oleander flowers, and begged. I knew in that holy place if one began giving there would be no end of it, so I politely bowed the reverend gentleman out, and as fast as I got him out of one door he appeared at another, so I had to shut both, and endure the stifling want of air till he was tired out.

At last I started off to see the most lovely little temple, not more than eight feet long, resting on the backs of tiny elephants, like a miniature copy of the great Kylas at Ellora. The whole building was a mass of rich carving, but I saw no Greek beauty in the figures; they were as ugly as possible. The elephants were quite natural, and in high relief, with half of their bodies detached from the wall. All the other temples were of the usual order, looking best at a distance, when mixed up with fine trees and backed by gray mountains and rain-clouds.

The next morning we ascended a river-bed to Kyera, a pretty but feverish spot full of lovely flowers, then climbed the ridge, and looked down again into Naini Tal, descending among its villas and civilised ways to be told that it had rained incessantly ever since we left it a month before. I was nearly at the end of my money, so I went to the bank (there was one on Coutts' list), showed my letter, and asked an old gentleman there if he would give me some money. He read the letter of credit slowly three times, and said deliberately, "It cannot be done." "How funny. Why not?" said I. "Because it is a most irregular proceeding." So I wished him "good-morning," and went up to Mr. G. and told him. He said, "Like him, the old idiot!" and lent me fifty rupees tied up in a handkerchief; and the next day I descended to Karledone in torrents of rain (I was not sorry to leave it all), and was dragged on all day and all night in a garry till past twelve, when the road came to an end in the river opposite Muridabad.

The bridge was washed away; there was water in front and on both sides close up to the road, and several garries were waiting there, with the buffaloes half in the water. My man unharnessed the horses, and let them trot back again to their last post-house. There was no boat, and nothing for it but to shut one-self up in that box on wheels and wait till morning. Storms of rain, thunder, and lightning came on, and when dawn broke I found only a few inches of road above water. The river was rising steadily, and I watched the last blades of grass disappear under it at the edge of the road. At last the waters closed under the wheels. The natives, apparently content to wait the possibility of dry weather and of the bridge mending, sat under mats on the tops of the garries, and would have gone on so for a week. I was soaking, and so was everything else. The world seemed to consist of isolated trees and hedges in the great waters, and I saw the houses of the city on the other side, and that there was no ferry or other rescue from it expected. Then I discovered one old boat, full of water, and ordered it to be emptied, getting into one of those rages which are sometimes necessary when dealing with semi-savages, and fearing all the time the boat had a hole in its bottom, but it had not. Two men set to work with a bucket made of matting, slung between them on ropes. Themselves standing on the seats, they slung the bucket cleverly in and out, and in about an hour the boat was empty. All the other wrecked travellers begged a passage in it. They stuck up a kind of thatched fan to shelter me from the rain, and moved in the luggage.

We started with my shivering coach-man and guard,—the latter a terrible personage with a big sword, and his upper lip cut in two like a bull-dog; but he was most kind and careful of me. We had to go a long way round by the lee side of islands, and the men pulled and hauled to keep the boat out of the great currents. At last they landed it below the town, on a mud-bank, and we scrambled on shore, finding our way over the slippery banks and lanes to a kind of square or open place. Here we rested ourselves and our things on the wall of a well to wait for a garry which the guard had sent for; when a tidy official appeared and coolly demanded toll for the bridge and barrier which did not exist! I refused, and laughed in his face. He insisted, but at last laughed too, and brought a slate and pencil for me to write my reasons for refusing, which I did, and have little doubt "the sahib " also laughed when he read them, for I heard no more of such myths as bridges and barriers. The hotel I expected to find was shut up, so I drove to the railway-station, and after much search a key was found to the ladies' room. The door was opened with a good thump, and I found a comfortable dressing-room and a most kind station-master, who sent me an ayah to dry my things, saying, "he saw everything I possessed was mortal wet," and he told the Khansamer to feed me.

I felt safe at last, and was just settling myself to rest when Dr. P.'s "baboo" arrived. He had borrowed a Rajah's fine open carriage, and was so genial I could not refuse to go with him and see the lions of the place, so started in a pair of slippers and a ragged old dress all splashed with mud. He was a very fat old man, dressed in pure white calico, with a big stick, gold spectacles, and black smallpox marks all over his face. His son was with him, also in white, but with the addition of a shooting-jacket over it. He rode on in front on a fine horse, but after a while, finding what a dowdy old thing I was, he gave up the painful process, sent his horse home, and mounted the box beside the coach-man, when his father repeated for his benefit all my wise remarks, including the dictum that very little meat and no wine was the secret of health in India. He himself had lived all his life on rice and a little vegetable curry, drinking nothing but water, but I could see the son was inclined to laugh at his father's oldfashioned notions, and to imitate the bad example of young England in those matters, so I was quoted as well as General R. and Dr. P., for his benefit,by the famous "baboo,"—a rare old man, full of original ideas on most subjects.

He took me first to see the beautiful metal-work made in the bazaars, for which Muridabad is famous; the brass is first tinned over, then engraved in beautiful patterns, and a black composition made of five different materials rubbed in, then the tin is removed from certain parts, leaving the brass exposed. It is said to last for ever, and can be cleaned with a little lemon-juice. The "baboo" offered to lend me any number of hundreds of rupees. He took me to the houses of some of his rich native friends, among others to that of the Rajah who had lent me his carriage, and who himself did the honours of his house. In one marble-floored little room were a round table and arm-chairs, and a "debating society" held its meetings there, they told me. There were plenty of books, both English and native, and a look of cleanliness and comfort was about the house. The son of that Rajah had taken a degree at Calcutta, and was going to finish his education in England. In most of the native houses there were odd collections of European rubbish, and duplicate coloured prints on the walls, opposite one another,—two ladies with camellias in their hair, two hunters, two dancing-girls, two little Samuels, two Lord Beaconsfields, all in gorgeous gilt frames, with quantities of glass chandeliers and looking-glasses, generally cracked and almost useless from damp and dust. The things were little worth looking at, but the baboo's talk about them was most amusing. At last I was taken back to the station, and at five the son came back in an entirely European costume to see me off, and to repeat his father's offer of money or anything else he could do. "It would make him so happy to be of any use," he said. I had a good night's rest in the train, and got most comfortable rooms in the native hotel at Lucknow.

The graves and the stories of the mutiny here sickened me, but the gardens were beautiful, and I found several new flowers to work at. I saw some odd things in Lucknow; one of the oddest, twenty elephants taking their bath, each with his attendant scrubber. I tried to paint this, and also the lower storey of a palace, which seemed to be all baths. The silverwork was fine. I bought some bits as specimens, and got much amusement out of the buying, sitting on a shop-front and looking at all the pretty things without hurry. But even their silver was mongrel, the ornamentation taken from Cashmere designs, cream-jugs and milk-jugs of European shapes taking the place of their pretty lotas and chatties. I got some breakfast at the station, and the Khansamer advised me to take some cold chicken and toast on with me, as I could buy nothing between that and Benares; and when I offered to pay he said no, I had eaten so little breakfast he was ashamed to let me pay for that, and would take no more. These Muhammadans were a delightful change after the Hindus; they were so much cleaner, more independent and civilised, and did not perpetually yell for backshish.

I found a capital hotel at Benares, with a most attentive brown landlady, and went the next morning in a boat, up and down the wonderful facade of incongruous and picturesque buildings which line the river's edge. They are all built one over the other, with grand flights of steps, but the lowest of these, as well as half the temples, were then buried in the swollen river, only the tops of the latter sticking out. Of course the buildings lost much consequently from their want of foundations, and of the terraced platforms. The great mosque towered grandly above all the Hindu buildings. On the very highest point above the river the whole frontage must have been quite two miles in extent. Some were most noble buildings, with fine old tamarind and peepul trees amongst them. Under one of those trees a goat was standing on a pedestal like a statue. I asked if he always stood there, and was told he was a holy goat, and got his food there, and that the Hindus liked him. I saw some women dressed in drapery of apple-green or red and gold shot silk, only seen among Orientals. I asked if the silk were made there. "No, mem sahib; that silk came from England," which ended another pretty ro-

mance. Then I went to see the famous Golden Temple, and the well into which the god jumped when his temple was turned into a mosque,—a most picturesque place which I determined to work at on my return,—but my nose warned me that it was not the season to linger longer in Benares then, and that saints are a dirty race; so I took the rail again, and was half smothered in cinders for eighteen hours.

About sunset we came to whole forests of palmyra-palms, like those of Tanjore, set, as those were, in the water. They looked particularly fine against the sunset sky. Half the population was "keeping crows," sitting on raised platforms on four bamboo sticks, with palm-leaves or matting for thatch. I saw some beautifully-dressed women, covered with bangles and other ornaments. The parrakeets which took the place of the crows were gorgeous too, while the blue jay sat and glittered on every telegraph-post. It got gradually dark while I was thinking of all this, and the next morning I woke up in a swamp worthy of Ceylon or Java, with cocoa-nuts and bananas which did my heart good to see, and soon found my way to the huge cosmopolitan hotel in Calcutta. I had a suite of great rooms given to me, with all sorts of curious creatures running over the floor. Six huge adjutant-birds were sitting on the top of the tall house opposite. I had seen them also on trees as I came along, which did not suit their long toes. They helped themselves about with their beaks as old gentlemen help themselves with their walking-sticks. I was followed into the hotel by a native done up in white calico, who said he wished to be my servant as long as I stayed, and the English steward said it was the custom for strangers to be possessed by one of those "ticket-boys," so I submitted; and he sat at my door, fetched my food, carried notes, and knew no English, which looked honest, though it did not add to his powers of usefulness. Nearly every one was out of Calcutta, and my only friends were Mr. K., the manager of Newman's (the great bookseller), and his wife, whom I had met in the steamer coming out. I

could not have had kinder or more efficient friends. I met some of the most agreeable and best educated people at their house, and seldom have heard better talk. There was also some exquisite part-singing, reminding me of our home glee-union. A young English lady who was staying there had undertaken the employment of teaching the wife of a Rajah of high rank, who had himself gone to see Europe. His poor little bride (a mere child) feared he would come back with a perfect contempt for all native ways, and she wished to educate herself and be taught the ways of Europe, so as not to disgust him on his return. Miss S. was a very bright, lively girl, and said it was a most amusing and interesting occupation teaching the poor little Rani, and telling her about the outer world. She even took her out sometimes (well veiled and incog.) to see sights. She had a brougham of her own to take her backwards and forwards every day to the Rani's country house, and on Saturday had a holiday. She took me one morning to see the Viceroy's present, which he may receive on giving an equivalent back, but is obliged to sell and not to keep. If he fancies anything very much he can buy it back at auction. The jewels were elaborately set with enamel-work, though, being cut flat like bits of glass, they had little brilliancy, but to me the way they were set in different patterns and colours was very attractive. The shawls were most gorgeous, and I saw some volumes of the *Memorials of the Prime Consort,* which I suspected were gifts returned, the original receiver not having probably been able to read.

The famous botanic gardens are six miles from Calcutta, but the whole drive is full of interest and wonderful vegetation. A German was director of the gardens in Dr. King's absence, and went heart and soul into my work of hunting up the Sacred Plants. He put me into the hands of a learned baboo who said "it pleased him much that I should take so much trouble about the flowers that Siva loved," and he told me many things about them. One plant, the "Bah," a famous cure for dysentery, he said never passed without bowing to, and always put a leaf in his pocket every morning, then nothing could happen to him,— he must be safe, as Siva loved all who were near these trees. He also told me that when he felt old age coming he should go to Benares and die there, and so be quite sure of going to heaven.

The flowers I was in search of were still out of bloom, so I left Calcutta again the next morning at 7.30, and soon had to change trains, then got into a steamer and crossed the great Ganges river, then into another overcrowded train. The plain of Bengal is wonderfully rich, full of sugar, Indian corn, indigo, arrowroot, hemp palms (toddy), and bamboos, in magnificent luxuriance. The cottages of the people were neater than any I had seen before; they are built like those of Java, on stilts, made of neat matting and bamboo frames instead of mud, the roofs rounded, which gives them a beehive look.

That night at Siligoru was not agreeable; torrents of rain came down, and I soon had to leave my soaked bed and clothes to wrap myself in my waterproof, and sit all night on a chair under the one yard of roof which kept the water out. I had tied up the door with bits of string to keep it from banging open every moment, locks being unknown there, and through the chinks in my floor I saw water underneath. It was almost as bad as that night near Muridabad, only there was no swollen roaring river. At last, about nine o'clock, the palki came with the most magnificent set of men to carry it,—real models of humanity, so different from the poor starving specimens in Kumaun. They carried me over all kinds of patched bridges and causeways, under fallen trees and over them. The road would probably have been impassable for weeks, but for the happy chance of the Lieutenant-Governor being expected hourly, so every one was working day and night. I saw Mr. Lear's subject, "The Plains of Bengal," even the very trees he had put into the foreground,— the pandanus and bamboo, which grew very large there. They were loaded with creepers and parasites, like everything else. Brazil could not beat the luxuriance of the vegetation there, with the cissus discolor in great beauty, ipomceas, a large white thunbergia, begonias, and ferns.

I had breakfast at the very dampest dwelling I ever saw; inside and out, all was dripping. When I mentioned an egg, the man rushed out at a small chicken, and as I had no time to have him cooked, I still tried to get eggs. At last I was taken into the storeroom and offered a choice of jams and pickles. I found a pot of potted ham, very spicy, which did well to fill the gap; and they gave me good tea and toast even in that damp hole. Then we went floundering through the mud and over the broken bridges again, reaching Kursim just in time for dinner. The next day took me over the most glorious road, among forests and mountains, to Darjeeling, the finest hill place in the whole world; and I brought my usual luck with me, for Kinchinjanga uncovered himself regularly every day for three hours after sunrise during the first week of my stay, and I did not let the time be wasted, but worked very hard. I had never seen so complete a mountain, with its two supporters, one on each side. It formed the most graceful snow curves, and no painting could give an idea of its size. The best way seemed to me to be to attempt no middle distance, but merely foreground and blue mistiness of mountain over mountain. The foregrounds were most lovely: ferns, rattans, and trees festooned and covered with creepers, also picturesque villages and huts.

The people, too, were unlike any I had seen before,—natives of Butan and Thibet, who come every year to make money, during the season. They are rather like Chinese, with flat faces, long eyes, and long hair. They are intensely goodhumoured, laughing and singing, very industrious and strong. They invest all their money in ornaments; and those also were most fascinating,—inlaid with great lumps of turquoise, coral, and amber, and a bright scarlet bead made of rhinoceros horn, which felt soft like india-rubber. The devout among those people go about twirling little silver praying-wheels in their hands, or they paint the prayers on flags and let the wind "do it" over their huts. They have also bells, and metal thunderbolts, and shells, in their worship; musical instruments made of human thigh-bones, and half skulls with human skin stretched over them for drums. In spite of such barbarisms, those Buddhists seemed a gentle, harmless race, fond of pets and of their children. They wore rich colours, pretty striped scarves, and long pigtails, with long loose sleeves, often red.

The flowers about Darjeeling seemed endless. I found new ones every day. The *Thunbergm coccinea* was perhaps the most striking; it twined itself up to the tops of the oaks, and hung down in long tresses of brilliant colour, the oak itself having leaves like the sweet chestnut, and great acorns as big as apricots almost hidden in their cups. There was another lovely creeper peculiar to Darjeeling,—the sweet-scented cluster ipomcea, of a pure pink or lilac colour. The wild hydrangea with its tricolour blooms was also much more beautiful than the tame one. I worked so hard and walked so much that, after a dinner or two with Sir Ashley Eden and other grandees, I refused any more invitations. I could not keep awake in the evening.

How I longed to spend a spring in Darjeeling, and to see all the wonderful rhododendrons and magnolias in flower! They were such great old trees there, and of so many different varieties. One hairy magnolia was then in flower, and the Lieutenant-Governor had a branch cut down for me one day; it was very sweet. Major L., the head of the police, was kind enough to lend me his interpreter—a most grave and responsible character, with long eyes and a pigtail. He wore a brown dressing-gown and a Chinese cap turned up like a beefeater, and whenever I made the slightest remark, he got out his note-book and made a memorandum of it, like an M. P. in search of facts. His name was Laddie. He spoke excellent English, and declared it necessary for me to have twelve coolies and a cook to go about the hills with me, bringing up my expenses to over thirty shillings a day. I started in a dandy the Governor lent me, carried by a fine band of ragamuffins; it was almost worth the extra pay to see their picturesque figures and independent air of insolence. One of them had nothing on but a striped blue and white scarf worn under one arm and over the other shoulder, where it was fastened by a skewer with a great silver ring in its head. Even the dirtiest were covered with bangles, and had turquoise in their ears. All had the flat Chinese face and long eyes. I had to take an old cook, with all his machinery and food, which made the luggage much heavier.

It was late in the morning before we got started, and ascended the steep hill through the camp, when the young officers darted after me, "Where are you going to now, Miss North?" for they all knew me by sight, though I did not know them. Much of our way led through the forest. At one place a great fallen tree filled up the path, covered with rhododendrons and other parasites, and I saw my old friend the aralia again. Rangerom is a mere clearing in the forest on the steep hillside, which some insane governor had once made to grow cinchona in. It was then turned into a botanic garden of native plants and pines, and a poor Scotch gardener was slowly dwindling away with fever and ague among them. There was only the one small bungalow besides, which was used for picnics chiefly, and was quite quiet at night. There was a grand view of Kinchinjanga when it showed itself, and the forest-studies all round were endless.

While hard at work at that fairy dell I felt it was raining, and before I could get over the fifty yards of steep descent to the bungalow with my things, I was soaked through and through, and came back through a running stream of water to find the house occupied by a large picnic-party—a regular ballsupper, cooks, coolies, and other litter all over the passage floor, and half a dozen ladies all drying their things and themselves in my room, using my towel and

soap, almost too much company to be pleasant. I escaped as soon as I could to my poor soaked painting. "You only sketch it on the spot and paint it indoors?" one beauty said, pointing to the poor thing which was so covered with raindrops that it looked as if it had the smallpox. "Yes," I said, "that's what I do. Then I take it out to be rained on, which makes the colours run faster, and that's the way I paint, as you say, so quickly." Those unthinking, croqueting-badminton young ladies always aggravated me, and I could hardly be civil to them. I had not met a single person at Darjeeling who had seen the great mountain at sunrise, and few of them had seen it at all that year. Kinchinjanga did not keep fashionable hours.

There seemed to be a superabundance of the foxglove and snapdragon kind of flower. One balsam was of a cream-yellow, with a deep claret-coloured throat inside and out, and there were lovely turquoise berries on another plant, shaded from blue to green, as the real turquoise is. I found, higher up, a beautiful blue creeper, like a gentian — Crawfurdia *speciosa,* with its buds set between two leaves. The bells were two inches long, shaded into white at the neck like the common gentians, and of the same waxy material. Another new idea to me was the poppy, *Meconopsis Wallichii,* the flowers as large as our field-poppy, but of the most lovely pale blue with a gold centre, growing on branches from a central stem of brown velvet a yard or more high. As they faded, all the leaves and stalks turned from green to gold and brown, and were covered with hairs.

From the hill above Jonboo one saw the plains of Bengal like a sea, and mountains on the other three sides. The clouds rolling in and out of the valleys and up into the sky at sunset, quite took one's breath away with their beauty and colours. They were perfect pillars of fire on some evenings, and one thick cloud with a gold edge, just in front of the setting sun, cast wonderful shadows and rays opposite; but the sky was entirely clear overhead on both nights. The road up passed through grand rhododendrons

with gigantic leaves with brown and white linings. The hydrangea, too, grew into quite a tree here. All the rhododendron trunks were pinkish, some of them quite satin-like and smooth; no moss or ferns could find a hold for their roots in them. Others were covered with creeping things, and the dwarf bamboo came up to the very tops.

It was then too cold for tents. Frost was white on the ground round me when I began, at sunrise, to paint the highest mountain in the world—Deodunga, or Mount Everest as it is now called. It forms quite a distinct group, detached from Kinchinjanga by a hundred miles at least, and its form is much less graceful and definite. I did not myself feel sure which was the actual highest point, while no one could make a mistake about the other. The trees were scraggy and leafless, and hung with lichen. There were bluish pines (webbiana, I believe) with blue cones; blue monk's-hood, and blue poppies—that same preponderance of the colour one finds in other alpine countries. The view was perfectly clear for two hours; all the rest of the day it was smothered in cold clouds. The second morning I saw a curious effect. While the great mountain was still in cold blue shade, the rosy light coloured the clouds above it, and made them glow with fire; then the clouds in the valleys between myself and the mountains caught and reflected the colour from those upper clouds, carrying it down into the world below. In the afternoon I tried to drag myself up to the highest point near, only a few hundred feet above the house, but found I could not do it. I sat down once or twice and tried again, but found it too difficult to breathe. It was very cold up there, and there was no furniture in the house, so I piled all the logs close to the fire and within reach of my hand without getting out of my quilt, in which I rolled myself close to it, so that I could poke on the logs and keep the fire alight all night, feeling sure that if it once went out I should be frozen to death. With my hot-water bag under my feet, and the bag which held my clothes for a pillow, that was comfort!

I took possession of my paintings at Jonboo the next day, and saw a most curious reflection of myself and the sun's disc in the mist, opposite the setting sun, with a gold halo and rainbow tints round it. It would have made a good suggestion for a Madonna or saint's picture. I saw red begonia leaves amongst the ferns, and other parasites among the treebranches; several pretty lilac and white orchids also, but it was too cold to enjoy anything, and I was glad to get down to 8000 feet above the sea again. Darjeeling was still crowded, and Mr. and Mrs. D. squeezed themselves to take me in, most kindly, for a night; then I went down 2000 feet lower on the north-east side of the hill to Mr. H., the manager of several tea-estates. His bungalow was delightful: roomy and full of luxury, surrounded by the most lovely flowers, with gorgeous blue pheasants walking about a large aviary. Nothing could be seen for miles but tea-terraces and a little cinchona; the beautiful forest had disappeared to make way for it.

The famous meeting of the waters is more like English scenery than Indian, and that is the true reason why AngloIndians always rave about it. The river rushes on like a whirlpool, and the night air is delicious. It made a pretty moonlight scene, with the men round the fire for a foreground. The most picturesque thing down there was a swing-bridge VOL. II D made of canes and rattan, rather higher up the Rungheer. At a distance it looked like a slice of spider's web. I got a sketch of it from two different points. All the ends of the rattan webbing were fastened to different boulder-stones and trees. The bridge was reached by a crazy ladder, and required some nerve to walk over, as the footway was very transparent and loosely put together. The whole thing swung up and down over the surging torrent below. We returned next day and took large doses of quinine in sherry as a preventive to the fever we ought to have taken, after which I rode back to Darjeeling and on to Kursion—a very beautiful place, but spoilt by the tea-clearings all round. I got a palka on to Shornabutty, and arrived just as the red

sun disappeared behind the great plain horizon. All was so warm, and all the brightest colours seemed there melting into one another in one harmonious whole. The large pandanus pines were very graceful in front of all the colour. I could not sleep in that fever spot. I had a long time also to wait at Silligoru, and was none the better for it, so I took twelve grains of quinine. A good English general and his A.D.C., whom I had met at Sir Ashley Eden's, sent me in a cup of the strongest tea and biscuits, which gave me new life, and I blessed them as good Samaritans. It was quite dark when we reached Calcutta, and I was again picked up and taken possession of by a stray servant at the station, who fed me and locked up my door when I went out. I went off to the Botanic Gardens at daybreak, and got all I wanted at last. It is a very lovely garden, and I had more leisure to enjoy it than I had before. One great banyan tree was perhaps its greatest pride.

It was delightful after a long night and day in the dusty train to find myself again opposite Benares; and the weather had become perfect, neither too hot nor too cold. I hired a carriage for the week, and went every morning to sketch on the river, where there was such a mass of picturesqueness that the attempt to paint and reproduce it almost drove me to despair. Sitting in a boat anchored by a rope or a stone, with a fidgety man holding an umbrella between me and the cloudless morning sun, is not a comfortable mode of painting. After two days' work I began to hope the first sketch might give an idea of the thing, though a very superficial idea; and I began another with the Nepaulese pagoda in it, and some of the sliding temples, which had come down the hill quicker than they intended. There were large palaces half buried in the river, and all out of the perpendicular, which had dropped down bodily from the treacherous banks above, greatly adding to the picturesqueness; and on those fragments pilgrims had perched themselves. Some of their modes of worship were curious. One man came at sunrise every day to practise a number of gymnastics

over and over again. He rubbed every bit of his body on a particular stone of the pavement in turn, picking himself up again perfectly stiff and upright,—an art it must have taken years to acquire, —all in honour of a little god he made fresh every morning out of a lump of Ganges-mud and some flowers. He used to finish the performance by throwing some rice on to the crown of his mud-god's head, and then the whole into the river, where it is supposed to germinate. The whole seemed too childish.

I went for a grand rummage through the bazaar with Mr. C. It was amusing, but I came back half dead from the heat and smells and crowd. We had half a dozen policemen to clear the road, and I did not enjoy doing things in such a grand official way. We went to the shop of the great man who sold kincob, and I saw many gorgeous materials, but bought nothing. The next morning I went with my little guide to the place where it was made, and saw the looms at work. I bought some things at half the price asked by the other people. On the night of New Year's Day I went with the R. C.'s to visit a Rajah, and we two women were taken to see his wife and the wives of his sons. They were all dressed most gorgeously, but lived in the dullest of dirty rooms, up a shabby ladder. After we had made a few remarks and been well examined, we were put into jampanys and carried through the narrow bazaars to see the illuminations,—every shop had little saucers of lighted oil. The streets about Seven Dials on Saturday night are brilliant compared to Benares illuminated; but the next night I went in a boat on the river, and the effect of even those small attempts at illumination was fine when reflected in the water. The Rajah was a remarkably handsome man, and talked perfect English. Mr. R. C. introduced him to me, told him he must come and see my drawings at the hotel, and then coolly told me he was the greatest rogue and blackguard in India! He did come, and was very agreeable, and gave me some letters to friends at Mathura, telling me it was well to have two strings to my bow. When we went to see his wife he sent his nephew in with us, as we might then see her face and those of her daughters-in-law, which would have been covered up if the husbands had been present. A widowed aunt was dressed in black with no ornaments. All the women looked the same age, and were loaded with bangles, nose rings, and other ornaments, and dressed entirely in kincob. I told the Rajah I was going to the old palace of Ramnagar the next day, and he said he would send and order a boat to wait for me opposite it; so I drove off up the river, past the monkey temple, and saw the amiable apes rush down from the trees and walls in hundreds at the sound of wheels, expecting cakes and fruit. They all sat down and bit their own fingers when I did not stop, chattering loudly their opinion of my character as I passed on. They had such red faces that they looked as if they drank.

We were stopped within a few hundred yards of the river by a party of men and a jampany; then a finely dressed young native gentleman made me get in and walked beside me. I thought he was one of Rajah Siva Prasado's sons, but he was indignant at the idea, and said they did not even belong to the same caste. He pulled out a bit of his string to show he was a Brahmin. The other was a parvenu Jain, only made Rajah by the English since the mutiny. A paddlewheel boat was awaiting us on the bank, worked, like the treadmill, by men's feet. The old palace looked noble from the river. On the opposite side the High Chamberlain met me,—a gentleman-like old man, with lank gray hair, and no whiskers or beard, who talked perfect English, and looked like a beneficed clergyman of good family. He put me into another jampany, then into an open carriage with fine English horses, and said as it was cool then I had best go and see the gardens first; after that the Maharajah would receive me. I was only in my old sketching clothes, and had not expected any such honours, but I always do as I am told, so I was taken to the temple, tank, and garden, and after making a sketch of the rather hideous strawberry-cream-coloured

gate, went inside, up the great marble stairs, where the old Maharajah met me, in a green embroidered dressing-gown and a gold cap. We went out and sat on a marble balcony hanging over the river. The little grandson was brought out and put on a little arm-chair between us, and the Chamberlain entertained us with a display of curiosities, very ugly but meritorious. Curious armour, and a revolver on the end of a spear, were also shown me, as well as a famous clock which told the hours, terrestrial and celestial, the moon's changes, and I know not how many other wise things. The maker was there, and I told him he must be a very proud man to have made such a wonderful thing. I got away as soon as I could, but the Maharajah did not catch an Englishwoman every day, and always had some fresh excuse to keep me as long as he could.

I was sent back in the boat down to the landing in the city four miles below, where my carriage had been ordered to wait, but it never came, and I had to return home in an ignoble garry, after giving backshish to a Silver Stick and other great men's great men. The old Maharajah had read of my Kensington Exhibition and knew my name, and directly he heard of my arrival in Benares he was anxious to see me, making me send my sketches for him to see also. The next day the Chamberlain arrived in a brougham, with two beautiful dresses of kincob and a request that I would send him pictures of English fruits and flowers as well as a copy of my sketch of Hardwar when I returned home and had time to do them.

One afternoon, just after their New Year's Day, I drove down to the river and met a procession of all the Maharajah's horses, led with gay trappings, his little grandson on a pony, all in kincob, and a band of gongs, drums, and real shells used as trumpets. In the middle was a figure of the fourarmed god, with red beard and black face, and two large fans of peacock feathers flapping on each side of him, while a huge elephant was tramping behind him, all painted and hung with gaudy clothes. It was a most barbarous group. The gods were

made fresh every New Year and kept in the house till the time came round again, when they were brought down in state to the river, rowed out to the middle, then dropped over and drowned! The terraces were crowded with people, and I saw many other gods go into their watery graves. It was a funny sight to see some thousands of unreasoning human beings playing in all gravity at god-making, as other children make dirt-pies all the world over. At the same time they went on washing their pots, pans, and selves, drinking the water, putting their dead into it, and gossiping and laughing over it. The burning-place looked picturesque after sunset, when the daylight was going; one could see the flames and smoke and dark figures against it, all reflected in the river, with the great odd-shaped temples standing out in the background, against the twilight sky, and all the big umbrellas against the walls, looking like targets. As it got dark the river front was lit up with oil lamps and fireworks, and was a splendid sight.

One morning I landed at the steep stairs leading up to the Nepaulese pagoda—a building which looked like a bit of Japan, and had a bell and cover of pure gold on its top. It was built on the top of a high platform guarded by towers and turrets. A huge tamarind and some peepul trees were planted round it, making a fine subject when seen from below, with boats of all sorts of odd shapes on the river in the foreground, the water being strewn with floating flowers, chiefly yellow ones. Some of the streets behind the river-frontage were so narrow, one could touch the walls on each side as one walked through them. It was difficult to avoid coming in contact with other wanderers, who were thereby rendered unclean, and had to return to the river and repeat their morning ceremonies and washings. We went on past many small Hindu temples covered with elaborate carvings, but very dirty and neglected, to the great mosque which once domineered over all the Hindus; now, it stood alone on the highest point of the city, a noble monument of fallen greatness, kept in repair by the charity of strangers, as the Hindus seem to have all their own way in their sacred city.

A thousand steps led down from Aurangzib's mosque to the river, so steep that it made one almost giddy to look down them. Looking up at the minarets was nearly as bad, for they rose 140 feet above the ground they stood on. The Hindus showed their spite and revenge for former illtreatment from the Mussulmen by surrounding their beautiful building with every kind of rubbish and untidyness up to its very walls, with Brahmin bulls and cows, gods and goddesses. In the very middle of all the confusion sat a holy Fakir reading his book of prayers with great solemnity. I hunted through the bazaars till I found some real Dacca muslin. It was not cheap, but wonderfully fine and soft, and it is difficult to get now. English stuff is so cheap and strong that they are leaving off making it at Dacca.

I left Benares on the 2d of November, and passed through Khanpur at midnight, when I woke up to the delights of a cup of good coffee, poked in at the window, together with knives (open), toys, and pith models of the Memorial, reminding one of that awful mutinytime. It made me wonder if it would not some day come again. No one can tell; we really know nothing of what natives think, and few make real friends among them.

On reaching Mathura, I found the one garry had been taken by the one Englishman in the train. I sat on the weighing-machine and waited amongst all the howling rabble till it returned. Such a lot of savage-looking faces.

The streets here were Moorish; even Cairo could not show more elaborate outside carving, and in Cairo all was wood or plaster, while in Mathura all was equally fine and lacelike, but carved in black and white marble, brown or red stone. It had the addition of Hindu oddities as well as Moslem. All the women and children were sitting on the house-tops and balconies to see the bulls led past for some ceremony, dressed in beads and flowers, with peacock-feathers stuck upright on their heads and daubed over with ochre and vermilion. Monkeys and birds abounded everywhere, and the fronts of the temples and chief houses looked as if they wanted glass cases put over them, they were so finely and delicately ornamented. It seemed a most thriving, busy place. The edge of the Jumna was lined with temples and steps, and was a sort of petty Benares. My coachman was a good guide, and left his old horse standing unprotected in the streets while he went up mosque steps and by-lanes with me.

Mr. L., the collector, took me in his own carriage the next morning over the eight miles of road to Brindaban, and we went again through the old streets of Mathura on our way. The temples of Brindaban were magnificent,—every variety of architecture and all sorts of fanciful styles surrounding a poor mud village. The right bank of the Jumna was lined with rich marble steps and balconies hanging over its waters. Many of the buildings were more like palaces than temples; others mere toy things with baby gardens— holy plants, with rice, shells, idols, and other curiosities inside them. In the water were sacred turtles and crocodiles sunning themselves on the sandbanks opposite, looking the same colour as the sand. Do they change their tints like chameleons? The finest of all the temples was still in process of building, in the form of a Maltese Cross of the richest ornamental work, sharply cut in red sandstone, on which the green parrots looked like real gems of colour.

Pilgrims were going in an endless procession from shrine to shrine, having fifteen miles to walk to visit all their holy places about Brindaban. The dresses were very gay, the women wearing full skirts, instead of the scanty drapery usually worn in India. I preferred the latter. Red-nosed apes were swarming up every wall and tree, carrying their children on their backs. They were a real curse to the people, stealing the very food out of the children's mouths. The humpbacked white oxen were noble beasts, and drew most aristocratic chariots ornamented with brass and red curtains, under which the great men sat in solemn grandeur, seeming above the weakness of feeling themselves shaken. They all salaamed to my jolly English companion with a greater air of respect than I had seen elsewhere. We met plenty of camels and even elephants.

I fancied I would as soon settle at Mathura as any place I had seen in India for subjects for painting. It was so full of strange sights and curious groups of people and creatures. We went at five o'clock down to the Ghauts to see the turtles fed. They came paddling slowly across the river in hundreds, stretching their long snake-like heads out of the water and scrambling over one another eagerly after the food. The still more eager and adventurous apes came down also and jumped on their shells, trying to snatch at the food before the turtles had time to get it, and occasionally got their fingers badly bitten in their thievish attempts, for a turtle's bite is no joke. They even bite the natives occasionally when bathing; but the crocodiles did not seem to care for Hindus, and I heard of none being eaten by them. The apes were very amusing, chasing one another from house to house like mad things, then without any apparent cause suddenly collapsing into pious imbecility, with their arms crossed and their eyes turned up as if they could not move without help. They did not know what fear was.

At last I got to Delhi, which I had passed and resisted twice before, and Colonel and Mrs. D. kindly took me into their beautiful house for a week. The Royal City was a grand place, and quite came up to all I had heard of it. The first afternoon I was driven round Delhi I saw the grand simple form of the huge mosque against a deep orange sunset sky, also the exquisite marble halls within the fort, with its massive red sandstone walls and gates. Also, alas! the hideous barrack buildings and other atrocities introduced by my countrymen. I worked regularly in the famous old marble palace which used originally to hold the peacock throne. The shell which held it was so rich I could easily believe any tales of its original splendour. It was built of pure white marble, inlaid with coloured stones, elaborately carved and gilt in intaglio, and the general tone was rich, from the quantity of gold used. A young English officer looked out at his barrack window, saw me painting it, and asked Mrs. D. what I was doing—"Was I drawing the railway suspension bridge *1*"

I drove out to Hamayur's Tomb, through four miles of country dotted with domes and fine gateways, like the Campagna of Rome or the Plain of Thebes; and on the way was another fort or walled city with bits of blue tile still left in its noble gates, and with a most beautiful mosque. The streets of Delhi were very lively, and I had one afternoon's shopping in them with Mrs. D., picking up a lot of interesting and highly ornamented rubbish. We finished our expedition by a visit to the great stone monolith outside modern Delhi, which was set up by Asoka three hundred years B.C. It is over forty-two feet high, and its long inscription is sharp and legible still. The pillar had been originally near Dehrah Dun, and an eccentric emperor had moved it all the way from thence to stick it on the top of his three-storeyed palace, now, like all the others at Delhi, a ruin, and a mere molehill amongst twenty miles of other molehills and exquisite remnants of buildings gradually crumbling to dust. Before the mutiny some of the old magnificence remained around the native princes. Now Delhi is a very poor place. 1878.—After a week here, I went on eleven miles, and settled myself in the bungalow which had been made in one of the old gate-towers, under the shadow of the Kutab, the highest tower in the world (250 feet), which reminded me of the American sequoias or big trees in its general proportions and colour. It has the same swell at the base, the same gradual tapering to the top, and I think it is one of the few buildings which really looks its full size. But all its surroundings are mere dwarfs, except the great pointed arches, built with horizontal stones overlapping one another, and no keystone. Near them was a forest of small Hindu pillars collected from six different temples, each pair of pillars of a different pattern. Many of the pillars are carved like cameos, but the conquerors decapitated most of the figures. The Gate of Ala ud Din was the gem of all; the details and lacework of stone and marble, and the beauty of general design, surpassing any building I had yet seen in India. Beyond the actual Kutab ruins is a completely ruined city, with tanks and tombs and mosques without number scattered over some miles of ground, now left to the mercies of vultures and eagles. Some of the tanks have four or five storeys of galleries and chambers below the level of the ground, richly arched and ornamented; and the natives were in the habit of jumping into the water from the top for backshish. I had the place to myself for a week, except for chance visitors who came over for an hour or so, mounted the great tower, made a picnic meal, and drove away again; but after the first week the Davies arrived with their camp. Such a tribe of people, tents, camels, and horses! The Colonel had a regular court there, and all the neighbours (including beggars) turned out to meet him and camp round him. At night the place was lighted up with their fires.

Mrs. D. and I drove one day to Tughlakabad, the whole population having been ordered out for the last two days and nights incessantly to patch up the road and make it passable, which they did principally with no tools but their hands, tossing handfuls of dust and stones from the side of the road into the holes to fill them up. Plenty of bullock-carts passed that way every day, but no one ever attempted to fill up the big holes till we came; they got over them somehow. Tughlakabad was a wonderful old fortress city crowning a high cliff or isolated hill, with many miles of ruined walls and towers, many of the stones fourteen feet in length, and laid together without cement.

After three nights the D.s rode away, their camp disappeared, and I remained in sole possession of the dead city and enjoyed its quiet. But the mornings got almost too cold for me to hold my brush, and I wandered about the ruins instead of attempting to sit and work, till the sun warmed the day. I found endless beauty in the old ruined city of Siri behind the Kutab. Some of the mosques were most elegant, with marbles and coloured tiles let into their walls and ceilings. In one building were exquisite medallions in fine plaster-work, which I longed to steal; nothing could be more beautiful than their designs, and they were only crumbling away there. Every dome had a big bird sitting on its point, generally a black vulture with a white head, and so motionless that they looked as if part of the stone-work; but the whitened bones which strewed the ground explained why they haunted that place. Nearer me, the camp-horses had left an abundant harvest for the squirrels to gather in. They came in crowds to the place, and were most tame and pretty to watch. I nearly caught one litttle fellow, head downwards on a branch of a tree, nibbling at one of its pods as it hung. The cold also brought the minabirds and doves down on the ground, with their feathers all ruffled up, making believe they had fur coats on. It was sometimes rather lonely and awesome among those tombs of the old city, with the wild dogs, vultures, and bones. One morning I did not like the looks of the people. First a child came to beg, then a woman, then a fierce man who ordered me to give them backshish. I always pretended not to understand, and never had any money to give, but I did not like the scowls I saw, or the looks of other men who mounted up the towers, and seemed to be looking out to see if I had any friends or was watched. I thought discretion the best part of valour, so went back to the shade of the Kutab, and within reach of its guardians, and began a sketch of the big arch and iron pillar from under the Hindu colonnade. The old trees must have been as old as the Kutab itself, possibly much older. The iron pillar is supposed to be the pivot on which the earth turns, and to go down to its very centre; and though some English engineers dug down underneath it some two yards, the Hindus did not cease to believe the story, and said the English thought they dug underneath it, but the gods muddled their brains.

On the 24th I drove away from the Kutab and across to Nizamudin,—a most lovely little tomb and mosque of white marble, with richly coloured praying-carpets hung up as blinds, and a grand old tamarind-tree over it. A fine old Moslem was keeping a school of little boys in the court, all the children gaily dressed, and standing on bright carpets spread on the marble pavements of the court as foregrounds. What a subject it was, if I could but have done it as I wished to do it! Another picture close by attracted me—a deep tank with tumble-down old buildings round it, and another old tree on the top of the steps, the faithful doing their prayers and ablutions on its edge. It was difficult to tear myself away, but at last I did, drove on to Delhi, and put up at a hotel made out of a collection of old tombs strung together, my bed being under a beautiful dome. I called at the post-office, and wanted to pay for a parcel of paints from Bombay—twelve annas. I had none, and offered two six-anna stamps bought at the same office, and was told by a native clerk "it was not a legal tender "! I felt inclined to box his ears. The priggishness of the educated native is most odious and ridiculous. The next morning, after getting my money from the bank, I went on by rail to Alwar.

CHAPTER XI RAJPUTANA

All the faces and costumes had completely changed in a few hours, and I was among a new race. The Rajputs were finelooking men, with very marked features, long whiskers and moustachios, the ends of which they tied at the backs of their heads. They delighted in dyeing them red or orange too, which gave them a very odd look. They wore cashmere shawls on their shoulders and gay caps. Major L. met me at the station. He was most genuinely hospitable and goodnatured (though peppery). His wife was in Canada with her own family. He took me the next morning to see the old Palace and its lovely tank before breakfast. The buildings were all of marble, with coloured lines and scrolls of mosaic work let into

it. We went inside and saw the hall of audience —a fine room full of European rubbish, including eight marbletopped washing-stands — and on the marble-paved terrace outside there was a plaster fountain furnished with a pink Cupid with green wings. Peacocks were the wild game of the country; I saw hundreds on every road, eating up all the newly-sown corn, but they were never allowed to be touched. The holy tank was full of ducks, geese, and swans. The latter looked most dignified, sailing under the red sandstone arches. Above the beautiful tank with its marble pavilions rose rocky hills with forts, and domed buildings half hidden amongst the bushes and trees. Oranges and other fruits grew in abundance in the gardens, wherever there was sufficient irrigation. All the water was brought from a lake ten miles off, artificially made in the hills. We went there twice, and the second time the barouche was drawn by four thoroughbred camels, with a rider on each, who were tossed about from side to side in a way which made me giddy to look at. They went at an even trot all the way. Each of the camels had draperies of red, green, and yellow; the men had red turbans and sashes, and white dresses, and looked very gay. The lake was surrounded by low stony hills with no trees except in one or two sheltered crannies, with an island in the middle like a jam-tart, all of stones. Even the old Palace was not picturesque, perched on a steep shelf over the lake. But my host was happy, for there was a new cockleshell of a boat, lately imported by the Maharajah from England to try; and how he blew up all the natives, who had done their best to spoil it by the stupid way they put the different bits together! At last we risked our lives in it, and he rowed himself into a high good-humour and heat; then we had tea and trotted home again.

The Maharajah was a spoilt boy, and had some most objectionable habits. He thought he had a right to everything he fancied, and no one could refuse him anything. His Highness was the first full-blown specimen of modern "higher education" amongst the Rajahs, and had

been "finished" at Mayo College. I cannot say I was deeply impressed by the result. His stable was a sight worth seeing. He had a grand number of fine horses, and was generous in his way. When Major M. arrived with 500 camp-followers, he offered to feed and keep them all the time they stayed, and seemed really attached to him. They wanted to take me to see the Maharani, but I begged off, as I had no inclination to give her any of my paintings. Her Highness has no children,—a great grief,—and certain old hags in the zenana were supposed to be accountable for it. I saw a whole street full of hunting chetahs and lynxes. The latter are the most restless wild little animals, which jump at their victims' throats like bull-dogs and strangle them. I saw a man put a piece of meat on the end of a bamboo cane and hold it up as high as he could, and one of the small animals (not much bigger than a cat) made a prodigious spring from the ground to the top of it, took the meat, and was down again in an instant. Their ears stick up right over their heads and meet at the top. The chetahs are taken out in carts blindfolded and let out when within sight of the deer, when they creep up and spring upon them, holding them till the hunter comes up and kills them. They are so intent on their work that they are easily blindfolded and led away again. All those wild beasts are chained to trestle-beds in front of the houses down the street, their keepers sitting or sleeping behind them, and little children, peacocks, cocks and hens, wandering among them without the slightest fear.

Alwar was full of strange sights. I used to take my sketching stool and sit at the gate of an evening in the road, making studies of camels and passing travellers. There was an old ayah who, in the absence of her mistress, devoted herself to me and was constantly in my way, hiding my things and putting all the chairs against the wall, but she was so genial, it was impossible to be cross with her. She had been to England, and was much struck with the magnificence of the Albert Memorial, which she thought just like one of her own Hindu temples, she said, and compared its four-poster to the oriental dome—a high compliment, I thought.

One of the sights of Alwar was the great elephant-carriage, two storeys high, in which his Highness was dragged once a year by four elephants to a Hindu temple a mile or so off. Two long ropes were fastened to the machine behind, dragging as it moved, along the ground, and not even the VOL. II K biggest of the nobles dare go within that length of the Maharajah, except the one privileged to perch behind him, whose office it was to fan him with peacock's feathers to keep the flies off. The musicians went in the lower storey of the carriage.

After a week the big-voiced Major drove me back to the station, and started me for Bhartpur, telegraphing to the Maharajah there to look after me and send to meet me, which he didn't; so I found my way to the bungalow in a country "ekkah" with all my luggage, my feet hanging over the wheels, for I could never learn to sit on my heels like "other people." The ekkah was the common twowheeled conveyance of the country, with a shower-bath top, hung with crimson curtains, under which I have seen as many as half a dozen people packed, all squatting on their heels, and nearly lifting the one wretched little pony off its feet. There are double ekkahs, with two-domed roofs, and a sort of porch over the driver's seat; those are generally drawn by two bullocks—grand animals, with huge humps and coloured horns, one red and one green, or sometimes both alike. Bhartpur had not even a resident Englishman in it, and the Maharajah was in the country; but his bungalow was kept up for travellers, who lodged and boarded the first day there free of expense. It was in the middle of a pretty garden— a pleasant place to pass a day in, except for the excessive dryness and dust all around. The cold of early morning was as strong as the heat at midday. There seemed no dew or moisture of any sort in the air. The plain I had come over looked like a filled-up lake, with groups

of stony mountain heads pushing through its surface, and huge rounded rocks like the granite boulders of Brazil, here probably of some softer stone. When I heard the next morning that a large open carriage and horses had arrived in the night for me, I took for granted it was the carriage sent over from Mathura and I ordered it to take me to Dig (twenty miles); then I found out that the carriage I was in was not from Mathura, but was sent by the Maharajah. It had followed me to the bungalow, and was at my orders as long as I liked to keep it. The coachman did not appear surprised, though his horses were valuable ones.

When I reached that wonderful group of palaces, the guardian was asleep, and they could not find the keys. I was taken to a huge hall which looked very comfortless, all windows and marble; so I wandered downstairs to look at more rooms in another building full of exquisite carving, and suddenly found a big yellow snake in one of them, perfectly motionless, with his head up, looking at me! I was advised to keep in the upper rooms, as these elegant reptiles object to stairs and don't climb up them. Soon the keys were found, and I had the choice of any number of lovely rooms, with marble lacework for windows, and the finest carving on walls and ceilings. A huge tank of green water on one side of my particular palace, full of playful turtles, on the other the most exquisite artificial garden, with more fountains than trees in it. I had come before the provisions, so boiled up my own tea and ate my own biscuits and potted meat, and tried in vain to sketch. There were too many tempting bits, and the architecture was too hopelessly intricate and beautiful for hurry. Five exquisite palaces, and not a soul to speak to; plenty of guardians, who all begged for backshish if I even looked at them. After a time I was told the Seth's carriage and four horses had also arrived in search of me from Mathura.

So I sent the Maharajah's back. The new coachman attached himself to me and made himself useful, giving me hopes of getting some dinner after sun-

set, when some hundred cups of oil were lighted and placed in every doorway of the passages and hall, as well as in a dozen or two of rooms leading to mine, and tall silver candlesticks were lighted in the hall which had the lovely windows. I could almost clasp my fingers round the supporting marble pillars, they were so slender, and the deep tank below glittered in the full moonlight, which made the whole garden look clear as day. But at first, when I came in hungry, I found that rats had eaten my few remaining biscuits and left only some crumbs scattered about the table. I thought I should have preferred a dish of porridge to two hundred spare rooms. Soon after, however, gorgeous servants appeared, carrying in seven silver dishes full of capital food, with champagne, claret, coffee, etc. It was like a scene in the *Arabian Nights*,—even the poor fever-stricken guardian looked happy and gorgeous in a gold and silver livery. I stayed two nights there in the greatest magnificence, but was ashamed to stay longer. If I had had a quiet bungalow and bread and cheese I would willingly have stayed a month, the place was so beautiful.

I drove on to Gobardhan, which is even more picturesque, with many ruined palaces, and a large tank in odd angles and shapes, with marble steps and noble buildings near it. There was also a splendid tomb of the Bhartpur ancestors, which I attempted to draw, a tamarind-tree coming straight through a turret in the foreground having split the building right in half in the process. We met a mounted policeman just before reaching the town, who gave the coachman orders to take me to the Maharajah's own bungalow, and I was to sleep there if I liked; but I didn't, and merely wandered about the place and sketched for a few hours, then went back to Mrs. L.'s hospitable house at Mathura.

Mathura seemed even odder and fresher on my second visit than it did at first, and I went every morning down to the ghat or street, among all the odd people, animals, and buildings, in my friend's carriage, working in peace and no hurry. I found a quiet niche quite on the edge of the ghat from which I could get a good view of the Suttee tower of red sandstone, covered with old carvings and live monkeys, and surrounded by picturesque buildings, with a pretty peep of the Jumna at its foot, plenty of people and sacred bulls crowned with flowers lounging about, turtles disputing with the monkeys on the steps for the food the faithful were throwing them. The street scene I painted also on the spot, sitting in the collector's carriage in the middle of a street as full of people as Bond Street in June! There was a perfect block of ekkahs, bullocks, camels, horses, and people. Such gorgeous people; and now that the mornings were cold they had taken to wearing their bed-quilts over their shoulders and heads, while others went about in suits of kincob.

The "Seth" of Mathura was said to be the richest man in all India. He had a weakness for keeping beautiful carriages and horses and lending them to Europeans, and he had sent over to Dig for me. He came one morning and talked to me by the side of the carriage where I was painting, and gave me a photograph of the great temple he was building at Brindaban. He was dressed in a coat of black velvet over his silk sarong, and had a kincob cap on his head and a red cashmere shawl over his shoulders.

He sent me back straight to Bhartpur, twenty-three miles, with three pairs of splendid horses to relieve one another at different points in the road. From thence the rail took me to Jaipur, where Colonel B. received me most kindly at the Residency—a beautiful oriental house in a garden full of cypress-trees and fine shrubs. The Colonel was a model English gentleman and a great friend of the odd old Maharajah, who came to see him the afternoon after I arrived and made me bring in my Mathura work to show him, though he was nearly blind. He was such a funny little wizened thing, with his long whiskers pulled over the tops of his ears and tied together with his long black hair in a knot behind his head. It was parted on the side of his forehead and a bunch of chrysanthemums stuck in behind, with a lump of diamonds at the top of some strips of red rag which did duty for a turban. I fancied he was proud of his hair and did not like to hide it. He also wore gold spectacles, and was very intelligent. Colonel B. kindly translated all his stories for me. He had never been at Alwar; next neighbours never visited; and it would cost too much, as each Maharajah must give more than the other. One of his slave-girls once went to Mathura and spent three lacs of rupees on the visit! If it cost her so much, what would it not cost him! So he had never been even to Mathura. He had been to Benares, but only as a simple poor pilgrim who begged himself, so that did not ruin him. And he intended to die there, if he knew when the time was coming. He could not escape death, he said, and might as well go the easiest way. If there were any truth in the Ganges leading to Paradise, it was well; if not, it would do no harm.

I liked the odd old man, and he seemed thoroughly to like the Colonel, sitting on the sofa beside him with his hand on his shoulder half the time. He promised to send his biggest elephant in all its most gorgeous attire and ornaments for me to paint the next day. I was told by the doctor that the old man's idea of home comfort was very low. He found him one day in a state of high fever on the bare floor, with half a dozen mongrel dogs on a trestle-bed near him. The doctor told him he must go to bed, and went away to fetch some physic. When he returned he found him in the same room; but the dogs were on the floor, and the old man in the same costume in the dogs' bed.

The streets of Jaipur are all painted strawberry-creamcolour and built at right angles to one another, but the individual houses are most picturesque and oriental in shape, and the stone lacework of the windows is very finely carved and varied in pattern, stone elephants guarding many of the doors. Great fourpost bedsteads stood on the pavement in front of the houses, in which the merchants gossiped while they did their money-lending and gambling. Jaipur is famous for its dyers. One saw the trees (of which there were many in the wide streets and built into the walls) hung with magnificent pieces of crimson, scarlet, pink, yellow, and green calico to dry, with people shaking them about to air. There is a most abundant supply of water, and English brass cocks to all the fountains, which are not in the least beautiful.

The gardens are lovely, with the stony hills in the background. A drive of seven miles through picturesque suburbs and between gardens took me to the foot of the hills, where I had the option of a tonga with bearers or an elephant to take me up the steep road, and on by the side of the lake to Amher, the old capital of the country. It is all now deserted, but crammed with subjects for painting,—fort, palace, temples, tanks, and gates, among bare stony mountains, with distant views of the sandy plain. Near the lake were great india-rubber and banyan trees, with their roots twisted about in all sorts of unexpected places and hanging in long fringes from their branches. It is a grand place, and I could not understand why they ever left it for a low place like Jaipur, where a perpetual war is going on with the encroaching sand-drifts. Gardens and houses are often buried under them in a few hours, as Swiss villages are buried in landslips and avalanches. They are wisely planting great belts of tussock-grass and trees to bind the enemy and keep it off all round Jaipur. The ailanthus seemed particularly adapted for the purpose, and gave good shade too. Jaipur itself is the second largest city of India. I spent one afternoon painting the state elephant in the garden. He was covered with crimson and purple velvet heavy with silver embroidery and kincob. Two golden lions were sitting on the top of his head, his face was covered with silver plates and bells, while on his ears dancing-girls were painted. I wanted to paint him also kneeling down, but he moaned so much over the cramped position that I let him off. All the time he did kneel, his attendants held the gorgeous draperies out like a tent so that they should not touch the ground (four men's work, they were so heavy); the whole was only a few inches off the ground when he stood up, which saved me the difficulty of drawing his legs.

Four miles from Jaipur was a lovely crack in the hills, filled up by a summer palace and some fine houses. The whole way down the steep street was a succession of turrets and arches on the tops of the walls, on both sides alike, perfectly useless, but very elegant, with frescoes, some of them exceedingly well done. Some of the tanks in the gardens were very pretty, with flat edges, over which the water trickled on three sides, making them look like sheets of looking-glass, with the whole border of vegetation exquisitely reflected in them. The whole of Jaipur is lit with gas made from oil. I went one day with Dr. and Mrs. H. and their baby to see the tombs of the Rajahs, Colonel B. sending on an elephant to take us over the sand. He nearly rubbed us off when passing under the banyan-trees, against their huge branches and hanging roots. Mrs. H., who was a highly nervous lady, screamed, and thought the precious baby's eyes would be put out. Some of the tombs are really beautiful, one especially so, with an exquisite series of basso-relievos round it, representing hunting-scenes, all in white marble.

The Brahmin bulls were a great curse in Jaipur. They used to go up to the poor market-people's baskets and eat up everything without even saying "by your leave." They were noble-looking beasts, and everybody (who was anybody) went into mourning when one died. His heir was given, with a cow, to the ruling Brahmin of the place to keep; but bulls do not give milk, so the holy man only kept the cow, turning the bull loose into the streets to support himself as best he could by stealing from the devout Hindus around. In the famine time it was quite scandalous the amount that was consumed by the idle beasts. Colonel B. persuaded the old Maharajah to lock them up and put them on scant rations, thereby causing a small rebellion among the people of the place at the insult offered to the souls of their

ancestors. They swore that famine was caused by the way the sacred bulls were treated, so they were let out again.

When I reached Ajmere I heard at the bungalow that Captain L. had called an hour before, so I drove out to Mayo College, where I found him and his bride most hospitable, and they made me come that same evening to stay. Every other European was in camp. Captain L. had been one of Lord Lytton's A. D.C.'s. He had just married and settled as Head of the New College for young Rajahs, and his honeymoon was barely over. The place was on a sandy plain, surrounded by bare hills, whose tints were glorious at sunset. It was two or three miles from old Ajmere and its lake, but the college interested me too in its way, as an experiment of young Indian education. Nobody was admitted who was not of sufficient rank to make his Maharajah get up to receive him! There were forty pupils, and one of them was himself a Maharajah. He had a separate house, thirty servants, a tutor of his own, and lots of horses, and went out hunting every Sunday. The others were limited to four servants each and one horse. Captain L. did not teach, but only superintended. He said the great thing was to make gentlemen of the boys, and teach them to speak the truth and to be on good terms with one another. They learned lawn-tennis, croquet, cricket, and swimming, and they would no doubt rub off some of the old caste prejudices, but whether they learned much good remains to be proved.

The lake of Ajmere, surrounded by its bare stony mountains, is beautiful, and the desert look of the northern end, combined with the clear blue haze over the water, reminded me of the Dead Sea. All the purest and faintest tints of salmon and lilac were there, and sand came down to the very edge of the water, with great thick banyan-trees here and there, casting the deepest blue shadows on the ground under them. The outlines of the hills are very fantastic, and the highest of them are topped with old fortresses. There are many marble palaces at one corner of the lake. These are now turned into public offices. The

walls dip into the clear reflecting water, having pretty domes and other Oriental ornamentation, and behind them are lovely gardens. The old town is full of picturesque streets and bazaars. One very beautiful building—a Hindu temple—has been turned into a mosque like that of the Kutab, and, like it, is faced with pointed arches, built of horizontally placed stones.

I drove on across the great desert plain to the mountains on the eastern side of the lake, and over them by a fine zigzag pass, for seven miles, down to another lake (the original site of the " Holy Poker," Mr. Fergusson said). It is a very lovely spot, surrounded by elegant buildings of different ages and styles, and is much frequented by pilgrims. The water was clear (in spite of the continual bathing of the faithful), and full of tall lotus stalks, leaves, and seeds. It must be indeed beautiful in summer when the pink flowers are open. The great banyan-trees had twisted their roots in and out of the broken walls and buildings, and seemed to bind them all together, often also causing them to crack from top to bottom by their swelling and growing. I saw a most luxurious Fakir in the road, in a neat little tent about five feet across, sitting on a chetah-skin, with all sorts of beautiful silver ornaments and china on the ground beside him. He was as nearly naked as possible, covered over with yellow ochre and white paint, and wore his hair in long ringlets down to his waist. He was a very prince of all beggars.

The view of the lake in the sunset lights was most lovely, as I came over the top of the pass and sat down to sketch it. The gray-whiskered monkeys came out of the banyan-trees and imitated me—graceful creatures, with long curling tails, and silver-gray coats. As I passed over the road in the morning there was a huge buffalo breathing its last by the roadside. A few bones remained when I passed in the evening, and all the rocks around were fringed with great disgusting vultures digesting—big black birds with evil eyes.

One of the drawbacks to Indian travel

to me were the ayahs. In all Anglo-Indian houses they plagued me, they were so thoroughly useless and without tact. I was perpetually pushing them out of the room. They threw away the clean water and left me without any; they hid all my things; stared like wild cats; rubbed up against my wet paintings; if I gave them anything to brush they did not do it. I never felt safe from their intrusions, and all their picturesque flowing drapery required one hand to hold up, only leaving one to do anything with. Though often told I ought to have an ayah to take about with me, I never saw any good that would have come from the move. Much the contrary.

Captain L. got the native authorities at Ajmere to write on my behalf to the Governor of Chitor for a permit and protection when sketching in that wonderful old ruined city. He drove me over to Nasirabad himself, and arranged with the magistrate to send me a chaprasi and to get me a camelcarriage; then after a cup of tea together in the bungalow, he and his wife drove back and left me to my fate; and at night I started, those old beasts, the camels, preferring to tramp all night and munch all day. The carriage was as long as an English omnibus, with two low wheels, and an upper storey with a roof over it, in which my chaprasi slept. I had blankets hung along the open side to keep some of the cold out, my padded quilt spread on some straw with my trunks for pillows, and a sack full of chopped hay to fill up the entrance-door at the end and keep out the draughts. I slept as well as I usually do, and the camels tramped on slowly from eight at night till eleven the next morning. They did thirty-eight miles, never stopping for more than a few minutes at a time. The same camels went all the way. The very good-natured chaprasi was told never to lose sight of me till he handed me over to some other responsible official. The nights were very cold, in spite of my bagful of hot water, waterproof sheet, and quilt. I had plenty of room to stretch myself at full length, and soft hay underneath to lie upon. The first day I spent in a nice airy bungalow, on a rich plain, with five wells within sight, all working at once, with two pairs of bullocks pulling up the skins of water and filling the irrigation channels, while a great deal of creaking and talking went on round them. There were camp-fires and groups of resting travellers on all sides, constant traffic on the road in front,—some in ekkahs drawn by four bullocks, others were riding camels, or horses, or buffaloes, others walking,—and my own two camels made excellent sitters in the foreground. They were odd creatures. Directly we arrived they had huge pills thrust into their throats, made of some sort of corn and beans mixed; after that they continued to munch chopped hay, and I began to dread their emptying my door-sack before I ceased to want it. Whenever they stood up a man rushed at them, and made them double themselves up again. Their poor noses were horribly torn from the bridle, which was strung through them from side to side; and it was not pleasant to see the way the flies walked in and out of that tunnel.

Cotton was the commonest crop of the country. Women in long blue veils and dresses edged with red were picking it, hidden among its stalks, for it grew as high as themselves. Their arms were nearly covered all the way up with bangles, chiefly made of lacquer. The cornfields were also looking green, which was refreshing after the long desert we had come over, with nothing but euphorbias, and now and then a barbal or acacia-bush, to enliven them.

The second night's journey brought us to Bhilwara, to find the bungalow surrounded by a camp of English artillery, with guns, camels, and even elephants. The chief officer was sitting on the verandah and occupied the room next mine. I insisted on being friendly, though we had not been properly introduced; but a lady from one of the tents rode past, and would not even return my bow! I spent the day drawing their troop of camels being loaded, and saw all the tents packed on their backs, and the soldiers' wives with clean white aprons, arms akimbo, and helmets like their husbands to preserve their complexions, cooking their Christmas dinners, while the jolly English soldiers nursed the babies. I had a great mind to go and talk to them, but felt they might perhaps imitate their betters and snub "such a shabby old thing." At last they all cleared off, and the great vultures came and picked the bones left by the beef-eating sahibs, and I ate my bit of cold mutton and bread and cooked my own tea in my etna, enjoying it as much as most people do mince-pies, plum-pudding, and the "family party" it is part of the English religion to feed with, at Christmastime.

Another night's tramp and I saw the long hill of Chitor before me, arriving about ten o'clock at the bungalow on the plain beneath it.

Before I had time to get my hat off, a most genial English gentleman, Colonel C., was at my door, with his hands full of English letters and papers for me. He said he and his camp were close by, and he had expected me to spend a merry Christmas with him the day before. He was to leave the next day, but before he left he made all sorts of kind arrangements for my stay and future movements, and I had breakfast with a merry party of friends whom the Colonel had invited to spend Christmas with him. The Colonel's clerk accompanied me that first day and showed me the way through fine gates up to the table-land on the top of the isolated hill, which stands like a green island in the great burnt-up plain, quite covered with ruins of palaces and temples. There were two exquisite towers, covered inside and out with the richest ornamentation; and small clear lakes of limestone water, in which were huge crocodiles. How did they get there? In one of the lakes was an island-palace, which was entirely taken possession of by great gray herons and flamingoes—the roof was crowded with them. There were also plenty of bamboos and banyan-trees; custardapples grew like weeds, while a pretty dodder crept over all the bushes, covering them with bunches of white bell-flowers.

The whole hill-top was surrounded by strong walls, towers, and precipices.

At the foot of the steep ascent was a considerable Indian town, and beyond it a broad river, crossed by a noble bridge of pointed arches, approached at either end by a steep incline paved with great stones. The rest of the bridge was quite flat, and paved in the same way, with no parapet. It was so slippery that natives and animals preferred the safer course of wading through the water. The ferry beside the bridge was always crowded with splendid subjects for a figure-artist, the whole making an exquisite picture, with palms and different rich foliage on the banks, the hill behind covered with a kind of scrub, quite purple in its autumn dress, and looking even crimson at sunset: above all the old ruins and towers of Chitor, while great squared stones were strewed about the river's edge and bed. The women of Chitor had peculiar fashions in their dress, wearing black full skirts, with large sleeves, and flowers printed in blotches on them, dark red veils, with broad, black scroll borders, and about half a dozen great black circles on them containing writing. They sewed little silver bells at the edge, round the part which shaded the face. The more I saw of the old city, the more I admired it. One of the gates was richly ornamented, with numbers of elephants in high relief and every possible variety of position, not bigger than my hand. Near this gate was an exquisite group of old Hindu pillars, now used as a stable and black-smith's shop. It was sad to see how the exquisite buildings were neglected, the famous Jain tower having a ficus on its very top, which was steadily loosening the stones with its roots. Before very long it would bring the whole to the ground.

While I was there the Maharajah arrived with all his train on a hunting expedition. The guns announcing his Highness's arrival were fired just as I was packing my things to come down. So I met all his followers climbing the hill—a most gaudy tribe, leading fine horses with finer draperies, elephants with half a dozen impudent dancing-girls in boxes on their backs, and tightly closed palkas containing the real queens, any number of camels loaded with the most common furniture (there was none in the palace), and a lot of mongrel dogs led by the keepers, like wild animals. The Rajput nobles have a real look of "race" about them. The Rana is said to belong to the oldest family in the world, being descended directly from the sun itself. He passed the lake one day where I was painting, with all his hunting procession; but I hid myself behind the rocks, as such grandees have a habit of demanding anything they have a fancy for, and have no idea of being refused, while I had no idea of giving away the sketch I had come so far to make, to a half-civilised human being I had never seen before.

That night I was awakened at one o'clock in the morning by a great thumping at the door and calls for "Mem sahib." I had to get up in the cold, out of my warm quilt, and open the door, to see two tall white bundles and a still taller camel, looking all dislocated, as camels do when tired. A letter was thrust into my hands, and I did not bless them, but shivered and grumbled ungratefully till morning. Those natives never think, they only do what they are told; and of course they thought Colonel C.'s despatch of the utmost importance. In it he had written my exact programme of proceedings for the next day; and when such arrangements are made by great men in India it is wise to keep exactly to them, or one gets into trouble and difficulties. I had one more day on the old hill, and saw his Highness go off on a tiger-hunt, with a long procession of elephants and led horses. As I passed the chief temple the steps were running down with blood from some great sacrifice in his honour, he himself having killed the poor beast with his royal hand. The great feat was to strike off the head with one blow of the sword. I also went to see the most interesting spot in Chitor, the Ghar Mukle, a very holy spring and deep tank, with curious old carved buildings and caves all round it, quite surrounded by big trees. In some of those caves the brave women met a voluntary death by burning, rather than fall victims to the conquering armies of Akbar in 1580. The caves were still bricked up which contained their ashes.

At last Dr. S. arrived with the Maharajah's big open carriage and four, and we started together at a grand pace. He was a most genial little medical missionary, and had just been sent two days farther up the country to doctor a very learned and enlightened native gentleman, who, however, had a bad habit of eating ninety grains of opium daily. He had had a partial stroke of paralysis, but the doctor was trying galvanism and had hopes of his recovery. At Mandsera, where we slept, we heard the bad news that the bullock-cart which Colonel C. had sent away towards Udaipur with his spare camp furniture and baggage when he left Chitor had been robbed by twenty men on camels. Everything was lost; nothing was left but the cart and empty boxes. The china and glass, which they did not care to carry off, they broke. It had been proposed that I should send some of my luggage that way; but when the Colonel saw how little I had he said it could all go with me, and I had a lucky escape. Poor Dr. S. lost his portmanteau and all his clothes. He said drily, "I wonder who's wearing my preaching-gown now." The robbers were said to come from Ulwar.

We had a guard of the famous Bhils, who had sworn never to rob English officials, but to pillage the rest of the world in a decent orthodox manner, clad in our uniform and eating our rice. We galloped over sixty-eight miles, with four fine horses to drag us; and over one particularly bad bit of road we had six. We were delayed more than one hour at a river, waiting for some bullock-carts which had stuck fast in the middle to be got out of our way: the natives as usual in no kind of hurry and perfectly apathetic, Dr. S. working like a true Scotchman. We also stuck in the sandy stream, and broke both springs, over which all the heavy luggage had been tied, in getting out, and with the help of some bullocks were dragged up the opposite bank. We passed large tribes of picturesque gipsies wandering over the great burnt-up plain, with flocks and herds, which it is their particular profession to collect and tend. The women wore fool's caps of brass under their red cotton veils, and dresses heavy with their own coarse embroidery. We stopped one who was working as she walked, and made her show the work to us. She was quite pleased to do so when she saw we meant no harm. The Doctor had a happy, easy manner, and joked with every one.

At the last stage an elephant was sent out to meet him by the greatest noble of Udaipur, whose brother he had been to doctor; but Dr. S. preferred the easy carriage to the slow lounging pace of the more dignified elephant, and we passed through the great gate which fills up a chasm in the hills seven miles from Udaipur (and is the only entrance on that side) just as the last remnant of daylight faded from the sky. The rest of the drive was made by the light of the stars. Even in that light I could distinguish the city glittering like a group of pearls, with the marble palace above it, and the lake behind, surrounded by bare mountains. Then we turned up a sideroad to the Residency—a picturesque mass of Oriental buildings, fitted with English comforts, which I had all to myself, as the Doctor went to his own quarters, in a tent, half a mile off.

The next morning he came early and took me in the grand carriage, which was put at my disposal all the time I stayed, VOL. II F by the Rana, and we drove through the old gates into the city and through the busy bazaars to the grand Jaganath Temple in its centre— one of the richest bits of Hindu work I had seen in India, great elephants of stone guarding the top of the steep flight of steps which lead to it. Then we walked down a steep street to the watergate, and the full glory of the lovely lake burst upon us, with its distant islands of palm-trees and marble palaces, and its nearer orangery surrounded by white marble arches and pavilions with exquisite tracery. Still nearer, palaces, gardens, and gates, all reflected in the still blue waters, and over all the pale salmon-coloured hills, with their lilac shadows, so faint, yet so pure in colour.

The people who were washing and filling their water-jars in the foreground, were covered with the richest colours, every shade of red preponderating. We found the Rana's boat waiting for us, rowed round all the islands, and walked in their lovely gardens and courts. In one of these sixty English women and children had been sheltered, clothed, and fed during the mutiny by the good Rao of Baidah. He went with his drawn sword to the Rana, and said he would kill him if he did not help them; then took an escort and rode off ninety miles to Nimach, and brought them safely back with him. It was a small paradise, but no doubt they thought it a prison. This good old man had a great liking for Dr. S. He came and paid me two visits, looked at my paintings (and held none of them upside down). He was a most noble old man, full of intelligence, and he told me many things I did not know about the different plants whose portraits I showed him. His dress was exquisite, all black and gold, with diamonds and pearls all round his neck, and a snowy turban with a bit of turquoisecoloured silk twisted into it, his long black whiskers and moustache tied back over the tops of his ears. He used to send me a great basket of vegetables and flowers every day, as well as barley-sugar cakes and nuts.

On the island where the sixty women were lodged grew cocoarnuts, palmyrapalms, mangoes, bananas, pomegranates, oranges, and lemons, with plenty of lovely flowers, all kept in the best order, and stone elephants half under the water. At the landing-place the lake was very full, and we rowed up into odd corners and inner lakes, as wild as any in the Highlands of Austria, only inhabited by wild boars and peacocks.

We landed on the mainland, and mounted by steep terraces and steps to the very top of the huge marble palace. No views could be more superb than those from the upper storeys, over lake, city, river, and mountain. The marble lattice-work of windows and balconies was most wonderful. Sometimes it was filled in with coloured glass, which cast lovely tints on the polished white floors

and walls. The Durbar Hall was surrounded by inlaid peacocks in gray and blue, and I wondered if Whistler got his idea from Udaipur. The Rana was building an "English" palace beside the old one—a perfect atrocity of bad taste. He had about two dozen clocks in every room, all telling different time, and in the gorgeous drawing-room two carriage-lamps were hung on each side of the door.

The great Moslem fete of the Muharram took place while I was at Udaipur. The Doctor came and fetched me from the palace (where I was at work), and took me to a room over a gate in the High Street, where the chief banker, his boys and friends, were looking out at the crowd. He was an albino, as fair as any Saxon, though a real Rajput by birth, and a Jain by religion. He had white hair and red eyes, wore a bright emerald-green satin dress, and a red cashmere shawl over his shoulders. There were often fights, and lives were lost at this Moslem festival; but this time all went quietly. The Rana had taken off the most turbulent spirits with him to Chitor, and he was not allowed to come back till some particularly lucky day, ten days after the fetes were over. The streets below became crammed with people; all the housetops were overflowing, and looked like flowerbeds of bright colours. Then the models of the tombs of the Moslem saints were carried past, with extraordinary hobby-camels under them; men carrying long bamboos with garlands of flowers and naked swords hung on them, which they set twirling round and round. They stopped most of the cars under our window, formed circles round some drums, and began a curious dance, meant to represent despair and sorrow at the death of the saints, beating their chests, wriggling and groaning in chorus, and laughing at the same time. Then came some fanatic priests, with long lanky black hair, who went through sham tortures, very unpleasant to look at, though one knew they were only make-believe. The colouring of the whole was marvellous: every shade of red was mixed with black, with a sprinkling of turquoise, dark blue, green, and yellow. I made a sketch of the whole procession winding up the narrow High Street, with the Palace and great Temple against the sky above it. While I was at the albino banker's, a silversmith was sent for to show me some of the native ornaments. One of them was a shield of silver to rest on the back of the hand, or top of the foot, with chains going from it to rings on each toe or finger and a bracelet or anklet attached to keep it in place.

The Prime Minister came to pay me a visit at the Residency. He was a very different man from the Rao, and did hold my paintings topsy-turvy! He had been accused at the death of the late Rana of having conspired with the present one's father to poison him, and was banished from the country, but afterwards recalled, and he was then made Head Man. He was full of civilities, and said he had orders to be "entirely at my command in all things"! (He had an emerald necklace that I longed to command possession of immediately, or loot.) Dr. S. spoke the language of the country with great ease. The old chaprasi who had charge of me and of the Residency was a regular Caleb Balderstone. He used to ask the Doctor "Why you keeps counts always 1 While Mem Sahib is here she is the guest of the Kana. He give sheep, carriage, boat, bread, everything, and ask no questions. Why you want to know how much? English sahib always want to know how much. What good 1"

I found that twelve hours of work daily in boat and on land, without coming home to rest, was too much even for my strength. I had to take a day in the house; when the Rao came again and paid me a long visit, saying he hoped to meet me again, if not in this world, in the next; and the Doctor said that if he were not worthy of a good place there, no Christian was.

At last I left the wonderful city, so full of magnificence, and yet not three hundred years old! For sixty-four miles I was carried on in a great open carriage, full gallop, with four fresh horses awaiting me every twelve miles. After that

the chaprasi Col. C. had sent me, took his departure joyfully to rejoin his master, being fairly tired of the sketching woman. He muttered this sentiment in his tongue as he left me (in the very head-quarters of Thuggism), after having packed me into a bullock-garry.

We crawled on for six hours of moonlight, with two very irregular guards marching near us—sometimes on horseback, sometimes on foot. I was nearly dead when we reached Mrs. B.'s hospitable house at Nimach. She made me swallow a glass of sherry before she even asked me how I was; then gave me a good supper and a tent to sleep in, hurrying me off again in the bullock-cart the next morning, as I found a letter to say a carriage was waiting at Mandsaur. So we dragged on all day at two miles an hour, and reached the town at five. But instead of continuing on the great road, my driver turned off on a voyage of exploration. I got into a rage, and when a Briton does that natives become humble and submissive, and I got a man to show the way. We had to retrace our steps then over a long crazy bridge, which, like many others in India, dipped in the middle to let the winter floods go over it, not under it. It was quite dark when at last we reached the bungalow, and to my horror and despair I found that the carriage and horses sent by the Nawab of Jaora had left a few hours before, after waiting three days for me; so there I wrts in that solitary bungalow with no means of going on, except by bribing the sulky bullock-driver. I nearly cried with vexation and fatigue, but the good-natured Khidmatgar was kind, and managed it all for me, and I crawled on again the next morning. It was a weary mode of proceeding, but I always saw pictures everywhere over the great burnt-up plain. Every now and then we came to huge banyan trees with parties of gipsies encamped under them, encircled by their beasts, and I came upon one strange group of Cabul people in a ring of resting camels—wild Russian-looking men with long hanging black hair, and petticoats under their loose blouses. They did a deal of small trade in those parts, but were distrusted and

hated by the natives.

After eight hours in the bullock-cart we met the Nawab's carriage returning again for me, and the coachman with a flea in his ear for not having waited longer. He was outrageously kind and officious. The good old Khidmatgar had telegraphed of his own accord after I left, from the town two miles off. The carriage seemed to go at railway speed after the bullock-cart.

At last it put me down at a pretty little bungalow in the Nawab's garden, and I was received by half a dozen liveried servants as the guest of the Nawab. Soon after came the interpreter, who put himself entirely at my disposal, and asked if I was a member of Miss Carpenter's Mission. I asked in return if he was. He made a face and a shrug, and gave a very distinct "no." He then said that the Prime Minister was at the palace close by asking permission to come and see me, so I got out a bundle of sketches to set their minds at rest as to why I had come to India. I then showed them to one of the fattest men I ever saw, and we made speeches at one another. He said the Nawab would take me to see the Begum the next day, and send me to Ratlam if I persisted in going so soon. The big man had hardly gone when the young Nawab appeared, aged seven, with his governor and nurse, and all my sketches had to be shown again. I never saw a more thorough little gentleman (all in kincob). He conversed most affably, and quite understood even the small sketches in my pocket-book, pointing out with glee each camel, elephant, or bullock as he came to them, and accepted one of his father's pomegranates most graciously, though he did not eat it. At last they all departed and I had a bath, and tea and rest, and then a capital English dinner. I got a hundred-rupee note changed. I had wondered as I came on if the railway people at Ratlam (who never have small change) would have trusted me if I had come creeping up in my bullock-cart with none to pay for my ticket. This is one of the difficulties of Indian travel: the lack of small change is sometimes very inconvenient.

The next morning the Prime Minister's son and the interpreter took me for a drive round the place in a small open carriage drawn by a pretty pair of white Burmese ponies worth £70 each. The best things they showed me were the Arabs in the Nawab's stables—exquisite little creatures, with fine noses and small ears, grand tails and gazelle's feet. After breakfast I was taken up a set of dirty stairs, only a degree better than a stable ladder in England, on to the roof of the palace, where his Highness received me in a gray shootingjacket, knickerbockers, stockings, and turban to match. He was very ugly, marked with smallpox, and his eyes all nohow. He took me in to the Begum, who was most gorgeous. Her head was hung with great bunches of pearls and diamonds, with ropes of pearls round her neck, and endless bangles of precious stones. She wore the most gorgeous crimson silk train and veil, covered with gold embroidery, and a pea-green satin petticoat. She was older than her husband, with a sharp clever face. She was settled in the middle of a beautiful square carpet, which, with three other chairs, made the entire furniture of the pavilion. Women's faces were looking through half-opened doors all the time. The Begum catechised me most unmercifully, and believed none of my answers, her husband, who spoke good English, playing interpreter. "How old was 1? Was I married Had I any children? Why did I not marry?"—I said I was too old.—" Oh, that did not matter if I had plenty of money," etc.... I was a complete puzzle and comedy to her. The Nawab got enthusiastic on the subject of hunting. He had been out that morning and had a "splendid run" with his harriers, killing a fox and a wild cat. ... The young Nawab came again, and said his A B C to me. He was a dear child, and I gave him the old blunt knife off my chatelaine, to his great delight.

Three pairs of the Nawab's splendid horses took me on. Their coachman was a grand man in white gloves, with a guardsman's cap fastened over one ear, and a perfectly wasplike waist—a great dandy! I had been told the Rajah and Rani expected me at the palace at Rat-

lam, but I was too tired to encounter more native catechising and picture-showing, and escaped by the night train to Indor, where I found a really nice quiet bungalow to rest my weary limbs, for all my internal machinery seemed unhinged, and I felt that if I were taken up like the boy in Pickwick and shaken I should rattle! Indor did not interest me. I took a garry and drove about, then rushed on back to Bombay, where Mrs. R. C. gave me a most kind welcome and put me in the nicest of all the bungalows at Government House, on the furthest point of the cliff, with sea on three sides of me.

The old ayah Miss Bartle Frere has made famous as the story-teller in her *Tales of Old Deccan Days* sat on the doorstep. People there said, the old lady was quite guiltless of any of the stories imputed to her; that the only thing she was famed for was idleness and a habit of getting drunk on Sundays, when she said: "I Christian woman; I go to church." But Sir Richard Temple promised the Freres to keep her, and he did. I liked the old lady, as she never worried me by putting things tidy, but sat picturesquely on the door-step and told me of the wonderful things she had seen. She tried to persuade me to take her on my next travels with me: a female John! bottle and all!

After a few days' rest I took my passage home, then started by rail three hundred and nine miles northward to Ahmedabad. I had only twenty days more in India, and wanted to make the most of them.

My next move was back to Baroda, where Mr. M. met me at the station—a very grand gentleman, but extremely courteous and kind to me. I was sent out to see the lions with a fat native gentleman, who spoke good English, and thought Baroda had but one rival, and that was Jaipur, which city is to native Indians what Paris is to Americans. The streets were full of colour and carving, their overhanging woodwork and balconies being entirely of native design, and little spoilt by European innovations.

We went to see the gold and silver

guns, which had garlands of real flowers round their necks, and were worshipped as gods by the Hindus, incense being burned before them. Then we saw the gold and silver state carriages. One of them had a musical-box fixed between the wheels, which played whenever they turned round. The Maharani must have been the original of the old song, "And she shall have music wherever she goes "! Another carriage had its outer hood covered with matting: this concealed machinery by means of which little jets of water fell on it continually when it moved, to keep it cool in the hot season. All these wonderful vehicles were made in Baroda.

In the afternoon Mr. M. took me to the Palace to see the Maharani, the widow of the late Rajah. She acted as Regent for his adopted son, a lad of fifteen. She was very slight and graceful, with eyes like a deer, the ideal of an Indian lady, wrapped in a veil of carnation-coloured gauze with a green and gold border, a green and gold bodice underneath, and ropes of pearls round her neck. Her little daughter was with her. She came and received us at the door of the great room, like an English lady. I showed her a lot of my paintings, and she enjoyed the monkeys she found amongst them, but did not understand everything. She sent for her jewels, said to be the finest collection in the world—diamonds and emeralds as big as pigeons' eggs, and set transparently. One diamond alone was worth £90,000. There were seven strings of pearls in one necklace, varying from the size of a hazel-nut to a threepenny piece. The Maharani at first sat in an arm-chair as we did, but gradually habit got too strong for her: first one foot, then the other, was tucked up on the seat under her. Her feet were remarkably pretty, with rings on the toes, not too heavy to show their beauty of form.

When I first came to Baroda Mr. M. had thought it impossible for me to go to Champanir; but his wife helped me, and the Maharani lent me her own bullock-cart, in which I jolted through the bright moonlight, over thirty miles of bad road, reaching the ruined gates and walls before daylight. We changed animals four times on the way; all of them were real prize beasts, and snow-white. My expedition was an "affair of the State." I had a most gorgeous tent and bathtent, luxuriously carpeted and furnished, and a tribe of servants to cook and do for me, also a native gentleman to entertain and look after me. He talked beautiful English, and had read Locke, Stuart-Mill, and the *Vicar of TVikefwld.* He was full of philosophy, though very deficient in orthodoxy: a most genial, happy mortal too.

The city of Champanir is a purely Moslem place, originally built by one of the Rajput princes. The fortress on the hill above is a wonder to soldiers. From the perpendicular scarp of the cliffs it was almost impregnable, but is now entirely deserted, except by tigers! I was warned not to linger about after sunset, as they were apt to come close after dark.

I started the second day at daybreak with Mr. M., on seats slung to poles, with no backs and no foot-rest; but on my suggesting the latter, a turban was taken off and untwisted, and the stuff slung between the poles as a stirrup for my feet. My native friend sat after his fashion on his own heels. The road up the hill was wonderful, passing through at least a score of curious old gates and along natural ledges of rock hanging over perpendicular precipices. Halfway up we stopped to see the old granary, with five-domed rooms; much of the ascent being a staircase cut in the solid rock. When we reached the great flat top it was strewn all over with small Hindu temples of the richest stonework, but all tumbling about as if they had been the victims of earthquakes. Above that rose the upper mountain—a sheer perpendicular scarp, with a most lovely marble temple and two lantern towers on its summit. It was approached by a steep flight of steps cut in the solid rock, with two pretty lakes at their foot. The views over the great blue plain, distant sea, and hill-country, were extensive and lovely, and I was quite sorry when the time came to descend.

Many pilgrims were going and coming to the temple of the goddess (wife of Siva). They all brought cocoa-nuts for a fakir to crack under her shrine—in a miraculous manner, of course. The steep black limestone steps were bordered with exquisite little temples of Buddha and the gods. As we descended the lower hill we turned aside to see the King's Palace, which was four storeys high, with a single room in each, opening on a balcony, all excavated and carved out of the solid rock, with much ornamentation and domed ceilings. The windows and balconies hung over a sheer precipice of a thousand feet, only approached by the steepest of stairs of eighty steps, each over a foot high, from the hill above.

My friend the vakeel got very tired. He was, like all wellto-do natives of India, far too fat for locomotion; but he was a remarkable man, with most original ideas and thoughts. He said he had the power of hypnotising himself by concentrating his thoughts on one subject, and could then understand the deepest things.

The mountain we had been up must have been quite 2000 feet above the sea. When I asked him the height, he said, what a pity he had not brought a tape to measure it! and I found he had never heard of aneroids, so I promised to send him one, and have since done so. Strange that one who had read and thought so much should have no other idea of measuring height than by a bit of tape!

My journey back to Baroda was not without its dangers. Once we stopped, and I saw my guardian and the two mounted police and four odd running men with torches all drawn up in a row in front of my bullocks, which shied right round as two small donkeys trotted out of the jungle! And the drawn swords, bows, and arrows were put out of the way again, and my last chance of seeing a tiger was gone too.

At Baroda at sunrise large employment was prepared for me. First came the five gold and silver guns, drawn by noble bullocks with gilded horns covered with kincob and bangles, and a company of native artillery to assist the native artist to stare at me. Then came the Maharani's gold carriage, with silver wheels and gorgeous bullocks, quite hidden in silver draperies. Then the two State elephants, painted all over, carrying about £5000 worth of ornaments on their backs: all of them had to be drawn. I was very nearly dead when dusk came.

Before I left Baroda I received a letter from Major Nutt, saying he expected me to cross by the next steamer from Surat to Bhaunagar, where I should find the carriage of the Maharajah to take me over the eighteen miles to his house on my way to Palitana. At Surat I invested largely in the beautiful sandal-wood and ebony carved boxes, and had a perfect fair in the judge's house.

The steamer was a purely native vessel, but the Muhammadan captain was very kind to me. We started at four in the bright moonlight, but stuck in the mud at the mouth of the river, and did not reach Bhaunagar till five in the evening. I was met, on landing, by the Prime Minister and all sorts of officials. One fat A.D.C. of the palace, who talked good English, put me into a nice open carriage, and gave me much talk on local subjects.

The drive on to Palitana was not interesting, except from the distant view of that curious twin-hill of temples, which grew nearer and nearer, till at last I was put down at a grand painted palace at its foot, and taken up to the top storey through a big Durbar Hall full of gaudy chairs, sofas, and chandeliers, with a grinding organ, and vases of artificial flowers. I had a small army of liveried attendants, who employed themselves in admiring their own faces in the innumerable looking-glasses around them. The glass and china were all engraved with the family crest—a peacock with a flag in its mouth....

About one o'clock the minister came back with the two young Rajahs. Their trousers were of orange silk, made very tight, and they had some dozen yards of kincob ribbon wound loosely round their heads. One wondered how it kept in shape at all. They wore regular ploughboy English boots, with the orange silk tucked into their tops. They were both hideously ugly, but talked English, and held my drawings topsy-turvy. They "hoped they did not disturb my ladyship," and departed.

We were taken up the hill on two square trays suspended on bamboos. The whole way is a steep ladder of stone, but the men never seemed tired. The hill is divided into two summits. The valley between them is entirely covered with temples of all sizes and ages. Seven years ago there were four thousand statues of Buddha; now there are many more. Most of the temples are of dark gray stone; some are of marble. The next day I returned at daylight alone, with my bearers and a chaprasi. A room over one of the gates was got ready for me to rest in; but I had no time to rest, though very weary, and, after swallowing a few mouthfuls of food, wandered out to work again.

There were crowds of people that day on the hill, red being the preponderating colour. They looked like a long garland of flowers against the hillside, climbing the steep steps. The drawing was most complicated, and no shade was to be got where I wanted it. I felt thankful as I descended the hill for the last time that I should have no more temples to puzzle me, but it was a glorious spot, with wide distant views of the plain and sea beyond its temples. All the way down there were little temples every few hundred yards, like the stations of a Sacro Monte in Italy, with banyan trees shading them, and tanks of water.

When I got back to Songarh I found the whole place in commotion. The first agricultural show ever seen in the country was going on, and I accompanied Major N. to the opening lecture, in a big tent, and had the honour of sitting next his Highness of Bhaunagar—a good-natured fat boy of twenty, with a fascinating diamond necklace. He said in English: "Will you kindly come and spend three days in Bhaunagar? I hope you will be so good. I think you will be glad to see it; it is very good there." On the other side of the Major was his Highness of Palitana, my late host, with his two sons and a little girl. He was certainly the most hideous person I ever

saw, with great goggle eyes. He wore the simplest white dress and no ornament. The two Highnesses did not speak or visit, and had a hereditary feud, which had lasted for generations (like true next-door neighbours in more civilised lands). But that day a peace was made by the genial Englishman between them. Palitana xi *Agricultural Show at Songark* 79 asked Bhaunagar to "drink opium out of the palm of his hand," to which the other (who knew European ways) demurred, but offered to shake hands, when Palitana drew back, thinking it a trick or a newfangled notion; but after a while he consented, and they agreed to write to one another, and paid each other formal visits in their tents that afternoon for the first time.

It was an odd sight, that tent full of strange figures of all races and ranks, listening to an Englishman lecturing on "Soils," not one word of which they understood. Then an interpreter read the translation, and I wondered if they understood it any better. After this we departed, gold umbrellas and all.

His Highness of Bhaunagar came and wandered about the rooms like a tame Newfoundland dog, looking at pictures, and seemed quite at home. Then we all went to the show under the flowering mango-trees.

The horses were superb, of the purest Arab and other races: the king of all was of the Kathiawar breed, with little ears which met over the top of his head in an arch, and a stripe down his back like a zebra. He was a light chestnut, with a wild waving mane and tail of silver: I never saw any creature so full of grace. He pawed the ground and snorted, yet was perfectly gentle. He gained the first prize, and Palitana's noble Arab the second; but neither of the great men would take the money, giving it over to increase the next prizes.

There were some most extraordinary buffaloes, with overhanging foreheads, which nearly hid their eyes, and low curling horns. They were only to be found in Bhaunagar's stable, and were kept for milking. There were groups of camels with their young wild Arab drivers, and most noble bullocks, goats,

cocks and hens, and Major N.'s donkey— a perfect beauty and without a rival in Kathiawar.

It was funny for us two women, wandering about with the gorgeous princes, and all their strange wild people, including the very dirtiest and poorest.

Young Palitana in the orange silk trousers wanted me to draw his father's famous Arab, but I might as well have tried to draw an angel! He then offered to send it across in the little steamer with me to Surat, so that I might draw it all the way! But even then I said I could not do it, which he did not believe a bit, but thought me simply disobliging, for which I was sorry.

I was driven back to Bhaunagar after the Maharajah half the way, and smothered in his dust; then he ordered me to go first, which was a great relief. The next day I saw the famous horse again, and all his descendants, with the same arching pointed ears. They were cantering about as wildly as possible, but let us go up and pat them, seeming quite conscious of our admiration. We went into the stables and saw still younger ones with their mothers, all having the same characteristics. Then we paid a visit to the famous elephant which had been brought up with a goat, and could not bear to see any one touch his friend or even her two kids. He pawed the ground, threw up his trunk, and roared with rage till she was free again, then stroked her with his trunk, and pushed the hay and green stuff towards her, allowing the little kids to walk over his feet, when he seemed perfectly happy. He and their mother had been on those terms for seven years.

The Maharajah was doing some good things for his capital, building a fine hospital and a grand tank outside the town; also a country palace for himself, the outside ornamented with beautiful illustrations of the native fruits and flowers in terra-cotta medallions.

On my return to Surat I took a few days' rest with a kind Irish doctor and his family. Here I saw some common snake-charmers, who came one morning and showed their skill under the porch of the house, with no appliances beyond a few rags and old baskets like strawberry pottles (flat). They had five cobras with huge hoods, which sat upright on their own coiled tails, and danced their heads to the magic pipes of their charmers.

The mango trick they also performed. All the trees around were dried up and in their winter foliage, but the conjuror scraped some of the dust on the ground into a heap, planted a mango kernel, covered it for a few moments with one of the baskets, then showed a young seedling plant with two dewy leaves; covered it again, then showed it with four longer leaves. Then again and again till it stood a yard high with a young fruit on it. I could see no appearance of joining or artificiality in it. It has puzzled wiser people than myself for centuries, so why should I even try to understand it?

Again I returned to Government House at Bombay for two days' shopping and packing. The last morning that wonderful man Sir Richard Temple returned before daylight, after three months' absence and perpetual movement from place to place. He was often on horseback for forty miles a day, then talking and writing all night, never knowing what fatigue was.

That morning after his arrival he sent in at 6.30 for me to bring my sketches on to the verandah, and employed himself in looking over and criticising them till the second bell rang for breakfast. After that he wrote me a list of all the generals and ex-governors of India, whose acquaintance he wished me to cultivate on my return home. It seemed as if he never could accumulate enough work for his superfluous energy to accomplish.

On the 24th of February 1879 I went on board my old friend the P. and O. ship Pekin again, and, thanks to the kindness of its officers, got a good cabin to myself, and had a calm voyage to Aden, where the colours seemed more lovely even than my remembrance of them, and everything about it VOL. If G attracted me as before. Those wonderful young savages with orange mops on their heads, produced by covering them

with clay and then baking them, how amphibious they were! rolling about with their tiny canoes in the clear water like seals. I had written home some time before leaving India for a fur-cloak and a great parcel of new books, which arrived just at the right time, and I had quite an agreeable three weeks of rest. I also sewed 2000 beetles' wings on some silk to trim some future dress with, and found it a most lasting and entertaining bit of work, the colours being even more marvellous than the sea at Aden, and every wing taking three stitches. It was barely finished when I entered the Channel. Until then we had very tolerable weather, but that last night some big English waves greeted us most unkindly and washed right over the deck. I heard lamentations on all sides, as the smart clothes, just shaken out for landing in the next day, were soaked with salt water, which ran in under the doors and down the staircases.

Cold was the one enemy I dreaded, and I met it in the steam-launch which took us up Southampton Water the next day. What an icy wind it was! I gave my keys to some man on board who said he was an agent, just caught the train, and reached home with my little bag in my hand on the 21st of March 1879, leaving luggage to follow the next day. It was very luxurious being again at home and amongst all my kind friends, but I found the perpetual task of showing my Indian sketches very wearisome. Every friend brought or sent other friends, and so many were interested in India that my tongue got no rest from telling the same old stories.

At last I hired a room in Conduit Street for July and August, and General M'Murdo most kindly helped me to start an exhibition there. This paid two-thirds of the expenses by the shillings taken at the door, and the remaining third I thought well spent in the saving of fatigue and boredom at home.

While on a visit at Aldermaston I met Mrs. Ross, the daughter of my old friend Lucie Duff Gordon, and the exact repetition of her mother in appearance, voice, and manner. She asked me to come and see the vintage at Castagnolo,

six miles from Florence, on an estate belonging to the Marchese Stufa, which she and her husband managed. I had never seen the Italian vintage, and promised to go after the end of my London exhibition, stopping on the way to pay a visit to my sister and John Addington Symonds at Davos am Platz in Switzerland, to which place he had been driven in search of health three years before. The experiment had answered, and he could enjoy an out-of-door life and take long walks, as well as follow his much-loved hobbies of book-making and studying, with far less fatigue than he had done elsewhere. But it seemed extremely doubtful if he could ever live anywhere else. I found the ground white with snow when I arrived in the beginning of September. The cold did not agree with my old body as it did with the invalids, and after three days of discomfort my sister and her husband drove down the lovely valleys to Tiefenkasten and Thusis with me, and started me over the Spliigen.

A few days spent at the Villa d'Este in the genial warmth of the lovely Como lake soon restored me. Then my old friend Edward Lear came down from the Monte Generoso, where he had been living in an hotel full of uncongenial English. He persuaded me to leave the rail at Monza and take a drive with him up to Monte Civita, where there was a new summer-hotel, as yet undiscovered by the travelling English. Laughing and sunshine did more than any doctor's physic could have done to drive off the remains of my late illness. Before that day was over I saw Milan Cathedral again, rosy in the sunset. The next day we separated: he to San Remo, I to Florence.

Mrs. Ross gave me a warm welcome in the strange old rambling villa of Castagnolo. Her husband was at Aix les Bains, the Marchese in attendance on the King and Queen of Italy. The vintage was unusually late, so I had plenty of time to enjoy the beauty of the grapes, hanging on their long branches, festooned from tree to tree or over the shady pergolas in the gardens. There were many species. The Isabella or

Strawberry-Grape, with white lining to its leaves, which is found apparently wild in America, was the most delicious of all to my taste.

Mrs. Ross superintended the whole vintage herself, spending day after day among the vats and presses, noting every load of grapes that came into the yard, and every barrel which was carried into the cellar, singing and joking with the men in their own patois and keeping all in good-humour.

In the evenings we had a great deal of national music. Mrs. Ross had never been taught, but, having real genius, had "picked it up," literally by ear, from the peasants round her. Whenever she heard a song she fancied in the street or field, she bribed or coaxed them to sing it over and over, while she wrote the words down, and found out the modulations of the air by ear on her guitar. In this way she acquired a collection of national songs of rare beauty and character, singing them like the natives with a pathos or humour which could make myself and many other fools cry or laugh as she pleased. Surely this power implies more real genius than the endless weariness of the "Music of the Future" which wise men sleep over! All the neighbours seemed to play the guitar at Castagnolo; they used to stroll into the old hall and join in the general chorus. Count Marco was a well-known character, who had turned his old Florentine palace into a bric-a-brac shop, and he had a fat old sister, the Contessa Julia, who lived close by, and used to drive her little daughter in a small donkeycarriage to mass at the chapel attached to the house every morning—a carriage and donkey so small that it was a wonder, when the two high-born ladies were fairly tucked in, that the little beast was not lifted off his feet. There was an old priest of high descent who lived by the chapel and had a bridge across to the upper storey of the villa. He used to enter down the great staircase with noiseless steps in a most ghost-like manner, take up his guitar, and join in the general noise, with a powerful nasal tenor voice enough to frighten everything ghostly out of the

place at once.

No country is more enticing than Italy, and I narrowly escaped the folly of hiring the Contessa Julia's villa for eighteen pounds a year furnished! I turned home, however, staying a few days with General and Mrs. M'Murdo on their lovely olive terraces at Alassio, and going from thence to spend a day with Mr. Lear at San Remo. The laughing humour was over, and he was very grave, but had promised to avoid his great grievance if I came, and did so, showing me all his wonderful sketches of India, making me eat pellucid periwinkle soup, mulberry jam, and every other luxury only Mr. Lear could think of, till at last, as the train was moving off, he looked in at the window and moaned out lugubriously, "Hasn't somebody been good not to mention the Enemy all day /" I went round by Geneva to see my sister's little girls at their school; saw, too, the view of Mont Blanc from the high ground north of the lake, and thought it quite showed its relative height, compared with the Himalayan giants I had so lately seen. At Geneva the distance from the snow is about the same as from Narkunda, for instance, yet the depth of the gray distance here is slight in comparison with the height of the snow-peak beyond.

CHAPTER XII SECOND VISIT TO BORNEO—QUEENSLAND—NEW SOUTH WALES

Among the criticisms of my paintings in Conduit Street was one in the *Pall Mall Gazette,* which suggested that the collection of botanical subjects should find their ultimate home at Kew. I kept this idea some time in my head before acting on it; but having missed a train at Shrewsbury one day and having some hours to spare, I wrote off to Sir Joseph Hooker and asked him if he would like me to give them to Kew Gardens, and to build a gallery to put them in, with a guardian's house. I wished to combine this gallery with a rest-house and a place where refreshments could be had— tea, coffee, etc.

Sir Joseph at once accepted the first part of my offer, but said it would be impossible to supply refreshments to so

many (77,000 people all at once possibly on a Bank Holiday), mentioning, too, the difficulty of keeping the British Public in order. I asked Mr. Fergusson, the author of the *History of Architecture,* to make the design and manage the building for me, which he did to the end with the greatest kindness and carefulness. I chose the site myself, far off from the usual entrance-gates, as I thought a resting-place and shelter from rain and sun were more needed there, by those who cared sufficiently for plants to have made their way through all the houses. Those persons who merely cared for promenading would probably never get beyond the palm-house. There was a gate and lodge close to my site for those who drove there straight, and though that gate was kept shut then, I hoped to get it opened by means of the *vox populi* in due time—perhaps not in my lifetime. I also obtained leave to build a small studio for myself or any other artist to paint flowers in at any time, as there was no quiet room in the gardens in which a specimen could be copied, away from the sloppy greenhouses and traffic of visitors.

One day, after arranging all this, I was asked by Mrs. Lichfield to come and meet her father, Charles Darwin, who wanted to see me, but could not climb my stairs. He was, in my eyes, the greatest man living, the most truthful, as well as the most unselfish and modest, always trying to give others rather than himself the credit of his own great thoughts and work. He seemed to have the power of bringing out other people's best points by mere contact with his own superiority. I was much flattered at his wishing to see me, and when he said he thought I ought not to attempt any representation of the vegetation of the world until I had seen and painted the Australian, which was so unlike that of any other country, I determined to take it as a royal command and to go at once. Mrs. Brooke persuaded me to return with her and the Rajah to Sarawak, and make a half-way rest there; so I joined her party on board the *Sindh* at Marseilles on the 18th of April 1880, and arrived at Singapore on the 15th of

May, after an agreeable voyage in that most excellent French steamer in which I had once returned from Ceylon.

I had secured one of the few small single cabins before leaving England, but as I found it was just over the end of the screw, I appealed to the French manager at Marseilles to change it, telling him there would be almost too much music just between the pianoforte and the screw, to which he replied, "Ma foi! yes; I do not myself object to music in moderation, when it is lively and not too long, but in that case, and all the way to Singapore, ma foi!" and he gave me the best cabin in the ship all to myself. A joke was often my most useful friend in travelling alone, helping me far more than any quantity of money (or men) could. The Rajah and Rani had a regular suite of apartments on deck, and suffered in consequence, as they had to sit on each side of the French-speaking captain, apart from their less distinguished friends, while I had the good fortune to sit at meals next the most genial and talkative of Colonial magnates, Judge S., and used to pass my days on deck stitching and gossiping with Mrs. F. She told me a good story of her mother, who was extremely fat and fashionable, and wore only a strap over her shoulders of an evening. The old cannibal king of Fiji, when staying with them at Sydney, used to stroke that great arm and say, "Beautiful! beautiful!" to Mrs. F.'s great disgust and horror; for he was thinking of its taste, not its looks, the arm being the choicest morsel of human meat! The Rani was chaperoning a young girl to join her sister at Sarawak—a young lady with big eyes and an astonished expression of face, with marvellous ribands and furbelows. She sat beside the second officer, who did his best to entertain her, after this manner: "Vous aimez le poisson, Mademoiselle?"—" Wee! Warte 1″ Then he got the dictionary, and after some time of anxious study, "You like die feeshe, Mees?"—"Fish? Why, yes! Wee! of course!" and the eyes opened even bigger than before, and there was a long pause until he had mastered another English question. A German merchant

of Siam sat on the other side of me and pretended to admire Wagner's music. He said he was disappointed in the music of London, and thought the Philharmonic Concerts bad. I said the orchestra might be better, but the Popular Concerts were the most enjoyable of any; there one could hear Joachim, Piatti, and Strauss. 'Ach! Strauss! that is the real music, his valses are divine!" he interrupted me (and I believed less than before in his devotion to Wagner).

A refreshing drive on shore at Galle, and the sight of some old friends, including the original of all monkeys on his pole, then another week of sea, and we were at Singapore, where big natives, Chinamen, and other grandees, under umbrellas, greeted the Rajah; and he was told that all the new furniture he had sent on in advance was utterly smashed, and that his two best ponies were dead. He took it all most philosophically and good-humouredly, but when his chimney-pot hat was found crushed in the cabin the Rani said, "C. was quite awful and dangerous!" We had one night in the barrack-like hotel, and then a friend lent them a most lovely bungalow some three miles out of the town, where they kindly took me also, and I found a shady lane close by with an old cinnamon and a nutmeg-tree to work at in the early morning, and plenty of lovely flowers in the garden. Singapore is surrounded by pretty villas and gardens, each perched on its own little hill, and none more than 200 feet above the sea.

We had a policeman at night to beat a gong and show that he was awake, and all the other villas had the same, so that sleep was difficult at first in Singapore. One night a great mass of the roof fell with a crash close to my room, and the Rani and her nice English "Sarah" rushed in, much disgusted to find no thieves, but only the work of ants or damp; the Rajah smiling benignly and not even troubling to look, as he knew he had himself fastened all the staircase doors before going to bed. Such men are aggravating!

We were near the beautiful Botanical Gardens, and used to take a stroll there

in the cool evening, or sit and hear the band and scandalise our neighbours in the orthodox manner of the place. The ground-orchids were magnificent in that garden, with flower-stalks as high as myself. There are also a good many animals and birds; amongst the former a huge ape, who put his long arm through the bars of his cage without any warning and grabbed hold of anything he fancied with irresistible force. He only got the button of my umbrella from me, but had quite lately seized the watchchain and locket of a German gentleman, dipped them in the water, and then munched them slowly, while the German danced round and round like a madman, lamenting the portraits of his beloved ones on the other side of the world, helpless to save them, till a native seized one of the hanging ants' nests from a tree and flung it at the brute, which dropped the mangled treasures with a savage growl as the small creatures revenged on his body the injury done to their house. Those nests were as big as two heads, made of leaves sewn together most cleverly. One hung close to our bungalow on an alamanda bush, and made a pretty picture, surrounded with its bunches of lovely yellow bells. The Poinciana trees were in full glory of scarlet bloom, and I shall never forget looking down on the top of one from the verandah of Mr. R., the consul, at night, a group of lamps throwing down their full light upon it. I never saw any colour equal to that mass shining in the darkness: to see it was worth enduring the heat within.

Those long European dinners, full dress, with glaring lamps, are a mistake so near the Equator. We endured several. The new Governor and his family were most homely, kind people, with eight children, just come from Tasmania; and Lady W. took us to see all the younger ones sleeping in uncomfortable corners about that architectural but illarranged Government House. Poor things, how they were being eaten up by mosquitoes, whilst dreaming uneasily of the cool antipodes! Singapore was delightful for flowerpainting in one's shirt-sleeves, but not for so-called society. The Dutch and Germans were much more sensible about this, and did not attempt it. We were not sorry to escape in the Rajah's gunboat, the *Alarm,* to Sarawak, where we arrived on the 25th of May.

As we entered the great landlocked bay which hid the mouth of the big river, the rosy clouds were reflected in it, and the two guardian hills and wooded islands were golden in the sunrise. These hills (2000 feet high) are apparently the mere tops of mountains piercing through the rich swampy deposit of a more modern age. On one of them, Santobourg (covered with the densest forest to its very top), some giant figures of Buddha had recently been found, engraven on the surface of the rock behind the tangled creepers, of which no legend existed. The lower coasts of the bay are fringed with casuarina trees. After passing the hills, the river goes winding on through dense mangrove-swamps and nipa palms, till richer land is reached, with all the trees the Malay loves, and now and then a house on stilts half hidden among them; bread-fruits, bananas, cocoa-nuts, areca, and sago-palms crowding one another out. In about three hours we reached the two miles of almost continuous habitations and gardens which lined both sides of the river up to Kuching. At every ladder and platform in front of them were crowds of natives letting off guns and crackers: one could scarcely see the gay dresses and flags for the smoke. On arrival, the long canoe the king of Siam had given to the Rajah was paddled by twentytwo men over a space not much longer than itself, bringing his young secretary in a tremendous cocked-hat and gorgeous uniform to convey us to the steps of the landing-place, where we had to shake hands with all the officers, also in gorgeous uniforms, with fat Chinamen, Malay, Dyak, and other wonderful people, passing through triumphal arches made of palm branches and exquisite creepers, past the terrible music of the Rajah's band into the welcome shade of the comfortable Astana, and felt at home again in its large airy rooms.

To me it was even more attractive than before; for the plants in the garden were older and larger. Some of the views might be lost by that, but the whole effect was even more luxuriant. It was still surrounded by its rim of impenetrable forest-tangle, and the great trees made the most harmonious background to the gorgeous shrubs and creepers, on all but one side—that which bordered the ever-moving river, covered with its busy semi-amphibious people, in every variety of canoe or boat—some, long hollowed trunks with fifty Dyak paddlers, some, such tiny nutshells that the figures they contained seemed to sit on the water, with nothing but their pointed hats for clothing. After dinner we crossed the river, and walked in procession through the long bazaars, where they threw down gay cloths and carpets for us to step on, and squirted eau-de-Cologne and rose-water into our eyes, to show their genuine pleasure at seeing their ruler back again. Over our heads were curious Chinese lanterns, like queer fish with goggle eyes. It is wonderful that we were not burnt alive as we walked through all the odd specimens of fireworks. One was a hobby-horse all hung with white lights, having its tail and mane of yellow flames in perpetual movement. It was trotted along by four men hidden beneath it, immediately preceding the Rani and myself, who led the procession. On our return we were taken to seats in front of the Court-House, and a table of Chinese dainties was set before us, but not intended to be eaten: it was a mere symbol of hospitality and welcome. A long display of Chinese fireworks followed, an artist having been imported all the way from the Celestial Land to make them expressly for this occasion. It was a curious sight to see that strange mixed crowd in the strong light and shade, with the palm-tops waving over them— overdressed Europeans, Dyaks with no dress at all, gorgeous Malay men, and even women (for the Rani had broken down many of the Muhammadan barriers to their appearing in public), and the ubiquitous and practical Chinaman with his pigtail. One of the prettiest things was a tree which gradually lighted itself

up, the performance ending with two long dragons covered with silver scales and vomiting fire, which floated about in the wind for a long while. The whole must have been most costly; but all semi-civilised races delight in playing with fire, just as children do: they think it drives off the evil spirits. Crackers, squibs, and rockets continued the game more or less for three days, and looked pretty from the verandah as they were reflected in the broad river between us. The Rajah was as happy to be at home again as his people were to see him after his two years in England. His dominion got more prosperous every year. The last census was about 200,000, the income £45,000, the country about the size of Scotland; and this strange mixture of races submitted cheerfully to the mild despotism of one simple Englishman, assisted by twenty young men called "The Officers," none of them remarkable in any way; the whole machinery apparently hanging on the prestige left by that great man, Sir James Brooke, which even years had not diminished. In the quiet mornings I found delightful studies close by. My first was a boat-house, with trees and palms half-buried in the water at high tide. Children were running in and out, regardless of crocodiles, with no clothing but their necklaces, pouring the water over their heads with monkey-cups (pitchers of the nepenthes). They were full of fun, and such lovely round shiny little mortals. Why don't real artists go to paint them *!* The Malays are a gentle race, and many of the servants at the astana were with Sir James when he lived in the building now used only by the cows. How he would have wondered at the state and luxury kept up by his successors!

There was a state dinner of twenty-four one night, and four women besides ourselves at it. The last time I was in Sarawak there was only one. The Rani had covered the whole centre of the table with pitcher-plants enough to make the fortune of an English nurseryman, but they were not appreciated in their native country. The party was quite funereal in its solemnity; the beautiful hostess blazing with diamonds, her head so fixed in a ruff that she could only move it revolvingly; the other ladies equally uncomfortable; the thermometer 100! I got into disgrace by preferring to sit and look at the moonlight and lights of Kuching reflected in the water, on the cool verandah, instead of joining the dismal circle round the glaring lamp-lit drawing-room, with its splendid straightbacked chairs carved with Rajah-like coats of arms, and leather cushions which seem to invite the white ants. That river always attracted me, making me forget all manners. One evening I watched a man (quite clothesless) throwing his net from the smallest of canoes, and an infant of four years old paddling at the other end. Why did not the thing tip up? I could not understand; or why the man did not throw himself out as well as his net. His movements were so perfectly graceful and secure, far better worth studying than the everlasting Venuses and Apollos of so-called "High Art."

Whilst I was painting a view of the astana behind a hedge of great sweet gardenia-flowers, a group of children brought me a big lizard, leading it by a string, to look at—a smooth, fleshy, harmless thing which they called a crocodile. They would have made a good tropical group, with their great laughing eyes and no shyness. I was taken one day for a drive by the Rajah over the fifteen miles of road he has made on the Kuching side of the river. At present the road leads nowhere, and goes through no place; but Chinamen are expected to follow it, and to build themselves villages, and it does to exercise the horses on (which are about as useful in Sarawak as they are in Venice, the highroads being all water, with this one exception). We saw much fine forest, and I succeeded in getting at last a specimen of the clerodendron, with orange leaves or bracts, one of the most singular flowers I ever saw. I had seen yards of the orange leaves, but never a green one till then, and it unfortunately grew in such inaccessible places that I could not get at it myself.

Mr. B. again took me up the river in his steam-launch to Busen, and on with the tram and a pony to Tegora, through that wonderful forest, with its dangerous bridges. One broke in two just as my pony scrambled over, the strut under it having been washed away by a late swollen stream. I was on foot, so came to no harm. There were no flowers, but the coloured leaf-chains and rattans clinging to the trees were most lovely. I spent a day in a canoe, painting the red-stemmed Palawen trees, which grew only on that river. The trunks were quite flame-coloured in the sun; the bark hung in tatters from them, and from the branches, as on the eucalyptus. The leaves were like those of the laurel, with brown young shoots, but I could get neither seeds nor flowers. There was a white-stemmed variety also, and the wild pines hung suspended from its branches, like gigantic spiders or wasps overhead, by threads as fine in proportion as their webs. The old quicksilver mine of Tegora was at rest, as they had missed the lode for some time, and were anxiously probing in all directions, hoping to come to it again. The chairs in the bungalow had also dwindled down to three decrepit specimens; but I used to sit on the steps and watch the sunset, as I did before, gossiping with the two tired men there.

Mr. E. had a young orang-utan, only half-a-year old, and very human in its way. It had a bit of cloth which it wrapped round its body, and if strangers came in it dragged it half over its face, pretending to be shy, as the women of the country did. In front of the bungalow at Tegora was a group of tall trees, left standing alone from the original forest, which was gone. They were incredibly white, and without a knot or a branch for full one hundred feet, bleached by the sun, which they had never seen before their companions were taken from them. One had to go far off to see both bottom and top at once of these gigantic poles, which were straight as ships' masts, with rope-like lianes tying them together, as ropes tie the masts of ships. The two under-officers of the mines asked leave to come and see me and my paintings again.

They always called me Mr. B.'s sister (he said), and had often asked him when he was going to bring her up-country again. Such strong sensible Scotchmen both of them, it was no slight sensation shaking hands with them.

I began my return journey badly, for my pony displaced a plank in one of those horrid bridges, took fright, ran away, and tumbled me off, the Rani's new saddle having no off pommel, and I lost my spectacles in a bank of fern. My friends too were frightened to let me risk the other slippery bridges, and got a canoe with a mat and pillow, and two Dyaks to paddle and push; so I gained once more the pleasure of shooting the rapids, lying on my back and looking at the tangled branches overhead, with their wonderful parasites; sometimes shooting swiftly down through deep-green water and white foam, while the men clutched at the rocks and tree-stumps; sometimes being almost carried by them over a few feet of water. Once we stopped to cut through a tree which had fallen across the river only a few hours before; and they hacked away with strange knives—half swords, half hatchets. These men were gentle creatures, with soft voices, and skins as muddy as the banks. I knew not which was more lovely to look at—the tangled banks, or the lacework overhead with natural bridges of lianes and fallen trees. At last we reached the place where Mr. B. was throwing in big stones to make a dry landing-place for me; after which came a pleasant ten miles of forest-ride and no accidents, and I was left to stay three days with the young manager of the antimony mines at Busen, where I spent my mornings up the river in a canoe, sketching strange trees and a bamboo bridge. One large cane alone serves as the foothold, supported on either side by a cobweb of others bound with rattans. These form a lacelike fence upwards from the foot-way, spreading like the letter V, which gives a feeling of security to the person passing over, even though the bridge swings in the air with his weight or the wind. I saw people constantly passing over the fragile thing with heavy loads on their heads and backs; women too were carrying children, all apparently without nervousness.

We saw some grand specimens of the Tappan trees, with their smooth white stems, on which bees delight to build their nests. No beasts or reptiles can climb these trees, only the Dyaks beat the bees by building clever ladders with bits of bamboo. They drive in pegs above their heads, tying the other end of the peg to long slender bamboos, placed one over the other and lashed together with pieces of bark, till they reach the honey and wax. The latter being one of the great exports of the country, these trees are protected by the Government. I also saw several great trees hanging over the stream with their trunks and branches flattened like knives, the edges always towards the water. My head sailor was an albino, a very sharp fellow, fair as a European, and much admired by other Dyaks. They all thought it great fun dragging the white woman over the shallow rapids, and were quite as much in the water as out, pushing like devils, then jumping in with a grunt, splashing the boat half full of water, and paddling most furiously afterwards, ladling out the water with a cocoa-nut shell, or a bit of its leaf-sheath stitched into a kind of bucket. When they had tied my canoe to some stumps and saw me fairly at work, they waded on shore and lit a fire on the sand, cooked their rice, and had a smoke; but when I asked them to rub the sticks to get fire, they laughed at my old-fashioned notions and produced lucifer matches from the folds of their turbans. If I asked for a flower from a tree they all climbed up and chopped down a whole branch. A sort of ailanthus with long yellow bunches like millet was very elegant, and made a striking foreground tree.

There was a remarkable pair of Germans then living in an empty house and deserted mine—Dr. and Mrs. P. He had been a doctor of some eminence in his own country, but when the war broke out with France all the young doctors VOL. II II were sent off, and he was so loaded with extra work that his health broke down under it, and his hearing

went entirely. So he gave up his profession and took to wandering through the most out-of-the-way regions, collecting for a naturalist at Berlin, who paid him so much a year for all he sent. It was a provoking arrangement, as he could sell me nothing; but he showed me all his wonderful stores of skins and insects in the half-ruined, unfurnished verandah; making an interesting picture, with his intelligent head and long beard, his pretty young wife translating for him to the troops of native children who came up, some with three butterflies, some with only a bit of one, all expecting farthings, sometimes six children to one butterfly, with other younger children on their hips or backs! Madame P. talked both Malay and English; he, nothing but German, and he was very helpless and sensitive. They had an exquisite little Japanese dog, and the doctor had got into trouble by shooting a dog belonging to the magistrate of that district, which had been uncivil to his pet. He always seemed to have a talent for getting into trouble everywhere. I pitied the poor little wife in her lonely life with him. She was a real " verstiindliche Hausfrau," and gave me delicious coffee, made in a real German pot. I saw a huge bee going into its nest in the doorpost by its own front door. They often bore so many of these tunnels that the posts fall to pieces, but they are cunning enough to curve them so that mortals cannot poke in sticks and kill them.

The steam launch came up for me, and carried me far too fast down the beautiful broad river again. At one point we saw a water-snake full twelve feet long, with its head held nearly a foot out of the water, swimming across most gracefully. It was all red and green, with a sharp ridge down its back. My sailors wanted to steam across it, but it was too quick for us, and curved its beautiful head back to dart an indignant and contemptuous glance at us as we missed it, perfectly ignoring the odds and ends thrown at it. The old steersman told me it was very wicked and poisonous, but it looked all in character with the other surroundings of the great river. The tide was very high—so high that I saw over

the wide fields and gardens on either side, which had never shown themselves before, and gave me a new idea of the cultivation and abundant population there. I found the Rani delighted to see me back, as her husband had taken her brother and his shadow off, up one of the other rivers, in the gunboat for a fortnight, and she was very lonely, but busy all day trying to paint as I did. Bushels of rare flowers were brought in, and died in two hours in the attempt, but she said life was twice as bright since I had set her trying to copy them, and it was a comfort to think I had done her some good by coming, for her life was monotonous, the brightest days being those which brought the mail with news of her boys in England.

Sometimes a troop of native women clad in all the colours of the rainbow (looking like a bed of Waterer's rhododendrons in the distant garden as they came through) would pay her a visit, but they were mere dolls, all alike, well-mannered but curious as monkeys. Mr. Brooke said they were a bad lot, and that no respectable Muhammadan women would come out in that fashion with uncovered faces. Perhaps he was right, but Her Highness thought she did good by being hospitable to them, and she liked their admiration of her nick-nacks.

Vegetables suited me better. The bushes of petrsea were a perfect wonder of bloom, covered with blue sapphire-stars on the blue-gray bracts. In other parts of the world one saw only two or three perfect flowers on a branch, here there were masses of them. There was a great *Vanda Lawii* which had had a dozen sprays on it at once, each eight feet long, the year before, I was told. I watched it from day to day so anxiously; and one morning (after the Rajah returned), to my horror, I found the whole orchid-house (a mere skeleton wooden erection) flat on the ground, and the great groundorchids mown down also! The other lovely orchids and trailing plants, stephanotis, etc., in full flower, all fading or dead, by order of that "mild despot" the Rajah! I felt glad I was going, but as usual he was right. I heard that three months afterwards the mass of beautiful flowers was even more luxuriant than before.

One morning I picked a huge branch of the petraa, meaning to spend the day in painting it, though it was so common there, when I came on a lovely spray of a white orchid and picked it grudgingly to paint, then suddenly found that every tree was loaded with the same, and the boathouse roof looked as if there had been a sudden snowstorm. The air was scented with it, so I got more, and when I reached the house found the drawing-room full of it. They called it the Turong Bird, and said it came out spontaneously into bloom three times in the year, and only lasted a day, and that I must be quick and draw it, for I should find none the next day. It was true; the next day the lovely flowers were hanging like rags.

When I went to finish another sketch I was astounded at the sight of a huge lily, with white face and pink stalks and backs, resting its heavy head on the ground. It grew from a single-stemmed plant, with grand curved leaves above the flower, and was called there the Brookiana lily, but Kew magnates call it *Crinum mifjmtum;* its head was two feet across, and I had to take a smaller specimen to paint, in order to get it into my half-sheet of paper life-size. It was scented like vanilla. Another crinum has since been called Northiana, after myself. It has a magnificent flower, growing almost in the water, each plant becoming an island at high tide, with beautiful reflections under it, and its perfect white petals enriched by the bright pink stamens which hang over them.

One day a boat-load of Dyaks of high degree came down to see the Rajah, and, I suppose, were told they ought to clothe themselves before going to the great house, for they came up in wonderful garments. One had a bright scarlet scarf with long fringed edges trailing on the ground like a train, and his arms folded with prodigious dignity in it, leaving all the rest of his body *an naturel;* another had a short Chinese jacket, and no continuations. Many of them

had fightingcocks under their arms, too precious to be left behind or trusted to women. They always walked up in single file, and squatted round the verandah till they saw the Rajah, and even after they had seen him, for hours and hours, seeming to derive much satisfaction in so doing. One of them startled us with a most infernal yell one day, and the Rajah said it was merely to show that he was happy, and was the same noise he would make on his return from a successful head-hunt.

On the 10th of July I left the beautiful island again, the Rajah putting me on board himself, like the true English gentleman he was. All the eighteen white men came to wish a good voyage to my companion-passenger, an officer of the B company, who had been fifteen years there without ever leaving the place, and looked none the better for it. Healths were drunk in champagne, mine included, and I drank theirs in return. Two nights and a day brought us to Singapore, where I was kindly received by the colour-sergeant and Mrs. C. S. I passed a pleasant morning in the museum with the former, and with Dr. D. , who showed us a beautifully prepared skeleton of a cobra, like ivory-lace, and also the head of a snake which eats cobras, skeletonised, so as to show the marvellous mechanism of the jaw, and the spring which touches the poison-bag! The largest Mias1 in the world is there also, stuffed. The doctor knew him when alive as a pet of old Whampoa. One day the old Chinaman wrote to say, "Mahomet is dead," and sent its body all doubled up in a very small box. It had next to no body; it was all head and arms.

1 The native name for the orang-utan or great man-ape of Borneo.

We saw, too, the birds which make the long hanging nests. They are no bigger than canaries, the hen being far the finer in plumage of the pair,—a rare distinction among birds,—but those nests are so completely protected from all enemies that there is no need for the hen to be unattractive in her dress.

Mr. S. also took me to see the vanilla-gardens. The daughter of the house

played the part of the missing South American insect, and doctored the plants every morning, making much money by the beans. They had Indian coolies working on acres of mandioca, and I saw a gutta percha tree at last, after having been twice to Borneo without seeing it, though half the income of the country was derived from it. Lady W. drove me to "hear the band" in the gardens, but as the young ladies were surrounded by young officers, gossiping, I did not hear it. There is a curious fly at Singapore which apparently collects little heaps of dust or clay and makes spider-traps all over the houses. He flies in and out unharmed, and if one breaks up the nest one finds it full of young spiders. The corners of bookshelves, desks, cups, vases, and all unused ornaments, are full of these nests. Did the spider make them or the fly? The S.s said the fly ate the spiders: I should have thought the reverse.

On the 19th of July the *Normandy* steamed out of the harbour—the very smallest of comfortable ships, with a most agreeable and sociable small company of people on board. First, Mr. and Mrs. M., travelling for his health. Jenner had signed his death-warrant (as he did that of my brother-in-law) and sent him on a sailing voyage round the Cape. Since that they had gone to Japan, and now were returning to Sydney. He was much better: always busy and cheerful, sketching perpetually, with or without subjects. Then there was an Irishman, who had been for years in Japan, and never opened his mouth without making us laugh; a young doctor who had tried and failed as a Ceylon planter, whose physic I should have been sorry to try; and the jolliest of young sea-captains. The latter was always inventing fresh entertainments for us: one day it was gymnastics with the trapeze, potatoes, and chalk; another day exercising two small ponies up and down the deck in a gale of wind, himself or a big monkey mounted on their backs. There were a puppy, three cats, and three monkeys also to entertain us—one of the latter a most amusing little thing, never so happy as when on Mrs. M.'s knee.

I bought a boat-load of shells in Singapore harbour for three rupees. I could not resist their beauty, and our captain promised to pack them and send them home, which he did in three casks, very few being broken when they were unpacked. I asked friends to bring their children with baskets and take as many as they liked. I got a good return for the investment in the children's happy faces, and still had enough left for my own enjoyment.

We passed beautiful volcanic islands and three smoking volcanoes, full of bright light at night, and after seeing the mud ones of Timor, came into more tossing seas, which lasted till we entered the coral reefs and other dangers of the North Coast of Australia. Through these the navigation is most difficult, and all entertainments gave way to it. To be wrecked there would have been unpleasant, neither the country nor the people being hospitable. Our captain once landed with a party in search of curiosities, and was greeted by showers of stones from the rocks above, behind which the natives were hidden. He had to retreat faster than he came. The tints over these coral-lined seas were marvellous. One morning early I saw quantities of white birds hunting a shoal of silver-fish, which jumped in and out, flashing like a fountain of quicksilver, now and then made more lovely still by touches of rosy colour from the rays of the rising sun, and the sea exquisitely delicate in its pearly tints round them. We also saw flights of boatswain birds, with their long tail-feathers.

The calm days were delightful—meals on deck, and all sorts of fun with the monkeys. The big one was very solemn, but gentle, and his fights (sham) with the poodle-puppy were ridiculous. He would stand on his hind-legs and make grabs at the small woolly legs, and then roll over and over with it, but never hurt it, though the puppy got out of temper and bit with all its might with its soft teeth. Sometimes the monkey went through all this with a small monkey hanging around its neck; sometimes he had his hands tied behind his

back, and had to move on like a two-legged prisoner, doing it with apparent ease too, the baby still clinging to him. One might take any quantity of liberties, only not touch the baby, when he would turn furious; and yet it was no kind of relation, and even belonged to a different species! One day when the big monkey was riding the pony round and round, looking wonderfully upright and dignified, the pony began to kick, which caused it to make frantic attempts to escape up the rigging. It was always pulled back by the captain's rope, and at last was seized with a bright idea of escape: one frantic spring seated it on the merry little man's back, who went into fits of laughter, and was nearly strangled to death by the tight clasp of monkey's arms round his neck on one side, and the pony pulling at the rope on the other. That ship was a perpetual comedy. Another day the big monkey was discovered sitting solemnly on the captain's arm-chair in his dark cabin, reading Shakespeare, after having rubbed his face and paws in the fresh paint outside, smeared over all the photographs and pictures on the walls, and overturned the clock. When scolded he did not move, but tried to lick off the paint from his hands in the same way a naughty boy might have done.

We were a week out of sight of land, and it was so cool the day we crossed the Equator that we were glad to wear woollen dresses. At last we came in sight of the little round island with its cave, in which provisions for possible wrecks used to be put, as well as letters for ships to pick up and take on. After dark we got slowly into the harbour of Thursday Island. The governor, Mr. C., came on board for his monthly excitement. I gave him the bundle of papers Lady W. had entrusted to me, and all spare novels, and he asked the M.s and myself to come home and see his wife, so, in spite of rain, waves, and darkness, we scrambled over the floating warehouse into a rickety boat, and then over a long jetty of wet stones, and up the sand to "Government House," a sufficiently watertight bungalow, where we had a couple of hours prose with

their Excellencies. Their son had just returned from an expedition into New Guinea with the missionaries, and though he had been further into the island than any one before him, appeared to have brought back much fever and little else. But the father had collected at different times a most interesting lot of curiosities. One terrible death-machine struck me as curious. It was a loop of bamboo to be slipped over a fugitive enemy's head, with a spear in the centre which pinned him through the throat from behind, sliding through the hollow handle with perfect precision to its mark. The stone axes and other cutting things were exquisitely fixed at all manner of odd angles, each adapted for special purposes.

There were also many curiously carved ornaments of bamboo and shells, including the famous bracelets which can buy a wife or ransom a man. I tried in vain to make out what the flower of the huge rattling bean was like, but no one knew, though it grew on Thursday Island on a creeping plant like a scarlet-runner, they said. There were few flowers or trees, and one would have fancied the few would have been well known. Few butterflies also, but none were collected by the brainless islanders. They cared only for the big oysters, which yielded pearls, and therefore money, and its fishers were the chief visitors there. Our young doctor went round administering doses to all the residents, getting whisky and water from each in return. We had to swallow port wine, to satisfy the hospitality of our kind hosts, and perhaps it saved our lives, especially those of the two invalids, for we were thoroughly soaked through before we reached the ship, the boat being half full of water.

Five pearl-captains came on board and went on with us, and one of them gave a basket of orchids to the captain. I tried in vain to paint one flower, it being too stormy on deck and too stifling in the cabin. He had also a splendid specimen of a shell, beautifully clear and pearly, a long hand in width, with a fungus-shaped coralline growing on its upper half quite a foot across, and most elegant in shape.

The morning we passed through the Torres Straits was calm and lovely. We were so close to each shore that we saw all the trees perfectly: mangroves, casuarinas, brown granite rocks and red sand, with giant ants' nests like obelisks of the same colour, which they said were used, like those of South America, for making floors and lining tanks and drains. At Somerset we saw the big house on the hill, wittr the ground all burnt bare in front to drive away, or at least make visible, the deaf adders, which are the curse of the place. On the other shore were the few modest huts of the fishermen, their boats on the golden sand, and low hills dotted with dracama trees. Then came grandly wooded headlands and rocks closing the narrow passage which admitted us to the Pacific Ocean beyond, near which were quantities of coral reefs hardly above the water, looking yellow or deep purple among the breakers, and soapy water of clearest and faintest blues and greens. It was a day to be long remembered, that first day along the shore of Australia, and the five new passengers were types of the rough practical men who are fast making it into a leading part of the world, full of local information and almost Yankee cuteness.

We spent a day in the harbour of Cookstown, which is perfectly surrounded by wooded hills and islands, the town out of sight. If I had known of the place beforehand I would have waited a mail there, and got some paintings of tropical Australian vegetation, but no one knew anything beforehand. A charming old Roman Catholic priest came on board, Father Cana, who had just ridden across the country from the Gulf of Carpentaria, going for days without food or water and sleeping on the ground, afraid even of lighting a fire, which might betray his resting-place to the treacherous blacks. It seemed to be "If you don't kill me, I kill you," in those parts between the black and the white man. But this good Italian was a picture of health and good-humour, in spite of all his fatigues and deprivations, and, moreover, a thorough gentleman and man of the world. He was going all the way to Brisbane for only two days' enjoyment of his friends there, and would then have to return for another long expedition through the bush. He had no great belief in missionaries, and admitted that the whites were much to blame for the treachery of the blacks, as they treated them like wild beasts, and often stole their children from them. The little things were very cunning, and sometimes crept back to the bush again. One young girl he knew was being brought up by a lady in Brisbane, who made her so happy that she wished to become white. He told her that if she were very good and washed herself often the black would come off in time, and she not only washed but brushed herself constantly, in the hope of getting rid of the colour! His stories were funnily told in his broken English, with twinkling Italian eyes, and much pantomimic action of the hands.

The days were calm after passing the coral islands, the shore-scenery very fine, with grand mountain-outlines leading up to the highest, "Bellenden Kerr. " The names of most places are ugly, Townsville ridiculous—it must have been chosen by a lunatic. Our Chinese waiters were comical creatures, with a sort of halo of frizzy hair standing up round their heads at the roots of their pigtails, and an absurdly astonished expression of countenance. At Thursday Island we had taken on board a famous character, Captain H., the one pilot for 900 miles. He looked like a riding-master. His dress was always the perfection of dandy neatness, his face beamed with benevolence, he had never been ruffled nor out of humour, and his attitudes on the bridge and off it were a sight to see. When he came to talk to us he would wind himself in and out of ropes, and once he carried on a long conversation with Mrs. M., kneeling on one knee. He was a perfect Sir Piercie Shafton, and a man of property at Bowen, where we parted from him with much regret on all sides. He said he had only one weak point—whist.

Some bits of seaweed were fished up for me to draw, very like the gulf-weed, with the same bladders, but with leaves even more plant-like. There were bits of pink coral and zoophytes on it full of wonders for the microscope. On the 8th of August we reached Brisbane, passing the bar— a long treble line of breakers set in sapphires and emeralds— without difficulty: when rough the troughs between the surf nearly swallowed the ships, but that day all was easy. The cold was most bitter, and we were told there had been two inches of ice up the country. It was dark before we could leave the ship.

That strange mortal, Baron M. (a Russian), came on board in search of some promised skulls which had not arrived, and though said to be a woman-hater, he did me the honour of carrying my bag. He had the reputation of being a real cannibal and enjoying a human feast. He asked me which hotel I was going to: "Good? No! The most hateful hole in the universe, and the woman a demon. Quiet? Yes! Very quiet, with eighty men all eating and talking at once. Beastly food and rooms, but he believed it would do for a lady!" He had been seventeen years tossing about the Pacific islands in search of men with tails and men with oddshaped brains. Seven of those years were spent quite alone in the interior of New Guinea. He was now on the point of rushing off to see a family perfectly hairless, somewhere in the North of Queensland, far in the bush, and promised to come and see me on his return, but wrote me a letter instead, enclosing a rough sketch of a three-headed cocoa-nut tree, which he asked me to elaborate into a painting, and then photograph, sending him a copy. The task is not yet done.

Darkness hid all the beauty of the approach up the river to Brisbane. When I asked the Captain if there were porters in Australia, he clapped his hand on the shoulder of the great pearl-captain from Thursday Island, and said, "Yes, that was the man for me, he would think nothing of picking up both my trunks and carrying them a mile!" So I told Mr. C. I believed him capable of everything, but thought that rather much to ask him, on which he lifted my big trunk easily on his shoulder, picked up the other in his hand, and marched ashore. They all packed me into a cab, waved their hats, and cheered as I drove off. Not a bad start on the Australian Island.

1880.—The hotel was clean but unattractive, and over full. Next day I was not sorry to accept Mr. and Mrs. J. B. 's kind invitation to stay at Government House, whose garden opened into the Botanical Gardens. The old director, Mr. Hill, also offered me a room in his house, and put a paragraph about my paintings in the local paper, which induced a little boy to ask, "What will they do with you when you return to England, will the Queen knight you?"[1] The weather was [1] That little Australian boy's question was answered four years later in a letter from the Queen's Private Secretary, in which he expressed "Her Majesty's regret at learning from Her Ministers that Her Majesty's government have no power of recommending to the Queen any mode of publicly recognising Miss North's generous gift to the nation" (by knighthood or otherwise). The Queen therefore sent her own photograph instead—a graceful gift, which gave my sister (ill then and depressed) the keenest pleasure. The letter is printed in its proper place in the diary. too untropical for much out-of-door sketching, and the gardens were dried up and unattractive. Hot sun, cold wind, and dust. The famous araucaria trees in the Botanical Gardens were brown and dusty, and not larger than the one in the temperate house at Kew. The ferns and palms looked bare and cold. There were few flowers, though the Government House garden alone was rich with sweet home flowers— roses, carnations, heliotropes, etc., a few tecomas and tacsonias in addition showing that the present cold was rare. Dracaenas, strelitzias, and Norfolk Island pines also give a different look to the gardens, as well as wattle trees, yellow, with thousands of fairy balls and leaves mimicking the eucalyptus, though the young seedlings begin with the ordinary acacia leaves. There were some grand blue nymphseas blooming on the water, but shrivelled and deformed by the unusual cold; certainly the climate of subtropical Queensland was rather different from what I had expected.

Brisbane itself is a most unattractive place—a sort of overgrown village, with wide empty streets full of driving dust and sand, surrounded by wretched suburbs of wooden huts scattered over steep bare hills. Mrs. B. took me a long drive up and down the steepest roadless wastes, over which no English coachman would have dared to drive. Some of the shops had tempting things in them: the birds, both alive and dead, I longed to accumulate. No one can have an idea of parrots without going to Australia; they have colours in them I never even dreamed of before, and there were many varieties of cockatoo. One great black one with yellow ears and tail I painted eating the Queensland nut, whose shell is so hard that (like that of the Java kanari tree) he alone can crack it with his huge beak. The velvet rifle- and satin bower-birds are as remarkable for their beauty as for their habit of ornamenting their nests and the approach to them with any gaudy-coloured things they can pick up. Squirrels, and even mice, have the power of supporting themselves in the air when dropping from high branches to the ground, spreading themselves out like bats. One kind of mouse has a tail fringed like a feather. Opals are one of the wonders of Queensland: a great lump had lately been accidentally found which might have been bought for £12 if I had come in time. Now it was broken up, and the smallest specimen was quite beyond my means of buying.

The Governor had introduced a party of Chinese servants from Hong Kong into Government House, and when people went to see Miss K. one of these pigtailed gentlemen used to say: "Miss want see plenty people; come Friday see plenty carriage, eat plenty bread and butter, drink plenty tea Friday "; and on that day the butler might be seen with a big loaf in one hand and a knife in the other: "Missus want bread and butter *1* " The hospitality in Brisbane was of the heavy order,—great luncheon-parties, with soup and fish, and four corner-dishes, roast and boiled, etc., as it was forty years ago in England,—and I was glad to escape to the hills. Mr. and Mrs. B. got up at six to see me off, and had arranged that their cousin (who managed their property) should show me the trees I wanted most to see on it. The railway took me up by marvellous zigzags and engineering to Teoomha, through forests of gum-trees, with the yellow wattles or acacias just coming into bloom, and a few grass-trees here and there, whose trunks and wiry grass-like heads were blackened by the fires which natives make inside them in order to get a grand blaze at once, but which never really kill them. These trees are called "black boys" all over Australia. They are under ten feet high, and their flower-scapes resemble the spears the real "black boy" generally carries resting on his shoulder, the points, like them, high above his shock head of black hair. Stag's-horn ferns grow on the stumps. The gum-trees seem to have an aversion to touching one another, as if they feared infection by contact. On the high plains of Darling Downs they were more stunted, and certainly monotonous on the hard dried-up ground, off which great flocks of sheep found it hard to get a living.

At Dalby Mr. and Mrs. M. met me with a troop of nice children and a pair of well-bred horses, and after a good English tea at a pretty little wooden many-roomed inn of one storey, hung with cages of parrots all round its verandah, we trotted over the plains towards the hills, picking up a quantity of parcels on our way at "the store." Dalby was not a bad specimen of an Australian country-town, covering a large space of ground. All the houses one-storeyed, and mostly separate, with no trees and few gardens, surrounded by a dry desert sprinkled thickly with empty tins and picklebottles. Every shop sold everything, or nothing in particular. A church and court-house looked gigantic and hideous in the midst of it all. We passed acres of fenced-in desert, with huts in the corners to certify possession.

We drove for miles over the bare tree-less downs—sometimes on a road, of-tener off it. Two bustards and a huge pelican flew past us, and some other strange birds. After that we came to the scrub again, and I was taught the names of different trees—oak, box, apple, all entirely unlike their namesakes at home, but showing the love of home of the early settlers in keeping those names. We passed no inhabited house till we came to the M.s' cosy farm of many low wooden buildings, with two or three huge chimneys like pyramids attached, built round a kind of court, with a pretty mixed garden of fruit and flowers, and an oldfashioned barn and pigeon-house under the trees. The whole was on the top of a small hill, with fine views all round, and a small lake under it, from which all the water had to be brought in a cart. Here one could go and watch the cranes, storks, and water-fowl drinking of an evening. Every little room had a bath let into the floor, with a cistern out-side which could be filled from the wa-ter-cart, and one could only pass from one room to the other by the outside, which kept one fresh and cool in that weather.

Mrs. M. and her daughters were all model housewives, and quite indepen-dent of all servants or outside help of any sort; they waited themselves at the table. The farm-men ate with us, and everything was exquisitely clean and well arranged. Sam, the Chinese cook, and some black loafers, seemed their only servants. The blacks lived in their own tiny wigwams near, received no wages, and had no particular work, but made themselves generally useful, get-ting occasional presents and scraps in return. They were devoted to the chil-dren, liked looking after horses, and were entirely trusted by the family they had adopted, but did not think it wrong to steal from others; and when the rest-less mood seized them they would move elsewhere without warning, not return-ing sometimes for many months. Two of the men were grooms, and managed the horses most cleverly, chiefly by the voice, seeming to know their language better than whites did. I was only al-lowed one day of rest, and then we start-ed for the Bunya Mountains, leaving two fair young girls and the black peo-ple only on the premises. They said they were quite safe, but their companions looked a queer lot, with their shock-heads and short pipes. The tents and heavy things had gone on with a long team of horses the day before.

Mr. M. drove his wife, myself, and three children, in a kind of inside-car with a roof and four posts to hold it. More children and three gentlemen rode, and there was a spring-cart full of eatables and luggage which broke down in every gully. Those gullies were no joke to get down into, and harder still to get out of. No civilised driver in Europe would have attempted it, but Mr. M. never had an accident, and his black scouts moved frantically backwards and forwards, finding the road, or chopping down trees to make one, or patching up the unfortunate spring-cart. They gal-loped furiously, with their great toes stuck into a stirrup-leather, and their el-bows, indeed all their limbs, appearing perfectly dislocated and loose. They shouted and screamed like wild things. Many times I VOL. II I could see no way through the bush, but on we went, in and out, over stumps and under branch-es, never breaking a bit of anything. They told me Mr. B. drove by that road with four horses every year in the same way, but generally sent on men the day before to cut, which we had not done. We had our mid-day rest, all among the grass-trees, near a hollow, where a little bad water was found for the "Billy "—a huge saucepan, which we boiled and then half filled with tea. Into this our cups were dipped, after the primitive custom of the country. After that we went on again till we reached the steep ascent where we were to leave the car-riage. I was mounted on the best horse, and started ahead with Sam the China-man, who had been disagreeing with his horse all the way, and was in an awful temper now. It was his usual state: no one minded "Sam," who made the best bread in all Australia.

I soon passed him, and much enjoyed my entire solitude through the grand forest alone, especially when I reached the magnificent old araucarias. Their trunks were perfectly round, with purple rings all the way up, showing where the branches had been once, straight as ar-rows up to the leafy tops, which were round like the top of an egg or dome, and often 200 feet above the ground. Only the ends of the branches had bunches of leaves on them, and only a third of the stem had branches left on it. But these grand green domes cov-ered one hundred miles of hill-tops, and towered over all the other trees of those forests. Nowhere else were the old bun-ya trees to be seen at all; and at the sea-son when the cones ripened, the native population collected from all parts and lived on the nuts, which were as large as chestnuts. Every tree was said to be-long to some particular family, and they produced so great an abundance of fruit that it was also said, the owners let them out to other tribes on condition that they did not touch the lizards, snakes, and 'possums—a queer form of game-pre-serving, which reduced the hirer to such a state of longing for animal food that babies disappeared, and then there was a row, and no white person ever ven-tured on those hills while the bunya har-vest was going on. Under these giants there was a fine undergrowth of every shade of green, brown, and yellow, roped together by fantastically twisted lianes, and great creeping roots, like the snake-tree of Jamaica, dracsenas, ferns, and the sandal-wood raspberry. After half an hour of this scrub I came out to the clearing, where our tents were being put up, having arrived only a little be-fore us, owing to the difficulties of the road.

The rest of the things arrived in the course of the night, when the horses, not finding it comfortable, trotted off home, thirty miles without a house, and scarcely anything like a road, but no one troubled himself about them. We found many of the trees hung with whip-birds' nests—long hanging pockets of the greenest moss, the entrance often deco-rated with the feathers of the blue and red parrot, one of the commonest birds there. The whip-bird has a pretty bronze crest, and makes a call like the whistling of a whip. We climbed up to the top of the highest point, and got a grand view over the yellow burnt-up plains, with now and then patches which looked like lakes, and miles of forest-covered tops. I had my first sight of a party of perhaps twenty kangaroos, all hopping down the hill in single file, or feeding in the hollow below. I can fancy no more comical sight than a procession of these strange creatures, proceeding over the long tufted grass in the way I saw them then, using their big tails for balancing-rods. Another day we rode farther into the forest, and saw still bigger bunya trees, and great skeleton fig-trees hugging some other victim-tree to death, with its roots spreading over the ground at its base like the tentacles of some horrid sea-monster. We rested an hour at a partial clearing over a wood-shoot, from whence there was a far distant view over the distant Bunya Mountains and the plain below, with scraggy old casuarinas and a gigantic fig-tree as foreground, with tree-ferns and seaforthia palms (the most elegant of the whole family). Birds'-nest ferns were clinging to the trees, and a kind of dracama with slender bending stem leaned against them for support,

On the ground were violets with grass-like leaves, and a few yellow everlastings, but no other flowers. Great piles of sawdust and chips, with some huge logs, told that the work of destruction had begun, and civilised men would soon drive out not only the aborigines but their food and shelter. The gum from most of the Australian trees is beautiful, and I gathered pieces of yellow amber from these old *Araucaria Bidwillii* trees as long as my hand, but too soft to retain their polished beauty long in a traveller's trunk. Under the trees were many of the leafy mounds made by the brush-turkeys to put their eggs in, and in which these are hatched by the heat produced by natural fermentation, without the trouble of sitting on them. The flesh of the bird is brown, and has a game flavour. The second night our tents were nearly blown down by the wind, which changed suddenly

and became intensely cold. We dreaded a sudden rain, which would have made the road back almost impassable, and to stay amongst that long grass very unpleasant; though it made the most delightful spring-bed, with an opossum rug over and under one, and a skye-terrier on the top of all to keep it steady. To my delight we waited there an extra day for the missing horses. First a white man was sent on after them, who returned with the news that one only had arrived safely at his stable. He had not the sense to bring it or to look for the others. Then Mr. M. ordered his favourite black off in search, telling him to bring them all back, which he did in an incredibly short space of time. That man obeyed no one but his master, but I believe would have hung himself if told to do so by him. He broke in all the horses (and Mr. M. had about five hundred). He was devoted to the children: taught them to eat roast opossum, and every sort of bush accomplishment.

The very smallest of these children could climb on a big horse by its tail or mane and stirrups. They rode without the slightest fear, and went up the trees with the same ease. They knew all their names and uses, and where the different birds built, and were the most delightful companions. A poor little sloth-bear was shot for me before I could say "don't"— so soft and harmless, all wool and no body or bones. I felt so sorry for the useless murder. They also burned the grass, and the fire came alarmingly near the tents; but the trees are so full of moisture that they never catch fire till after many days of scorching, while the grass blazes up and is out at once. In this case care was taken to pull up a circle round us before the match was thrown in. When by accident the flames come too near, every white man, woman, and child has to take branches and beat it out, while the blacks sit down and sigh. The young grass is stifled by the dense mass of dry tufts above it. The only way of giving it necessary room and air is by burning off the old grass, and its ashes are the best manure for the young shoots. On our way down I again started alone on foot, stopping to enjoy and ex-

amine all the lovely things in the forest, and to make pencil-studies of leaves and plants.

The xanthorrhoea or grass-trees form perfect globes, and it was most delightful to pull the young centre spikes apart and let the thousands of fine green hairs free. The peeps through them on the blue world below were enchanting. When I got there I spread my pocket-handkerchief on a tuft of grass for a pillow, and lay on my back examining the Eucalyptus leaves overhead for an hour at least before the others came, in perfect peace. It is a libel to call them shadeless trees. Just at noon the knife-edges of the leaves are turned towards the sun, thinking more of keeping themselves cool by exposing the least possible surface to the sun's rays, than of shading the ground below. But in the morning and evening they give more shade to their own roots than European trees, and their constant movements fan the air pleasantly: the scent is delicious. There is rather a likeness to the olive in the commonest sorts, only the leaves all turn down instead of up. There is a vast variety of tints in the different species, and the bark twists itself off in a hundred lovely curves. The mistletoe, too, hangs in long golden tresses with pink stalks and flowers, making charming masses of colour against the gray trees and white stalks. I kept so quiet that a kangaroo came feeding close to me, and I could watch its comical modes of proceeding, till startled by the old Chinaman, with his Yankee tongue and perpetual grumbles. He stopped to converse: "It was a beastly poisonous place that mountain! He was always sick there, and could make nothing nice! Had I come off without breakfast *I* Wall! Some folks worked less, and ate more. He could get home in two hours, but he was riding that young colt not two years old. It was a beauty, and he must take care of it; Master would trust no one else on it. It would suit the fine ladies grandly some day," etc. Then came the others, and Black Sam was sent ahead to find the road to "Bottle-Tree Plains." "Very big fellow, bottle-tree!" and off he scampered, with all his legs and arms tossing about as if dislocated. After all sorts of Astley-like feats of driving, we got to the "big fellow." These curious trees are really like bottles, with a crown of willow-like leaves; the ends of the branches being tipped with ivy-shaped leaves, and the very youngest plants having their lower stems shaped like a radish. They are always found at the edge of the forest, and never more than one or two in a group.

Just as we had begun to settle, and I had got my sketchingthings ready, we were told to bundle into the carriage again, for they had accidentally set fire to the long grass in attempting to boil the kettle, and the wind was our way. In five minutes the ring of flame encircled half an acre, and it was spreading fast and could not be put out; we must pass it. The horses were put full gallop, and took us through without hesitation; they knew all about such things, and that they would be safe inside the magic circle, for burnt grass could burn no more. The girls rode over, and the big dogs jumped through, but the poor little Skye felt he could not jump high enough and cried piteously till he was sent for and lifted out of danger; then we settled again for our luncheon, and I never got a really good sketch of the bottle-tree.

It was pleasant resting at the M.s' farm again. They were an ideal family for bush life. But the pet of all was "Jo," a young lady of eight years old. She actually offered to climb to the top of a gum-tree and bring me down one of the tiny native bears alive, in spite of scratches and bites! The whole family had a wondrous power of eating jam. Three pots were emptied every morning at breakfast. There are few cases known of delicate appetite in the bush, and the amount of meat consumed was appalling. Mrs. M. complained of the few advantages her girls had up there; but it would be difficult to find nicer ones, more unselfish and sensible, and I should always recommend all young men who want good useful wives to seek them in Australia. Even there an attempt was made at accomplishments. There was a piano (to my sorrow), and

a request was made by the head farming-man, just as I was leaving, for the loan of its case "to pickle the pork in!" The best labourers there got seventeen shillings a week, house, and food; their boys, if old enough to work, got ten shillings, so that it was not a bad livelihood. Mr. M. said he soon found out what they were worth, and sent them off at once, or kept them for years. We watched some kangaroos feeding or hopping after one another in single file, as we drove slowly round them, across the hedgeless fields; and I was shown more bottle-trees and bushes of gum-apple bearing bunches of dull-red cherries and bright-green leaves, also the "pomegranate," which bears a green velvet berry something like the outer shell of the horse-chestnut.

The return drive across Darling Downs was bitterly cold. The railway took me on to Harlaxton, a house on the very top of the zigzag railway, with a glorious view over "the Range," as the hills are called between it and Brisbane. They are covered with unbroken forest, having a peculiar deep bloom on them seen only on masses of the gum-trees. At sunset the view was particularly lovely, when the gray branches and white stems of the near trees were tinted with rose-colour like the sky itself. Close by were gardens full of oranges and peach-blossoms, and we had strawberries in abundance from the garden. Mr. G., my host, was one of the first explorers in Western Australia. He told me a story of his having to speak at the Geographical Society on his election as a Fellow, and how there was a map of Australia on the walls which he did not then know was the work of Sir Roderick Murchison himself. He began by telling his hearers they must carefully erase from the map the big lake in the middle, a good many rivers, and other mistakes, and that perhaps on the whole it would be as well to whitewash it all, it was so full of blunders! He said he saw a good many persons round him trying to smother their laughter, but he went on innocently to the end of his story, when Sir Roderick good-naturedly apologised for the map, to his sur-

prise and confusion. His children were very charming, as most Australian children are, from their early and close acquaintance with the natural things round them. They had a catapult with which they shot small birds for me, skinning them too, but not successfully. Mr. G. remembered Mr. Darwin's visit in the *Beagle,* and said that he was the most agreeable and the ugliest young man he ever met.

My next move was westward by rail to Gumbara, where Mr. W. met and drove me from the station over eleven dreary miles of plain to his luxurious little house and pretty wife. The hills were on fire, and the foreground was black with a fire that was only just over. All that was unburnt was browned by frost and want of moisture. Stunted whitestemmed trees were dotted about, and not a flower was to be found. The garden was full of imported bushes and plants, dying a lingering death of thirst. There was a tame wallaby, a small species of kangaroo, which was very bewitching, and so tame that it was difficult to keep it at a sufficient distance to sketch. It came up close, folding its short little hands and examining me with as much curiosity as my own. It would jump on the table like a cat and off again without turning over anything. The M.s had shot one of these pretty creatures, and they pulled a little live baby out of its pocket to show me; the poor little hairless creature shivered, and crawled back into the accustomed refuge again, then no longer warm, and made me almost cry. It seemed so cruel to have murdered the mother, harmless and trusting as all animals in Australia are. I was told if I heard noises on the roof over my head at night I was not to mind them; it would only be a snake hunting an opossum which lived there. How did the snakes get there? The laughing jackasses (a giant kingfisher) pounced down on the snakes whenever they had a chance, but often dropped them on the roofs when they could carry them no farther, and then the 'possum suffered.

We watched a native bear a long while, curled up in the fork of a gum-tree, and very sleepy. After we had flung a lot of stones at him, he cocked up his big ears, rubbed his eyes, and gave a great yawn, but did not move. He knew he was out of harm's way. He took his constitutional at night only, and was not going to alter his habits of life to suit surrounding strangers any more than the black men did. There were also platypus in the clear little river, but they were so shy that they had to be watched and waited for whole days before they were seen above water: the slightest movement sent them under. My next move was to Warwick. Here Mr. G. met me and drove me on to sleep at an old house where there were fifteen daughters and nieces assembled, and I began to think that I had misunderstood the accounts of the country, and that women, not men, preponderated there. It was a thirty miles' drive on through the bush to Maryland, mostly without a road; but I was told that buggies could not turn over, and was taken in and out between the trees and up and down steep ditches and banks in the cleverest way. We passed many fine trees, some with stems quite pink or salmon-colour, or white and shiny, with the most delicate lilac shadows, some with dark much-grooved bark, called "iron bark." Some of the young trees had leaves nearly as dark as the copper-beech, and we passed curious granite boulders piled about, with a dendrobium they call "rock-lily" amongst them, but not then in flower.

They were making a railway to the famous tin-mines, and the bark-huts of the navvies looked picturesque amongst the trees. We also met great English waggons, with teams of eight horses each, taking down loads of ore from the mines. A noble old "carragong" tree stood near the house at Maryland. It had a rough reddish bark, with bright-green ivyshaped leaves, which made it very conspicuous among the gray gum leaves, with their smooth marble-like trunks. The apple-trees were another exception to the gray leaves, though less bright than the carragong. Their trunks and branches were twisted into the most fantastic shapes, and in their knobbiest

corners water could always be found by tapping. The richest tree in point of colour is the "mountain-ash." It has crowns of green leaves like an india-rubber, with yellow midribs, five leaves on each crown, a reddish stem, and the upper branches perfectly barkless round it. I saw also fine casuarina trees called oaks, but looking like feathery cedars. They have a peculiar mistletoe which mimics them. The appletrees have another with round leaves, and the ordinary gum has one with leaves exactly like its own.

I also saw the first banksia bush there, called honeysuckle, because of the sweet honey which may be sucked from the base of its flower-stalks. It grew about thirty feet high, and the male cones had a lovely brown plush inside, used as wicks for lamps. I saw hundreds of cockatoos, with snowwhite backs and yellow crests and breasts, which flew before us screeching for a long while, resting on the trees for a gossip, then flying on again. They ate up all the grain, and farmers paid a halfpenny a crest when brought in, so that before long those lovely natives would also cease to exist. The "stringy bark " was another conspicuous variety of gum, whose cork-like slabs were turned by the blacks in a few moments either into a house or a canoe. My host was a real lover of all these things, and a most agreeable companion, his only grievance being that his uncle at home would not see the advisability of buying the best land at first, and now small settlers were taking up the choicest bits at a pound an acre in every direction, and becoming legally possessed of what he had been working for years to improve. We passed several of these little "cockatoo " wooden houses of two rooms each, on nice patches of green meadow, close to precious "creeks." It was quite impossible to teach horses and cattle not to eat in such places, and then they got pounded for trespassing, and the people at home, who had originally "taken," not "bought," the land, could not see the necessity of buying it now. One heard the same grumble everywhere.

The swallows had just returned, very

tired, and were sunning themselves in crowds on the house-roofs. They were very small, with red beaks, and made a grand chattering, tidying and repairing their bottle-shaped clay nests under the eaves. If we broke one of these fragile habitations it would be mended again in a day or two, I was told; and it might be broken over and over again as often as possible, it would always be rebuilt; they would have the spot they had chosen. I saw a pretty black and white bird with a fan-tail, apparently trying to get into the house through a broken glass window. He went always too high or too low, but was untiring in his efforts to get in, and I left him at it. Mr. G. thought he was trying to see his own reflection against the dark room, he was so vain, and he had often seen him admiring and pluming himself before a looking-glass when he had put it purposely in the bird's way. I was taken to Starthorpe to see an aviary full of parrots in an old lady's garden there. She had a dozen different sorts, some guinea-pigs, quails, doves, and a New Guinea cockatoo with red points to its white plumage—all in one big cage, and all living in perfect harmony. The dove seemed the most pugnacious character, and was making violent assaults on the cockatoo, which merely opened his big beak at him and looked frightened, having apparently no idea of his own superior strength. Some gaudy little lories, called rosalias, lived in the box with the guinea-pigs, and all were in magnificent plumage.

Starthorpe was a long straggling street of the usual onestoreyed detached shops, and seemed a busy place, owing to the tin-mines all round. A few miles farther took us to the principal one. The metal was found mixed up with quartz, about eight feet under the surface, and we saw the washing and sifting, all done in much the same simple manner that Noah's sons might have done it in, the principal workmen being Chinamen, who worked from sunrise to sunset upon four meals of rice a day. Their common cooking-shed and huts were all made of bark, and they looked merry and contented. The tin looked black and shiny, and was all in grains smaller than the smallest partridge-shot. We saw hundreds of casks full of it, and then, after the inevitable tea, which is always ready and offered to visitors all over Australia, we waited at the bridge till Cobbe and Co.'s coach came, with Miss B. keeping my place on the box, where we were shaken and pounded till after dark. We passed much grand forest-scenery, and one romantic bit between walls of huge granite boulders, called "the Gap," was full of ferns. The whole day's drive was through greener bush than I had ever seen before, white heath bushes and yellow wattles making it more lively. We saw three dead black snakes, and one live one, rearing its ugly head and neck out of a low bush to watch us as we stopped to look at it. The driver wanted to get down and kill it, but said the horses would be mad if they saw it. He said he would only give it a slight knock on the head with a stick, and it would then bite itself and die of its own poison. The blacks, when they want to eat one, take good care to kill it off at once, not giving it time to do that, as the flesh would also become poisonous—an odd story, if true! A few days before, one of the horses had shied at one of these snakes, which had twisted itself round his leg; but the animal had long hair, and had not been bitten, and the driver jumped down and killed the horrid reptile. Their poison is deadly.

At Tenterfield I had the usual fuss when two persons travel together, and was told only one room was to be had, butoI was obstinate, and ultimately got another. It was what Australians call "a very pretty place," meaning that there was not a tree within a mile of it, and that it had a little water within reach. The inn was good, and the food most abundant: hot beefsteaks for breakfast, roast beef for dinner, boiled beef for tea, and tea always going, with good bread and butter. What can English people want more? My friend liked the beef, I the bread, so we got on well. We were said to be the first ladies who ever travelled on that road alone by Cobbe and Co.'s coaches, so Cobbe and Co. were proud of us, and telegraphed be-

forehand to all the haltingplaces to have an extra quantity of beef ready for us, as well as that horrid double-bedded room. Cobbe and Co. coaches all Australia, with extraordinary vehicles of every shape and size, and really splendid horses: I hardly saw a bad one belonging to the famous company. They had the best possible harness and no breeching, and yet they went down the steepest descents, and over the roughest ground, in and out of the trees.

While wandering along the street, we saw a lady with her baby on one arm and a cockatoo on the other. Every now and then she said, "Cocky, kiss the baby," and the bird put its great beak to the baby's lips, who crowed with delight, to my horror, but the mother laughed at the idea of danger. At Tenterfield a gentleman offered me a collection of ferns he had made on the Richmond river; another, a collection of photographs of Australian scenery. Nothing could exceed the kind interest people took in my work. There was an odd custom, not only at inns but in private houses, of supplying the guests with brushes, combs, and sponges. Miss B. told me her sister's girls, when they went out anywhere to stay a few nights, never thought of taking luggage, but depended for everything on their friends, and were thought rather particular if they even took their own tooth-brashes.

The next day's journey took twelve hours, and I was so stiff that I fell flat down in the street when I attempted to get off the box. But the day had been most enjoyable, in spite of the squeezing and jolting. Soon after sunrise we overtook a tiny native bear on the road, sitting calmly within a yard of the wheels. We stopped the coach, and the driver made him a speech beginning "little man," which the small woollen ball thought impertinent; for after staring a few minutes, he suddenly got on his four feet and scrambled off towards the trees, faster than I thought possible on his funny clown-like feet. He had huge furry ears, and a most fascinating expression of face. The scarlet and blue parrots were very gay, morning and evening, in the trees. We passed some

white gums called "messmates," and many varieties of acacia. A pretty purple pea was running over the ground, called sarsaparilla by Australians. The dryness was sad to see. We constantly passed poor dying and dead beasts by the roadside, which were left to be devoured by wild dogs and cats, and afterwards had their bones cleaned by the ants. One saw them whitening all over the country, and one's nose was constantly suffering from this custom. But on this third day's journey in the coach the rain began, and though it made the roads heavy, we all rejoiced for the sake of the dried-up, thirsty country.

We passed groups of strange boulders scattered over a plain, and heaped one on the other, which they told us were called Stonehenge; and we had our dinner in a bark house of two rooms, most certainly not watertight, but the pretty little woman and her girls had an excellent hot meal ready for us, and the great chimney was full of blazing logs. A boiled leg of mutton, potatoes, parsnips, tea, bread, and cheese, all extra good, well worth two shillings apiece. And that house was thirty miles distant on either side from any other habitation: all was bush—"monotonous gum-trees," as they are often called, but to me so full of variety in form and colour. We were 4000 feet above the sea, and very cold, but were well covered and dry. We passed a long lagoon or lake which is famous for its black swans. These, like the emus, are fast disappearing before the killing race from Europe. Government, however, is at last making laws to prevent them from being shot at certain seasons of the year. The eggs are peculiar—long, gray, and rough—and people spoil them by painting landscapes on them. The lake is called "Mothery Ducky," or "Mother of the Blacks." Some of the reasons for names are amusing. Some one said, "Ain't this a queer place 1" —"Believe yer!" so it was called "Bolivia." Another place was called Boonoboono, a native name, and we passed over a smooth boulder.-top in a half-dry creek called "London Bridge."

Armadale we reached after dark—a

considerable place, with some stone houses in it, and a bishop. An English clergyman met me at the door as we entered the hotel, with a note from Mrs. Marsh. The hotels were all good, and the charge, ten shillings a day, included a sitting-room and good fire. Meat cost a shilling for ten pounds. We started at eight, outside a large coach, with four noble black horses to pull us over an excellent road, as straight as a piece of Roman work, to Uralla, where we descended from our high perch, had a good breakfast, and waited till Mrs. M. came for us. We had passed some acres of orchards,—peaches, pears, apples, etc. ,—all fenced in with a regular quickset hedge, sweet-brier, and blackberries. The owner made £500 a year by that garden. We had also passed a good many huts of free selectors, or cockatoo settlers—people who only take forty acres on loan, at a pound an acre, borrowing money for the purpose. They buy more sheep than they can feed, and soon have to give up, having improved the land for the lenders, poor things! The cold was awful, with not a cloud in the clear sky, and the rain had hardly wetted the ground.

Salisbury Court was a pretty old house, but the number of European shrubs and leafless trees made it look extra wintry-like. The gums were all "peppermint," the slender old leaves hanging on red or orange stalks, the young shoots full of opalesque colours. Mrs. Marsh, a sweet old lady, was most hospitable and kind, bringing us a delicious tea into our rooms with her own hands, and leaving us to rest in perfect peace after all our jolting. She lived in the house her brother-in-law, Matthew Marsh, had built and made his fortune in. Her sons and daughters were all settled about the country near her, and the place looked like an old-fashioned English home, with old books, and some pictures on the walls. She sent us on in the buggy to Bendemere—a pretty green meadow with a clear river running through it, bordered by casuarina trees or "she-oaks," so called from the original Indian name of shiock, which had been again varied into "he-oaks,"

"swamp oaks," and even "oaks" alone, all being species of casuarina, a tree as unlike the English oak as it is possible to find. They looked golden in the setting sun, and made a pretty picture, with the gray companion-birds stalking in and out of the water. The Bendemeerites were much amused with the sketch, and thought I must "make a heap of money by them things "; they added that if they had a lot of money to spend, "they would sooner buy any amount of them sort than gaudy chromos, they would," which flattered my feelings. The inn was an ideal one, and we longed to stay a week—till the night came, and then we wished ourselves elsewhere. There was "any amount" of fleas and noise: first coaches and supper; then drunkenness and gambling till three in the morning in the bar, which was only separated by planks of wood from our pretty little rooms. I had heard of such unquiet nights, but seldom met them in Australia, and we were not sorry to be off, fortunately getting the inside of the coach to ourselves on that day of constant rain.

We passed through pretty scenery, with huge boulders scattered amongst the great trees, distant views of purest blue seen under them, and foreground pyramids of yellow acacia. Many of the gums were sprinkled with white flowers, and a few purple and pink peas grew amongst the scanty grass. One sort, called the poison pea, has a wicked attraction for sheep, which will run far after it, eat it greedily, and then die of atrophy in consequence, unless killed when the habit begins, and before they become worthless as meat. We descended steadily all the way to Tamworth, where we found a warmth we had not felt before. From thence the railway brought us on to Musselbrook, over a richer and wetter country, where imported green willows marked the stream's course, and patches of white iris and sweet-brier were growing even more luxuriantly than in their native homes. How it rained when the rain did come! It was no easy task for four strong horses to drag our heavy coach over the black mud, the road winding

round the base of an extinct volcano wooded to the top, with basalt and other lava scattered about it. We had left the Queensland granite and reached lime and sandstone, and the VOL. 11 K black soil sheep-feeders delight in. We passed through miles of dead trees with rims cut round their bark on purpose to kill them. Some were covered with white cockatoos, which glittered against the slaty-gray rainy sky like huge white flowers. How they screamed! We saw an amusing little game played by some small brown soldier-birds with fan-tails, chasing a big black and white cat. A crowd of them were flying from tree to tree and jeering at it, clinging on to the trunks with their tails spread out, and hopping almost on its back: it was a funny scene. We also saw graceful gray cranes with crests, called native companions, and curious scrubby trees like heaths, with twisted white trunks, called tea (or ti) trees.

We did not reach Merriwa till nine at night, when C. C. met us at the little inn and drove us over the deep black mud to his home at Collaroy, on the top of a steep hill, from whence he had a view over the rich cleared country dotted with gumtrees, and winding river, bordered with so-called "oaks," to the Liverpool range. His wife was a Sydney lady of the most energetic and practical nature, with a lovely little girl of four, and a baby which considered everything in life to be a joke made for its amusement. In the afternoon Mr. C. found an opossum in an old stump and pulled it out by its prehensile tail for me to paint. We put it in a cage, and in a few hours it was lapping milk out of a teaspoon and having its head scratched, without the least fear of us. While I was there one of the shearers came in to Mr. C. and said, "Please sir, we was talking of commencing a union, and wanted to consult you about it." Mr. C. had his head full of trades' unions and said, "Well," with no great heartiness. "Well, sir, me and that girl down at the overseer's, we was thinking of commencing a union. You know, sir, it's very hard to come in tired to a cold hut, have to blow a fire, and to cook rations after a long day, all oneself, and I was thinking that girl *could* cook, and she could blow, and she would be as good as any one else to commence a union with" (an Australian way of announcing his intended marriage!) All servant-girls went the same way; Mrs. C. was quite worn out with drilling fresh ones.

On Saturday night a parson came over from Merriwa, driving himself in a buggy and four. He kept twelve horses, and was perpetually on the move, marrying, burying, and preaching over an enormous district. He was very deaf, and could only hear through a long trumpet and an india-rubber tube, and he spoke so indistinctly no one could understand half he said; but he was a real good fellow, and bore me no malice for not going to church. He looked over my work, and said, if I had had time to stay he would have shown me many curious things about the country no one knew but himself. I painted a pretty swallow's nest there, which was built in a tin funnel hanging to a nail in the cellar. When I hung it up again, after taking it away for some two hours, the owners (which were in a terrible fuss to know what had become of it) flew to it at once, and in five minutes time the hen was sitting on the eggs as quietly as before. That afternoon I saw a pair of the small birds called shepherds' companions, or Billy cocktail, chasing two big magpies all about the garden, pecking and chattering at them, and seeming to laugh at the fun of frightening such big creatures. Some fuss was made about starting again, things being somewhat untidy at Collaroy, roads being so bad, and our two portmanteaux considered heavy (I could lift and carry them both without difficulty); but at last horses were caught, and we started in two buggies with two horses each, and slept at Cassilis, ten miles off (a village half buried in silver thistles—another introduction from the old country, which throve too well to be appreciated, though the young shoots could feed cattle when grass refused to grow during the long dry season).

The inn was over full, but they all crammed together to give us room, English ladies being rare visitors. One of the men was a brother of A. F. and an inspector of police, who went over an immense amount of ground every week, and cared more about horses than about flint implements and articles of vertu. He had been twenty years away from home, seldom heard of his family, and was very curious for news. Mr. C. said he was a good fellow, but no one dare take much notice of a government inspector, or the rascals around would say you bribed him! Every one seemed afraid of his neighbour in that free young country. We all went after tea to the Court House, where we women had two armchairs given to us, while the men sat on the table, to see some acting, songs, and dancing by nine young girls the school inspector of the district had been training in his leisure hours, to give entertainments for charitable purposes. It was very dull, I thought, but might be meritorious. Our two pairs of horses crawled over sixty-three miles of uninteresting scrub the next day, with only one hour of positive rest, and we were glad to get to the smiling valley of "Mudgee," with its lovely river and large straggling town, with (strange to say) fine groups of large trees left here and there to shade it.

We were most kindly received by Mr. and Mrs. L. in a really comfortable new house on the top of a hill. The clever old grandfather had been one of the first settlers in New South Wales. The children, as usual, were very nice, and one little boy found me the double nest of the yellow-tailed tomtit—a very dirty specimen, but good enough to paint from. The cock sat on the upper nest to entertain his wife below while she was hatching the eggs, his nest being open to the sky, hers entered only by a small hole in the side. They showed me a tame emu which was walking about with some turkeys. It looked supremely dignified, but was said to be pugnacious. We also went to see the sheep washed —a cruel process. They were first half-boiled in mud at 107, then soused over and over in a cold shower-bath by men standing in the tubs, who swung them by horns and tail underneath it, and then they were pulled up to dry half-dead with fright and exhaustion, but marvellously white. A thousand were washed in a day, and it would take more than six weeks to finish the flock, with eighteen men. Mr. L. went down at six o'clock every morning to watch the work, and did not return till night. We drove down to see it in a smart barouche, with a grand coachman in livery, called George, who had to be back at a certain hour, as he was also the butcher, and was wanted to kill a sheep.

It was not easy to get away; nobody seemed to know how to go, so we went on and on by coach, and on reaching Wallerawang found no buggy, so continued our progress to the railway, where, at one in the morning, we found no rooms. After a weary hour, we started by train up the zigzags to Mount Victoria on the Blue Mountains, which we reached at 3.30; here left our portmanteaux at the station, and walked by moonlight to the hotel, and after some knocking at a window where we saw a light, were let in, thanks to a monthly-nurse, who was sitting up with a baby. She roused the "butler," and we at last found rest in two clean little rooms, and had a wonderful drive the next morning, six miles along the ridge, through forests of many wonders, the gum-trees having a darker foliage than any I had seen before, the young shoots of a bronze or copper tint loaded with berries of a purple bronze, the younger shoots very blue. Under the tall trees were all manner of flowers; but the waratah, just opening, quite took my breath away with its gorgeousness. It is like a large peony in size and colour, with its petals formed like English honeysuckles, the buds like gray shells. Each head stands on a separate stalk of four or five feet high, with splendid thistle-like leaves. Many other flowers were just beginning to come out. We drove to Govall's Leap, the top of a high cliff, with a wonderful view of an inaccessible valley under it and distant forest hills steeped in the deepest blue. The cliffs were hung with quite a different set of flowers from any I had seen before. After our drive my travelling companion had to travel down to Sydney to join her nieces on board the English mail, to my great regret.

The rain came down in such torrents that, after a quiet day of painting and rest, I also went by rail to Sydney, to stay with my friends of the Torres Straits, Mr. and Mrs. M., and found they had changed characters, and that Mrs. M. was the invalid now, and her husband ready to go anywhere with me. I went to get some birds I had ordered from Goldie, the New Guinea naturalist; he had left them with some friends. One of these gentlemen was so much struck by our enthusiasm over the beauty of the birds that he asked us to come and see his treasures at home, and we drove to his address, five miles off, over ploughed-up roads, rocks, and common, till we came to his four-roomed cottage and pretty little garden. It might have had a good view over one of the many landlocked harbours, but another little brown house had grown up "quite promiscuous" and hidden it. That was the case all round Sydney; each individual house seemed to grow up like a fungus, wherever it fancied, without any reference to its neighbours, or any particular advantage to itself, and an enormous tract of country was spoilt by ugly buildings. After seeing some pretty birds and some equally barbarous weapons, we jolted back again to visit some warehouses on the docks, and up ladders and lifts after spears and tomahawks which Mr. M. collected. I got one of the clay masks stretched and painted over a real human skull from the Solomon Isles, and a chalk head from New Zealand, after which I went to see a most agreeable man, Dr. Bennett. He was about eighty, but took me all over the Botanical Gardens, showing me with great delight how much bigger the *Ficus Bennettii* was than the *Ficus Moorii*.

The gardens were lovely, but I longed for the country, and escaped to Camden, thirty miles off, by rail and road—one of the oldest settlements of New South Wales, and certainly the most lovely garden in Australia. Three generations of Macarthurs had devoted themselves

to it. The present Sir William had spent thousands on its orchid-houses, and had exchanged plants with every botanical garden in the world. I shall never forget my first walk in that garden. The verandah which ran round the house was one mass of blooming blue wistaria; close by were great jubaea-palms from Chili, a monster I had never seen before. There were quantities of Japanese and Chinese plants, and quite a grove of camellias in full bloom, strawberries with ripe fruit, lemons, bananas, apples, figs, olives, every variety of climate contributing to fill that garden. There were acres of bulbs and different herbaceous plants scattered about the park in different directions by themselves in unexpected places, and large vineyards for wine-making, which I feared would not be kept up when the old gentleman died. They don't pay as yet, and the younger generation often thinks more of that than of patriotism.

They lent me a buggy with a fat horse and driver for a week, and I went through pretty scenery till I reached the top of the Illewong Mountains, and went down the wonderful bit of road to Balli. At the top I saw many specimens of the great Australian lily or doryanthes, but they were not in flower. I watched a spike of one, seven feet high, off and on for two months at Camden, and it never came out (the one I afterwards painted at Kew took five months after it had begun to colour before it really came to perfection). There was a fine sea-view, and lower down the road took me through the richest vegetation, quite unlike anything else south of Brisbane. Tall seaforthia palms and cabbage or fan palms, full of flower, many of them of great height. Often one had helped itself up in the world by means of the branches of a giant gum-tree, resting its tired head against the trunk for support, quite 200 feet above the ground in the valley below.

But it was always raining in this unexpected bit of the tropics, and I had no easy task to finish a picture there. Three times I packed up my things in disgust, and at last brought home my paper wetter with rain than with oil-paint. People

were all related to one another, and all hospitable, and I drove from house to house, only regretting that the horse and buggy were not my own, when I could have stayed much longer with enjoyment. Another day I stopped to paint a gigantic fig-tree standing alone, its huge buttresses covered with tangled creepers and parasites. The village was called Fig-tree village after it, and all the population was on horseback, going to the races at Wollongong. At Mr. H. O.'s I saw a grand specimen of the "red cedar. " It had leaves like the ailanthus, but its wood smelt like cedar pencils, and was red as mahogany, which gave it its name. The tea-trees there were covered with tiny white bottle-brush flowers, and were rosy with their young shoots and leaves. Another sort was called the paper-bark tree, *Melaleuca leucadendron.* One could pull lumps of soft paper from it, tear it apart, and write on it without difficulty in a blotty sort of way. There were some old dead gum-trees left standing near the house to show the steps cut in them by opossum-hunting natives, who now no longer existed in those parts. The notches were probably only cut big enough to rest the great toe in, but the bark and tree had swelled as it grew older, and the holes were now large enough to hold the whole foot. Some of them had been enlarged into nests by the laughing jackass. Lots of those comical birds perched on those trees and gossiped about us, as we sat and watched them.

The garden at Doondale was a sight to see: pink and white *Azalea indica* fit for London shows, bougainvillea with three yellow blooms at once in their purple bracts, flame-trees *(Sterculia),* gorgeous Cape lilies, and all our home-flowers in perfection. I was offered the loan of this lovely house for a month, when they were all going to another house on the cooler side of the hills. It had a valley of ferns a mile off, and one could see miles of cabbage-palms below like gigantic Turk's-head brooms, such as housemaids use to sweep away spiders with. The road along the coast to Kiama (pronounced "Kye-aye-mar ") was dreary enough, through miles of tall dead trees all ringed or burnt to death purposely by civilised man, who will repent some day when the country is all dried up, and grass refuses to grow any more.

At the lake of Illawarra we again found ourselves in the tropics, all tangled with unknown plants and greenery, abundant stag's-horns, banksias, hakea, and odd things. I put up at the house of a pretty little widow, who apologised for having a party to say good-bye to some friend. They danced till morning, soon after which she was up to see me off. Before this I had wandered on the lovely sea-sands, seeing and hearing the great waves as they dashed in and out of the blowholes. Rocks and giant fig-trees grew close to its edge, and I found basalt pillars as sharply cut as any on the Giant's Causeway itself. The road up the Kangaroo river and over the sassafras mountain is pretty. I tried to make out the sassafras leaves by their scent, but nearly all the leaves were much scented on that road, and it was not till some time afterwards that I made out the tree. After turning the top of the hill we came suddenly on the zamia or cycad—a most striking plant, with great cones standing straight up from the stem. When ripe the segments turn bright scarlet, and the whole cone falls to pieces, then they split open, and show seeds as large as acorns, from which a kind of arrowroot can be extracted, after washing out all the poison from it. The natives roast and eat the nut in the centre of the scarlet segments. There were no zamias outside that valley, which seemed to have no outlet. Like that of the Yosemite, it was discovered by a mere accident. It belonged, like the greater part of Illawarra, to the family of Osborne, who were building a large house there. It was certainly the most enticing part of Australia, and I wished I were an Osborne.

We came upon another high platform or cliff with a great waterfall falling from it into the blue depths some thousand feet below, and a distant view, like that at Govall's Leap, over endless misty forests of gum-trees. At the station we found no horse-box, so I left the carriage and walked on through three miles of Camden Park in the broiling sun, not blessing the three generations of Macarthurs who had taken such pains to make such a quantity of shadeless turf round their isolated English homes; but I forgave them when I met B.'s warm welcome amid her children, and saw her dear mother's sweet smile again.

I saw the advertisement in a local paper of a ship sailing homewards commanded by R. T., so I wrote and asked him if he were the "Bobbie" who used to ride the rocking-horse in our lobby while his father gossiped with mine at Hastings years ago? He answered, "I am that very identical Bobbie," and asked me to come and have luncheon on board his ship; so I went, and sent my bird-skins home with him. After a day's shopping, the railway took me up into the mountains again to stay with the wife of the Prime Minister, a man of great talent, who delighted in collecting beautifully bound books, exquisite china, and other nicknacks to fill his pretty house. But he seldom lived there, leaving his wife and youngest daughter to keep house in almost complete solitude; and perhaps it was that very busy and unselfish life which made the daughter so attractive to me, and such a delightful companion. She knew so much of the plants and birds and beasts around her, and loved the beautiful views over the sea of blue forest and real sea beyond as much as I did.

I found twenty-five different species of wildflowers in ten minutes, close to the house, and painted them. The garden was cut in terraces, descending into the real virgin-forest, with fine gums and banksias left standing amongst the imported flowers. One could hardly see where the wild and the tame joined. The view was especially gorgeous in the sunset, when the many miles of forest beneath us became a rich plum-colour, with the bloom of the same fruit on the edges of the different heights against the golden sky, brightened by the stars of tree-ferns, ridge over ridge. But though it looked so bright, it was far too cold for out-of-doors sketching or dawdling, and I worked on steadily in my room. The native pear was in both fruit and flower. I painted it, and also a pretty little kangaroo-rat which Lily had had as a pet. She had a lame seagull, too, which had broken its legs, and she used to carry it in her arms while its brothers and sisters swam about in a small pond in the garden. She delighted in bringing up and taming strange birds and then letting them loose in the forest. Gorgeous foreign pheasants used to come and look in at the window occasionally, former pets which wished to see her again. There was something quite touching about her isolation and her devotion to her mother.

On leaving them I returned to Sydney, to the fine old house of Sir G. M. at the head of Elizabeth Bay, which was then occupied by his nephew and his wife. Mr. C. spent his life in arranging and collecting the most perfect museum of Australasian natural history in the world, in a temporary building in the garden. This was to go to his College of Surgeons at Sydney when he died. It was a great delight to me, and he gave me some duplicate butterflies, and a rare red parrot from the Solomon Islands. He had a splendid specimen of the long-nosed ape with the natural fur tippet from Borneo, looking like a medieval clown. His miniature opossums and flying-mice were exquisitely stuffed. The garden was lovely, the bay as blue as an Italian lake, with headlands crossing one another at the end, and three islands covered with woods and small houses. That famous Sydney Harbour! Every stranger is so much bored everywhere by the question, "How do you like Sydney Harbour?" that some English naval officers at a picnic printed up over their tent, "We do like Sydney Harbour!"

I did not care for the town, and was glad to be in the fine old comfortable Queen-Anne sort of house in such miserable drizzling rainy weather. Here I could work on quietly; but I returned for a night to Camden to pick up my box and take leave of dear B. and her mother, and then was picked up by an express train and stowed away on a shelf in a real Pullman car. We reached the end of the rails at eleven next morning, and I was crammed into an omnibus with thirty other persons, and with nine horses to drag us. The party were all most good-humoured, and the country was richly cultivated, with orchards and corn. It was Sunday, and they deposited us at a place called Albury, where there was a considerable scramble to find rooms. I was showing my free railway ticket to prove my respectability, when a gentlemanly young man told me he had seen me at Singapore three years before, and he turned out to be the valet of Sir W. G., playing courier to Lady F. and her daughters on their way back to Adelaide. My respectability was established by my being on speaking terms with such a great person, and I got a room. Albury is a neat little town, with blue hills behind and hedges of pink and white roses, with white robinia trees planted in its streets for shade, now covered with bloom and looking like snow-balls.

We started on Monday at six o'clock with the same troop of good-tempered people, and crossed the fine running river Murray, the one big river of Australia. It was very full, and there were still lakes left of its overflow, with pelicans fishing on the tops of their long noses, their heels in the air, many smaller birds also dabbling in and out of the water, and big trees standing out of it like islands. Many of the gums had a weeping habit like willows, and their long bundles of leaves were blowing about in the wind. Three miles brought us to the end of the Victoria railway, where my free pass ended, and I had to pay like an honest woman again. I had another talk with the *G.* valet, who said, "You must come and see our new place in the hills; directly I saw it I said it would just suit you!" We passed the two chimneys which marked the place where Kelly and the other bushrangers were taken—all the rest was burnt.

As we got nearer Melbourne we saw miles of pasture, covered with a kind of coloured dandelion *(Crypiosiemma cal-endulacea),* whose seed was brought over from the Cape only a few years be-

fore and now grew everywhere; but it did no harm, for the cattle ate it. Dear old Mr. C. met me at the station at Melbourne, and drove me home in his nice close carriage with splendid horses to the most comfortable of stone houses, with two storeys and a lift, as well as a beautiful marble staircase. It had been made for an invalid daughter, and was easily worked by water-power. Mrs. C. was nearly blind, and seldom went out, but was as kind as her husband. They had two nice maid-servants and a good cook; they never gave parties, but had their table always laid for twelve. All near friends and relations knew they were welcome whenever they liked to come, and the seats were seldom empty. With those kind people I stayed whenever I was at Melbourne, in the greatest peace and comfort and perfect quiet.

Melbourne is a noble city, and its gardens are even more beautiful than those of Sydney, with greater variety of ground, and lovely views over the river. The distant city towers make an imposing group from all sides, standing as they do on the top of an isolated ridge of high ground. Fine atmospheric effects are produced, as in London, by the abundance of smoke which hovers over the busy town. It is by far the most real city in Australia, and the streets are as full of quickly-moving people as those of London. The dracaenas in the many gardens about it were loaded with great flower-branches, and the ti-tree was everywhere gay with bloom, reminding one of the May bushes at home. Mrs. C. drove me down to her pretty house at Brighton, eight miles off, where I saw quantities of another less showy variety planted along the edge of the sea to bind the sand: the whole shore was lined with it. The same tidy comfortable establishment was kept by the C.s in their country house as in Melbourne, so that they could drive friends down at any moment, without notice or luggage, and find all ready for them. They had a few roses and carnations close to the house, but had the good taste to leave the rest to nature, and it was full of pretty low shrubs and sandflowers. I had a delightful drive and scramble round the low

cliffs and headlands, finding quantities of long spiral sundews and other treasures.

Baron von M., the great German botanist, gave us a great deal of his company at Melbourne. The Great Exhibition was going on, but as tiring as those things generally are, and I did not often go into it. There is a fine public gallery of pictures containing many good modern paintings: a huge duplicate of Herbert's "Moses," Long's "Esther," and another by him of a dancing-girl performing before a lot of Spanish monks. Melbourne is anxious to become musical also, and went mad over a highly gymnastic pianist, Ketten, of whom, they were all astonished to hear, I had never even heard. We went to hear the " Elijah " performed, chiefly by amateurs, and old Mr. C. went too and said, "Yes, he didn't mind it, but he preferred the bagpipes!" The old gentleman took me down to see the races on the famous Cup Day, and we walked about amongst the crowd looking at the marvellous dresses, some of them so loaded with pearls and other precious things that they were lodged at the banker's till Race Day came again. It was a very good-humoured crowd. There were more than 10,000 people in the reserved part; we were outside, which was more entertaining. My old host enjoyed going out to sights, "if he could be of any use. " I took the hint, and pretended he could be of great use, and it certainly added to one's pleasure to see his benevolent happy face near one. He had had a hard life. When he came out at first he disappeared into the bush for some years, and was called the "lost sheep." When he came out he was a rich man, having "taken up" ground and picked out trusty agents to look after it in all directions, with a discretion which cannot be taught.

I went to the Zoo at Melbourne one day, which possesses perhaps the finest living lion in the world, and a tremendous and most hideous baboon from Africa, with a long nose, eyes on the top of its head, and a furry tail curled over its back. It sat on a stool with its feet down like a Christian, getting up now and then to roll its stool about, then leaning its chin on its arms against the bars of the cage. It stared at us outsiders as if we were a show got up for its amusement, and thought what stupid beasts we were not to wear fur in such cold weather. I heard a good story of a cockatoo in those gardens which lived near the porter's lodge, hearing him say constantly, "Walk in, ladies and gentlemen. Don't come all at once; one at a time." The bird escaped from its cage, and was discovered with a troop of wild cockatoos attacking it, lying on its back, defending itself with its feet and beak, and crying, "Come on, ladies and gentlemen, come on; not all at once—one at a time, one at a time."

Mr. C. put me into a coach one morning at eight o'clock. It was crowded, but I had a decent kind of woman next me, whose husband was a Chinaman! I made friends with both, and though I could not help wondering if he had lost his pigtail in an official way, *i.e.* by the cutting of the prison barber, he seemed to me a much nicer neighbour than a rich squatter, who refreshed himself at all the wine-shops, and took doses of whiskey between whiles. Once the Chinaman caught my eye at the moment, and made a most comical face at him. We left him in a forest, where a groom was waiting with two saddle-horses— real Australian saddles, with pads in front to keep the men on "buck-jumpers," whose performances all the world has heard of. When we came to Healesville we changed coaches for the second time, and found all the men of the place eagerly waiting for news of the Cup Race, the telegraph not having reached those parts. At Lilydale I had a talk with a magpie in a cage, and the master came and showed it off—a real wonder of a bird. It laughed, and cried, and sang, with every word distinctly articulated; quacked, crowed, barked, and talked like a human being, while its master stroked it like a cat.

After leaving Healesville I got on the box-seat, and saw the lovely forest as we mounted the steep ascent. The driver said he did not believe any of the trees were 320 feet, and that they could make

the Baron believe anything they liked; but it was a noble forest. The trees ran up like gigantic hop-poles, with thousands of tree-ferns under them, also straight, and thirty feet high, swelling much at the base of their stems, a nice undergrowth of young gums and other shrubs under them again. The little inn at Fernshaw was perfect quarters, with a lovely little garden of sweet flowers, surrounded by the forest, and with two nice girls and their brothers to take care of me, their only guest. One of the girls took me out for a walk at once, crossing the stream by a long straight fallen tree for a bridge; then we walked under the fern-trees to another fallen tree, of which I could not see the end, but which was being sawn up bit by bit to use in building some new rooms at the inn. We found our way under the lace-work roof of fern-fronds to a small stream, which was also arched over by them. Their stems were green with moss and parasites, wire-grass, ferns, and creepers; over them was a lovely tecoma, with white flowers tipped with deep red purple, hanging among its glossy green leaves. There was a delicate moss on the ground with flowers like Maltese crosses, and tiny white and purple violets without scent.

The musk-tree was just coming into masses of white bloom, its leaves magnificent, polished like those of the great American magnolia, with white linings. It is difficult to realise the great height of those gum-trees, they are all so much drawn up. It was two and a half miles up hill to get to the tallest group, and was very cold, with some rain. I was glad to warm my half-frozen fingers by a fire in one of the blackened treestumps now and then. Not a creature passed me all day, and there was no noise, except the songs of birds and the jeerings of the laughing jackass. The leaves of those amygdalina gums were much larger and darker in colour than the other sorts I had met with; its young shoots were copper-coloured, and the stems were just peeling off their old bark, showing all sorts of delicate gray and red brown tints. The tree-ferns (chiefly dicksonias) were unfolding their golden crowns of

huge crooks. Every step brought me to fresh pictures, but it was impossible to give any idea of the prodigious height, in the limited space of my sheets of paper. The Baron had said, "One thing I must entreat of you, Mees; when you will go to the forest, make a boy go before you and beat about with a stick, and please, you will always keep your eyes fixed on the ground, for the serpents are very multitudinous and venomous." But the girls told me the only place a snake is ever seen is on the high-road; there it is dangerous. Snakes here only like dry places.

On the 5th of November the loyal Protestants of Fernshaw made a circle of great fires all round the house. Their effect among those tall trees was a wonderful sight, but the trees were so full of moisture that there was no danger of fire spreading, they said. A woodman told me that he had often felled trees over 400 feet high. "When they was down you could easily stump them off, and there could be no mistake about that," he said. The highest the Baron measured was 365 feet, and I painted that very tree, a white gum. There are over three hundred of these giant trees.

I painted a lyre-bird's nest wedged between two tree-ferns, four feet from the ground, made of great dry fern-leaves. The VOL. II L hen puts her tail over her head as she sits, and goes in backwards. In front is a sort of shelf or terrace on which the old ones perch to feed their one darling, never letting it out till it is old enough to feed itself and protect its own most inconvenient tail. They only lay one egg a year, and I was given two eggs taken in consecutive years from that nest. They were very different in colour,—one purplish, the other greenish, —but both the same size, and mottled. The birds are very shy, and seldom seen, unless by chance a party of them is found practising the art of mimicry, which they enjoy, and which engrosses them so entirely that bird-hunters have then been able to get close up and watch them. I heard their notes while painting, but never had the luck to see them. My landlady had tried to bring up young birds, but said they died of fright. The eggs too she had put under hens, but they were so thin the hen broke them with her weight. The robins' nests were very lovely, and the honeysuckers wind cobweb round and round theirs, taking the end in their beaks and circling round them till the nests look like balls of knittingwool. They are fastened in the same way to the twigs they rest on.

I had a delightful day returning. The coachman started by picking up a lot of school-children, one after the other, with their slates and dinner-baskets, nearly filling the inside with the happy little creatures; then he tossed me the reins and jumped down and into the bush after a snake, which however escaped him. We picked up some black men near their settlement at Healesville, and all the rest of the native colony came to the roadside to see them off. Some of the girls were handsome, with long silky locks well straightened with grease or water, "to look like other ladies"; the men with huge whiskers and moustache. One of them was called Prince Albert; and they perched themselves on the top of the coach, and looked supremely happy, with their short pipes always in their mouths. We passed large vineyards, but coachmen do not think much of a wine which only costs a shilling a bottle. They also had hop-gardens, which answered well. It is curious how we have introduced all our weeds, vices, and prejudices into Australia, and turned the natives (even the fish) out of it.

CHAPTER XIII WESTERN AUSTRALIA— TASMANIA—NEW ZEALAND

I ONLY stayed a night at Melbourne on my return, and then went on board the great P. and O. boat, *Malwa,* and on by it to the harbour of Adelaide; but the sea was very high, and though I had written to warn Dr. S. that I would land and see his famous gardens, I gave up all thoughts of doing so when I saw how it was to be done. We took a whole day landing twenty-four passengers, as no steamer could keep within reach of us for two minutes together. All the twenty-four had to be let down over the side in an arm-chair into a tiny steamer,

which was tossing about and knocking itself to pieces against us in the most terrifying fashion, the waves washing over its deck every moment. One girl from the Melbourne Exhibition wanted to go down with a pair of glass vases in her hand. Most of the women fainted before they were stowed away in the little vessel. One little girl alone went down smiling and as if she liked it, close locked in the arms of one of our jolly ship's officers. It was fearfully cold, and we were all glad to reach the calm and sunny waters of King George's Sound, and to land on the sandy shore of Western Australia.

Mrs. R, the flower-painter I had heard so much of, sent her friend, the young manager of the bank, to meet me on board, and to bring me to the little cottage she was lodging in, where she had kept a room for me, and at once introduced me to quantities of the most lovely flowers—flowers such as I had never seen or even dreamed of before. The magistrate, Mr. H., came soon after, and wished me to go on to stay at his house, but I was too well off to move. He told me the only way of going to Perth was either by the horrid little coasting steamer once a fortnight, or by the mail-coach, which also went once a fortnight, travelling day and night, with passengers and boxes all higgledy-piggledy, any quantity in a sort of drag or open cart. It generally broke down and killed one or two people. If I hired a private carriage, it would cost me £25 for it alone, without the horses. I said "Thank you," and wrote to the Governor by the mail just starting, who telegraphed in reply that he would send me a carriage at seven shillings a day hire, and I might have the free use of policehorses and a driver as long as I stayed in Western Australia, to take me wherever I wished. Long live Sir H. R.!

So I stayed on at Albany till the carriage came, and found abundance to do. The garden of our little house led right on to the hillside at the back, and the abundance of different species in a small space was quite marvellous. In one place I sat down, and without moving could pick twenty-five different

flowers within reach of my hand. The banksias were quite marvellous, their huge bushy flowers a foot in length, and so full of honey that the natives were said to get tipsy sucking them. The whole country was a natural flower-garden, and one could wander for miles and miles among the bushes and never meet a soul. The difficulty was to choose the flowers. One was tempted to bring home so many, and as they were mostly very small and delicate, it was not possible to paint half of them. Mrs. R. did it most exquisitely in a peculiar way of her own on gray paper. She was a very pretty fairy-like little woman, always over-dressed, and afraid to go out of the house because people stared at her. I admired her for her genius and prettiness; she was like a charming spoiled child. There was one interesting person besides in Albany, Miss T., who had a weak spine and could hardly walk a step, but she could ride all day long, and knew where all the rarest plants were to be found; she kept Mrs. R. supplied with them.

At last the carriage came, carrying its own wheels inside, and having substitutes, which did not fit, in their place. The head of the Albany police assured me the axle was broken, and no one in Albany could mend it; the carriage must go back by sea, and I might hire another carriage at fifteen shillings a day, etc. I said, "No, I would rather give up Perth, and go back to Victoria by the next steamer." After an hour or two he came back to say they could put the back wheels on the front, and the front ones back, and he thought it might be ready in three days. I grumbled and growled at so much delay, and was next told it would be ready to start in the morning, if I liked, which I did, and started, passing wonderful things, though the best flowers were said to be over. The chief excitement was a group of hakeas, like a tall hollyhock with leaves like scallop shells, perfect cups growing close together round and round the stem. Every leaf had a flower or seed-pod resting in it; the flowers were pink, but the chief peculiarity was, that every spike of leaves was gradually shaded downwards—the leaves at the top salmon pink, those next yellow and orange, and so into brightest green, blue-green, and purplish gray. It is one of the remarkable plants of the world, but I heard of a far grander edition of the same, 120 miles off in the bush—the *Hakea Victoria,* which is coloured the same, but is three times the size, each leaf as big as a soup-plate, and veined in the most wonderful way with all the rainbow tints. We stopped to rest the horses near a large mere, where I found beautiful lobelias, utricularias, rushes, and plenty of boronias and other common Australian plants. After that we wandered over long tracts of sand, wearisome, except that it gave one time to see the endless variety of flowers, for we could only go at a foot's pace. We stopped to rest at a lonely house, where I asked for some tea, taking for granted it was an inn, and after an excellent meal the woman would take nothing! So we gossiped instead, and I watched the baby sitting on the ground playing with two kangaroo-dogs, a magpie, and a cockatoo. One of the dogs, a kind of greyhound, rested his head on the child's knee, turning up its long nose to lick its face every now and then. The magpie was not in the least afraid of anybody, letting the child poke bread and butter, not only into, but down its throat. And I stroked it like a cat, and Cocky also, with his funny long nose.

The coachman, as usual, sat down under the carriage, hammering at the wheels. After that we got on to a better soil, and turned off the road to Mr. H.'s large comfortable house. His wife was quite cross when I said I must go on the next day, though he understood at once that I could not keep the police horses. Next morning he took me to see the buryingplace of the black tribe that belonged to that part of the country. Each grave was hung with all the treasures the departed had valued most. Emu-feathers, boomerangs, wild cats' tails, pots and pans, pocket-handkerchiefs, a chimneypot hat, and wigs stuck on sticks; sometimes others were murdered on purpose to accumulate wigs for the decoration of a popular chief's grave.

Mr. H. told me a good many odd stories of those people. He showed me an old hag who was in mourning for her seventh husband. The custom mentioned in the New Testament is the same there, and the next related has to "take the woman to wife " when her husband dies, *nolens* volens. They are a hideous race, but they work well, and make good grooms and shepherds. The first thing I saw when I got up in the morning was my police-driver hammering under the carriage again. We had no accident, but the country got drier and drier. All the flowers seemed to turn into everlastings, as if they were determined to fill the gap left by so many other departed flowers, and to keep up a show till the others began again. One sort was especially lovely—a white fluffy ball, with pink satin spikes set in it, and no visible leaves or stalk. It looked like a gem on the white sand. Yellow, pink, and white, all the everlasting flowers were there in quantities, also the strange plants known as "kangaroo's feet." I saw some specimens of the curious gum-tree which grows at the edge of the Marlock Scrub. The latter has turned back many Australian explorers by its density, being almost impossible to penetrate. The flower of that gum is four-cornered, and of the deepest carmine colour.

We passed only three houses in a sixty mile drive, and could get no food, but my Irish police driver boiled his "billy" and made some tea at Black River, where the water was worthy of its name. However, we ate all we had with a better appetite than those who have abundance at home, and divided our few biscuits with Black Johnnie, the policeman's Man Friday, whose Irish was almost as incomprehensible as the language of the natives; but he was very kind to me, and managed to avoid the deep ruts, and to keep the old carriage very cleverly from accidents. It was a kind of "inside car" with two seats sideways—one for myself, one for my portmanteau, and a bit of canvas spread overhead on four poles to keep the sun off. I had a tin biscuit-box half full of damp sand on the floor to put rare flow-

ers in; but the sand soon ceased to be damp, many of the flowers drooped as soon as they were picked, and the whole carriage, as well as the box, became full of them. It was impossible not to try to keep the beautiful things for the chance of being able to paint them. At Rogenut I lodged at a police station, and was so surrounded by policemen calling me "your ladyship" that I felt like the Queen of the Cannibal Islands, and rather a dangerous character. The sundew grew into perfect little trees near there, and we passed a mile of everlasting flowers, one perfect bed of them in the burnt-up grass. Then we came to another marvellous sandy plain, and every kind of small flower—great velvety "kangaroo's feet," with green and yellow satin linings, exquisite blue or white lobelias, heaths, and brooms; the latter was very tall, sometimes bordering the road like a hedge, and whipping one in the face as the carriage pushed through.

We stopped to dine at a pretty inn covered with creepers. The empty fireplaces were filled with masses of everlasting flowers of the most delicate pink and white species. We met, farther on, groups of natives with bundles of long arrowheaded spears, which they throw at any animal they wish to kill. I also saw some sandal-wood *(Fusanus* spicatus) trees, one of the gums, which has the same scent and qualities as the real sandal-wood; this is exported to India and China to take its place in the manufacture of boxes and other pretty things. It grows to the size of an English apple-tree, and is hung over with a mistletoe which mimics its own leaves exactly. On that day, too, I shall never forget one plain we came to, entirely surrounded by the nuytsia or mistletoe trees, in a full blaze of bloom. It looked like a bush-fire without smoke. The trees are, many of them, as big as average oaks in our hedgerows at home, and the stems are mere pith, not wood. The whole is said to be a parasite on the root of another tree (probably the banksia). They have never succeeded in cultivating those trees in captivity.

After that we came to William River,

whose squire-landlord was a curious mixture. A man of the oldest English family, a perfect gentleman in sentiment, though rustic in education, manner, and speech. I saw him watering and grooming his horses, and slouching along beside them in the shabbiest of old hats and coats. He took his wool and sheep to market, had never been out of the colony, and had no ideas beyond living there from day to day; and yet one felt that the man was a gentleman, though keeping an inn, ploughing his own land, and talking as if that were the only object worth living for. After leaving his house we had a heavy drag over the sand with tired weak horses, as the good ones had to be kept back for the expected mail. It was slow work, but we saw a sight worth some weariness —twenty-five emus all in a group feeding. We got quite close to the monstrous birds, all amongst the grass-trees. They must have been nearly as tall as myself. It is strange how little native birds and beasts of Australia seem to fear men. The grass-trees were in enormous quantities, covering large tracts of country, with flower-spikes eight feet high, out of all proportion to the trees, and often curled in curious snakelike curves. We saw the largest pair of kangaroos I had met with, the old man over six feet high; and arrived early in the day at the little inn of Bannister, which stood quite alone in the forest, with a lovely garden of sweet flowers in front, and a most friendly landlady. I had a quiet afternoon at my ease, with her gossiping at my side, delighted to get a new talking-post.

The next day we had the same tired horses and a seven hours' drag over the sand. We passed several hollows filled with the "smoke-plant," looking like mist on the ground, and many curious rushes, sundews, and bushes of exquisite scarlet grevillea, which looks like polished coral; blue veronicas, with lovely sollyas and kennedyas over them, and plenty of grass-trees, varied by kingia, a still more striking plant, with a crown of balls like drum-sticks on its head. The grass-trees at a distance, and especially when seen with their backs to the light, were wonderfully like the "black boys," with bits of skin hanging from their shoulders, and wild wigs, their heads so much too big for their bodies, and spears held up high above them. The banksia-trees were then covered with their young leaves and shoots of rich yellow, brown, or white, and the native wigwams of bark or leaves looked picturesque under them. At two o'clock we got some food and fresh horses, and came on eighteen miles at full gallop, covered with dust, holding on for dear life. Many horses in Australia will either go full gallop or not at all, and when once they are started (no easy matter), the thing is to keep them at it by hooting, whipping, and shouting. My Irish policeman and Johnnie enjoyed that last stage: it was too fast for me.

I found a note at the next hotel from the High Sheriff, asking me to come and stop with him; but I had promised to go to Mr. and Mrs. Forrest, and met them in the road, they having come fifteen miles to meet me across the country from Freemantle. So I transferred myself and my things into their pretty little carriage, and returned over the white sand to the prison, whose temporary governor he was. The sea at Freemantle was edged with delicate little shrubby plants, then out of flower, but their leaves and twigs had a whitish look, and seemed to harmonise with the dazzling white sand in a way that green leaves would not have done. It was fearfully glaring there. Mr. F. was a very bluff specimen of John Bull. He had led one of his exploring expeditions into the interior, and had written a book about it, and married his charming little half-French wife in consequence. Eight years he waited for her, and at last, when he came back from so many dangers, she consented. I liked them both extremely, and they both had a real knowledge of their country and its natural history. I painted the flowers of the jarrah or mahogany gum-tree there; it was loaded with bloom like our wild cherry at home, and I put in their pink cockatoo amongst it. He and his wife came from a more tropical part of this west coast; the hen was very delicate and colourless. The pair walked all over the house as they liked, and it was amusing to see the way the gorgeous cock used to try to help his wife up and down the stairs, chattering all the while. At night he would leave her and fly up into the tall trees outside to roost, coming in for his breakfast in the morning.

Mrs. Forrest also gave me to paint a bit of the black velvet "kangaroo's foot" with yellow satin lining, from Champion Bay. I was sorely tempted to go there, and to Nicol Bay, but the hottest season was coming and the flowers would be over; so I went on to Government House at Perth, to thank the Governor for all his kindness in sending to fetch me, and then Lady R. made me come and stay with them. But when I heard that the *Eucalyptus macrocarpa* was to be seen in flower at Newcastle, horses were again ordered for me, and I was sent over there. Mrs. Forrest came with me, and we enjoyed our eight hours' journey, with three relays of good horses. We went only too fast through all the forest wonders, and I screamed with delight when the small tree came in sight close to Mrs. H.'s house. Every leaf and stalk was pure floury white, and the great flowers (as big as hollyhocks) of the brightest carnation, with gold ends to their stamens. It was well worth coming for. The tree had been common enough in old days, on the edge of the desert, but the sheep had taken a fancy to it and had gradually eaten it all up, and they were carefully saving the seeds of this one that they might sow them and raise up more food for the sheep! It stood close to the verandah of an old-fashioned house, full of small rooms, belonging to a very dear old lady, a Mrs. H. She was a great reader, and had a great memory for remembering what she read, and she was never dull. A long-beaked cockatoo sat on the back of her chair, making confidential remarks in her ear, with a curiously smiling expression, his head on one side; and she fed him with a teaspoon. She said he sometimes took naughty fits, and would peck off all the buds from her flowers; then she whipped him, and when he saw the whip coming he used to retire into a tree, and sulk all day till he felt good or hungry, when he would come down and approach his mistress most humbly, making low bows all the way, and seeming to beg forgiveness. She had also seven magpies, and a most odd bird called "more pork," with an owl's head, lovely tortoiseshell feathers, and blue eyes. It was only lively at night, when it caught mice better than any cat.

Newcastle is a mere village. The hills all round are covered with pretty green round-topped little trees, looking in the distance like Italian pines. They are really a sort of acacia, called "jam" trees, from their wood smelling like raspberry jam—the same plant as the myall-tree of Queensland, I believe. The wood is very hard and good for carving, and, with the so-called sandal-wood which grows near it, is sent out to China to make into workboxes and other ornaments. The latter has a leaf like a gum-tree, and a mistletoe which grows on and mimics it. The road to and from Newcastle was hilly, and gave us some fine distant views over the plain and broad valley of Swan River, with piles of large granite boulders in the foreground, and many curious plants amongst them. The grevilleas were especially beautiful: one of them had blue metallic leaves, and long flower-bunches of graduated tints, from pink through orange into green, but they would not keep an hour, so I often had to draw them at once, finishing them from a dried specimen and my notes.

We took a rest in a grand forest of big "black butts" and red gums, with grand grass-trees and kingias and zamias underneath. We turned off the road at Guildford, but were stopped by a broken bridge, so sent the carriage back to the inn and walked on to a ferry opposite to the house of Mrs. F.'s brother, and she cooeed for a boat, which came and took us across the beautiful running river: a most refreshing sight in such a thirsty land as Australia. We found the family at dinner, and had a share of their boiled mutton and potatoes. One of the children gave me a huge bunch of ver-

ticordia, looking like everlastings, but every tiny flower was a bunch of delicate fringe. This is a class of plants impossible for clumsy fingers to paint, but most beautiful and peculiar to the colony. Afterwards we were driven to the house of grandmamma, an old Frenchwoman in a wheel-chair, who was a terror to all her belongings except her sons, whom she had spoilt. One of them had had six hundred horses, but found them such a bother to look after that he turned them loose into the bush, and never inquired what became of them; and that poor papa forgave even that, and set him going again with sheep.

Two cockatoos and a huge mastiff were walking about the darkened room in perfect good fellowship, but the great attraction to me was a bush of white grevillea which had come from Champion Bay originally. It looked like a gigantic lavender bush, with a woody trunk, and stick-like branches all round, bearing lovely cream-coloured waxy bunches of flowers a yard above the leaves. At night the scent was so disagreeable that every one killed it, and this plant was the only specimen left. Mrs. F. had brought me on purpose that I might get a bit and see it growing. We had a charming drive homewards, but I lost my nice friend half-way, where her husband intercepted us with his pretty carriage and white ponies, and carried her back to Freemantle. I found Perth in all the misery of a fancy-fair; every one was selling or being sold, and all were worn out with the weariness of it.

After a day's rest I was packed into a new carriage—a box on four wheels, with two seats across and a bit of canvas stretched over four posts to keep the sun off; no means of mounting into it except by the wheel, and I was warned to be always well seated before fresh horses were put in, as they were apt to run away at first. The Governor and Lady R. packed me in themselves, and O'Leary said "he knew them well, he did, and there weren't no harm in them, there weren't, neither the man nor the leddy." Perth was altogether peaceful and nice to stay in; no ill-natured gossip,

and every one seemed happy and content. Much of this was owing to the simple kindness of those at Government House, who when they were sent once to Singapore petitioned to go back again to Perth. The situation is very pretty, with Swan River looking like a lake in front, and a most lovely garden sloping down towards it. We passed through glorious forests of big gums and mahogany trees, and plains of paper-bark trees, with their curious white twisted trunks and velvety green heads, sometimes sprinkled with small white flowers. We saw also the native pears, with long bunches of greenish-white flowers, and gray velvety fruit, the younger ones almost rosy, like the winged seeds inside. We passed swamp banksias with twisted gray stems like olives, and miles of grass-trees and kingias, looking like frosted silver in the mid-day sun. We nearly ran over an iguana; the horses' feet were almost on him before he took fright. He was beautifully varied in colour, and a yard and a half long. They are said to be very good to eat.

I found quantities of a lilac satin flower about the size of a primrose, with oily grassy leaves. Picking it made my fingers wet, though it was growing in the driest white sand, among other dry things, and was said to be *Byhlis gigantea,* a sort of sundew mentioned by Darwin, but not yet seen in England. The little inn at Pinyarrah was a model one, smothered in creepers, with great bunches of the *Ipomoea cccrulea* all over the roof, and a huge fig-tree shading it, loaded with delicious brown fruit—the best and largest figs I ever tasted. The landlady was most anxious that I should admire some worsted-work pictures of the last generation, and other curiosities. It was a heavy drag on to Drake's River. There O'Leary took out the horses for water and a feed and boiled the tea, and we had a good dinner at eleven o'clock in the morning. The grass-trees had a dozen heads of flowers from one trunk, each head bearing its long flower-spike. The zamias were on stems or stocks a yard high. They are said to be the oldest plants in the world, a connecting link between palms and ferns, and have been found in a fossil state engraven on the Portland stone of England. After leaving Drake's River we passed large clearings filled with thousands of kingias, with the perpendicular sun's rays shining down on their crowns and making them look like frosted silver. We passed also magnificent spreading gums, reminding me of old oaks at home, their branches equally full of knots and twists, their rough red bark most picturesque. But the kind called jarrah or mahogany is the best timber, and it has a smooth gray bark. We had six changes of horses, and the first set ran away at once for three miles,—it was all the Irishman could do to keep them straight, —then, when they had had enough he said he hadn't, and he kept them galloping for another three miles. They were really splendid creatures, too good for such a driver. All the horses jumped about at starting, and I held on tight and pretended to enjoy it. O'Leary did really enjoy it, I believe, and kept them well in hand, letting them run away if they liked. He had been twenty years a coachman to a real "leddy in Irrreland before he came out with his wife and sax children to this counthrie, and a fine counthrie it was." The last pair of horses were real beauties, small and swift, and not vicious. The wife of the policeman who kept them gave me a good tea, and kindest welcome, and would take nothing. Soon after that we came to a lovely bay of the sea quite landlocked, with ti-trees, peppermint-gums, and acacias, and met a mounted policeman with a kind note from the magistrate and Mrs. C, asking me to stop with them two miles short of Bunbury, in a charming large house by the side of a clear river, with olive-trees, mulberries, and other importations all round the garden.

Mr. C. had built the house chiefly with his own hands. He was a most energetic and liberal-minded old man with a pretty young wife and baby. His one weak point was his descent, and rightful claim to a lost title; his scheme was that the baby was to become Lord de C. again. He forgave me for not going to church, where he read a service and ser-mon in the absence of the clergyman, and, judging by the same performances, morning and evening, which he gave us, it must have been comprehensible to himself alone. Why did he do it? He told me he had been much taken aback by having to read a printed notice that "the offertory on Christmas Day would be devoted to the augmentation of the Bishop's salary, that being quite inadequate to his wants; and that persons not attending church were requested to send their contributions to the clerk!" Mr. C. quaintly observed that he "thought both he and the doctor had also a salary inadequate to their wants, and might quite as reasonably make a claim on other people's money."

The country was more English-looking in that remote part of Western Australia than anywhere else that I had been to on the vast island. We went for a drive through cornfields and meadows with noble red gums isolated like the old oaks at home, with hedges and numerous gates which had to be opened and shut in the same tiresome way as at home; and we paid a visit to Mr. C. 's two old sisters, who had a pretty old-fashioned garden and pets, and took care of their own health. Then we crossed the river by a footbridge and went to another cottage in a wood to see Miss B., an old hunchback lady, who was famous for her dried wildflowers. A dear old soul, who hugged me for coming to see her, and loving flowers as much as she did. She showed me exquisite collections of dried seaweed, and would have given all of them to me if I had allowed her; but I only took one fine specimen of sundew, and a green "kangaroo's foot." Her brother was an Irish baronet, and she had talked all her life of going home, but still lingered in the old tumbledown cottage, which was originally brought out bit by bit from England fifty years before and more. It was smothered in fruit-trees: oranges, lemons, mulberries, peaches, and figs; the river ran beside the garden. It seemed a perfect place for a peaceful old age like hers. Poor little woman! I felt quite sorry to leave her so alone.

Bunbury is a model place, with a long wooden jetty Vol. II M running out into the exquisite blue bay; at the end of it a ship was being loaded with "mahogany " and other precious woods. After leaving this pretty place we entered miles of sand, and such wretched land that even trees were stunted; only the swamp banksia, with its smooth slate-coloured stem and thin white leaves, was very large, but the orange bottlebrush and some other swamp bushes were in great beauty. Patches of lobelia and other tiny coloured flowers made the sand gay. We had two pairs of fine fat horses, which were to go on with me all the way along the coast to Albany, one pair being sent on half-way to rest till we came. Some hours ahead Mr. H., the Head of the District Police, had arranged most kindly to go with me on horseback, and to make his tour of inspection fit into my plans. He was a model of an active young English gentleman, and soon after arriving at Vasse he arrived also. Vasse is the chief port of that part of Australia, and the fortnightly mail steamer always touches at it. It was named after the botanist of *La* Perouse, who was lost in the woods when a party from the ship landed there, and after waiting awhile they sailed away without him. Nothing certain was ever known of his fate, but the natives told stories of a white man who went up the hill every morning and looked out to sea for some hours, and he seems to have "lived till he died," like people in fairy stories. While strolling on the sands at Vasse I met a troop of small birds with white waistcoats like snowballs, who all faced me till I got dangerously near, when they turned their long tails to me and retreated with dignity some twenty steps, then simultaneously faced round again and stood perfectly still while I was still returning their first stare. The sand was as white as the birds, but more dazzling; the water like blue opals. The peppermint gum is the commonest shrub there, with hanging slender knife-like leaves like our willows, and a tiny bunch of white flowers at the footstalk of each leaf, which are strongly astringent in taste and smell.

I had tea with the magistrate and his

wife, who had just returned from a month of camp-life in the new settlement north of Nichol Bay, where he had been investigating some cases of kidnapping the poor blacks and selling them as slaves. He had little doubt that the story was true, and that a regular system was followed there by men who called themselves English. He said the poor people hid themselves when they saw his party coming, and though laws could be made to crush those wicked practices, it would not be easy to enforce them over such a large extent of country and sea-shore. He had also heard of some bad cases of murdering natives, which were difficult to prove, but a bad beginning for a new country. From Vasse we had a long drive over deep sand and swamps, a rest, and a change of horses. O'Leary drove me off, and after a few miles declared not only that he had lost the road, but was on the one we had come in the morning, and that he saw his own wheeltracks and horses' hoof-marks. He turned right round, in spite of my entreaties; though I showed him the sun's shadows, he went due north instead of south, and was fortunately stopped by the bush. It was no easy matter to turn again, but at last we regained the road we had left, when he again insisted it was wrong, trying another towards the east, which came to an end, and again we turned with the greatest difficulty. Then I cooeed, and after awhile the man with the led horses answered me and came up, telling me, as I knew before, that the first road was the right one, but that O'Leary was only good as long as he did not think; when he tried to do that he lost his head entirely.

Just before sunset we reached the great wooden bridge at Blackwater in the midst of a splendid forest; the police station is in a lovely situation with sweet flowers growing round it, and has a very nice master and mistress, who made us most comfortable. Mr. H. was a welcome guest, and never came without a supply of barley-sugar for a lovely girl of three, which she received as her right, absolutely refusing to give up her cat in return. She sat nursing it on the verandah, with a big kangaroo-dog looking down on her with a proud air, occasionally licking the top of her head, for which he got slapped, and did not mind it, while she shrieked with laughter. I never saw such a beauty.

The next night was at a house of greater pretension but less comfort, belonging to the governor of Honduras. We started at daylight again with considerable difficulty, one horse declaring he never would, should, or could go uphill. The other had the same aversion to going down; he went sideways, sat down, and had to be held up, while I led the three loose ones. O'Leary lost his head entirely, and soon after that I found myself on my knees in the back of the carriage, and saw him, the horses, and the front part of the carriage, going off separately. Mr. H. and his famous policeconstable of Blackwater cut down some young trees, and patched the vehicle together. We started again, but O'Leary's nerve was hopelessly gone; he ran first into one tree and then into another, and finally completed the destruction of the carriage within a mile of the waterfall where we were to have rested, and just at the entrance to the forest of perhaps the biggest trees in the world. It was eleven miles from "The Warren," the place of all others I wanted to go to, but which the Governor had said was impossible; and I thought it a most lucky accident when Mr. H. decided on riding on and begging its owner to come to the rescue and take me there. I spent four delightful hours sketching or resting under those gigantic white pillars, which were far more imposing than the trees of Fernshaw; their stems were thicker and heads rounder than the amygdalina gums.

About five o'clock Mr. B. came (a cousin of my cousins of Beechboro'). He drove a heavy kind of drag, and I felt I had no more fear, his driving up and down and in and out of stumps and trees was so sure, going at a good trot all the while. We were under enormous trees, chiefly white gums, as smooth as satin, and sometimes marbled, with a few rough red trunks or "black butts " among them, and small casuarinas and shrubby bushes underneath. The Warren, a rambling, untidy house with farm-buildings, stood near a clear river, in a hollow, with two fields surrounded by forest and "ringed trees"; nothing ever seemed to have been repaired there. How could it be, with no servants and no neighbour within thirty miles? Mr. B. and his sons looked after the horses and cattle from morning till night, dressed in rags, and his pretty ladylike wife did everything that was done inside the house, with only an orphan from the Perth Orphanage, with long waving black hair over her shoulders, to stare at her; she put her arms akimbo and had a good laugh when she was told to do anything. The baby was thought to be dying when I arrived, but took a turn for the better, and the poor lady said my coming had brought good to them, and she did not mind the extra trouble. She made a first-rate plum-pudding in honour of Christmas Day, in spite of all her other work and anxiety. What a situation hers was, with miles of forest all round, and no doctor within a day's journey! under those enormous trees of valuable wood, that were safe to stand because there were no means of taking them away. The growth under them, large and small, was good food for cattle; even in the driest summers there was water in the hollows, and many actual running streams with maidenhair ferns edging them. One lovely plant grew quite high, with its leaves arranged in stages all the way up like stars of green, and tiny strings of flowers or waxy berries under each leaf.

My old carriage came on after we arrived, patched together so that it might be sent back to its owners at Perth, but not fit to go on with; indeed, they all said O'Leary's nerves were far too shaky for any one to trust him as a driver in future. So Mr. H. went on his tour of inspection eastward, and I turned west, with Mr. B. in the heavy drag. He did not even take an axe or a rope, and after a few hours his carriage suddenly broke down without driving against anything. He calmly said he expected it, gave me the reins, and disappeared into the wood. Soon I heard a cracking and crashing, and he returned with a young tree with forked ends just the right size, and bound it on the pole and axle with a bit of liane he had also found of the right sort, and some superfluous straps from the harness, and it lasted well for twenty miles! One of the police horses, "The Lunatic," tried in vain to get us into more trouble. It would not consent to go down-hill without a severe struggle, getting itself under the patched pole, and pushing down the other horse. But it had a masterhand over it, and no harm came. The horses had all odd names; another was called "Breach of Promise," because it was bought from a man who changed his mind. We found a lighter carriage at Mr. B.'s, and went on for the night to the pretty cottage of Blackwater again, with no adventure but Mr. B.'s nose taking to violent bleeding. I made him get out and lie flat on the ground, after pouring some eau de Cologne down his back, and he tied his little finger tight with a bit of string; and I know not which was the cure, but something cured it.

We reached Vasse the day before the steamer started, and it took me back to Albany round the stormy West Point of Australia. John H., the P. and 0. agent, met me on the pier, and took me up to old Mrs. T.'s, who had kindly offered me houseroom. She and her daughter would have made a good centre for a novel: the poor old hunchback lady with her stick and nutcracker jaws, taking such a keen interest in the outer world, and the delicate daughter, scarcely able to crawl on foot, but riding so bravely on her little horse, finding out where all the plants grew, and how. Every one knew and loved her; she had never been away from the place all her life. Her father, the general, was one of the first settlers there, but he had been ruined by his sons, who were obliged to fly to other colonies; and the old lady still lived on letters from them, as her daughter lived on her collection of dried plants. She had coaxed many of the most curious wild ones to grow in her garden too, and they consented to be tamed. She had a pretty little maid they had brought up from childhood; and a funny old con-

vict gardener had been thirty years with them, through riches and poverty, and considered them his own property. I stayed a week, hard at work painting, and offended half the good people of Albany by not returning their visits. The place was full of feuds and follies. The original old Captain H. kept the shop, and speculated in different ways till he made ten thousand a year. For ten years he and the C.s lived next door to each other, but never spoke; then Mr. C. made friends with the sons, and married two daughters to two of them, but the old gentleman remembered past affronts, and still swore he would never give a penny to either of them. John, too, married the C.s' governess, and was at first in the same disgrace, but was now getting gradually into favour again, as they could not well do without him. He was agent for the P. and O., and also manager of the shop, and the most active and thriving man in the place. He promised, if at any time I would return, and give him a month's notice beforehand, to fit me out a covered waggon, and engage Webb, the naturalist (convict), with his black wife, to go into the bush with me far away to the east, and find the *Hakea Victoria* and other plants near the Marlock Scrub! That man had many curious things to show, which he sold to the ships when they passed through King George's Sound. He would have been a delightful companion on such an expedition, and October was the best month to start on it.

I bought from him a pair of lovely green ground-parrots with spread fantails, and a curious bit of petrified wood encrusted with coral. There was another collector at Albany who showed me a shed full of live cockatoos. When he opened the door they all ran out screaming with their mouths open, expecting food. The blacks brought them to him from the nests; and each had a painted mark so that they should not be sold to him a second time if lost, like the sheep. He got two guineas apiece from the P. and 0. passengers for them. Mr. H. put me on board the big ship at midnight, after nearly three hours' row in the moonlight, having secured a cabin

all to myself; and when I was humbly creeping into the lowest seat at table the next morning, I was ordered up beside the captain, and opposite an Indian general and his wife, who had had the sense to buy a house and property at Dunedin in New Zealand, to pass the rest of their lives in, and to start their family, as they thought the old world too full already, they said, and after thirty years in India had few links left there to draw them home.

At Melbourne I was again most kindly welcomed by the C.s in their comfortable home, and even Baron von M. was excited over my paintings of the nuytsia and the Eucalyptus *macrocarpa,* which he had named, but had never seen in flower. When I showed him the bud with its white extinguisher cap tied over it, which I was saving for Kew, he said, "Fair lady, you permit I take that?" and calmly pocketed it! I found the first steamer to Launceston was so full that I could not even get a place on its floor, so I went up to Mount Macedon to see the R.s for a night. It is 2000 feet above the sea, with villas dotted about in clearings of the forest. The one I went to was very pretty, with a clear running stream and artificial fern-gully and gardens. I found Mrs. R., whom I had seen at Albany, at home with her father and mother, and a small boy who called her "Little Mama"; and he had as a pet a fluffy native bear or koala, whose portrait I took. He had huge ears and astonished eyes, and was not so big as a cat. He was the best of sitters, as his activity came on only at night, when we carefully fastened him into his box. How he got out no one knows, but the next morning he was found sitting demurely on the doorstep, waiting to go into the house, with his funny claw-like paws crossed, looking the picture of sleepy innocence. 1881.—On the 20th of January I crossed the Straits in a small steamer, outrageously crammed, and every one sick except myself: it was most horrible! We stuck in the river near Launceston, and a friend of a friend's friend came to meet me, but was so busy that I told him to go on shore again, waiting myself till the steamer reached the quay, when I got on shore, and on by rail to Deloraine, where he had telegraphed to the parson to meet and lodge me. Mr. E. and his wife were charming people, and really liberal. The bishops at home had refused to ordain him, so he had it done in Tasmania or Victoria. He never read the Athanasian Creed or anything else he disliked, and he proposed Buckle and Herbert Spencer at the lending library. His wife was much disappointed at hearing the latter was a fidgety old bachelor, instead of the father of a dozen children; she had brought up hers on the principles laid down in his books, and looked up to him with the greatest reverence. I really enjoyed being with Mr. and Mrs. E., but I pitied them, for they had not one congenial neighbour. The country was not in the least attractive to me; it was far too English, with hedges of sweet-brier, hawthorn, and blackberry, nettles, docks, thistles, dandelions: all the native flowers (if there were any) were burnt up. One lovely flower I heard of and was taken a long drive to see. It was—a mullein!

Some of the hills looked like volcanoes, but were not, and beautiful lakes were said to lie beyond them; but I was not tempted to explore and to encounter difficulties at that season of drizzling rain and cold. After three days' rest I came over eleven hours of slow railway across the island to Hobart, crossing a mountain pass by clever round-headed zigzags, through a rich country of corn and grass, all burnt up, past stations with scriptural names, down to the Derwent River, which was like a series of lovely lakes, leading grandly down to the capital of the island, backed by its forest-covered mountain, the sea in front. Here Mr. S., the clever schoolinspector, had taken a room for me in a boarding-house at the back of the town, near his own house. I was not allowed to stay there, though I had no formal introduction to the acting Governor, Sir H. Lefroy. When I went to inquire for letters he and his wife received me like an old friend, and insisted upon my coming at once and making Government House my home while in Tasmania. They took me round their garden to see the lovely

views over sea and river, and were full of plans for my seeing the Island, which, however, were never carried out. They had a tree loaded with dark apricots like purple velvet, crimson inside, but tasting as other apricots do: it was very beautiful. The mulberries too in that garden were most excellent, with a comfortable ladder always under the trees to pick them from. Cherries, raspberries, every kind of fruit which grows at home grew better than at home. Half the jam in the world is made in Tasmania. It is sent on to the colder parts of New Zealand and Australia, where enormous quantities are always consumed.

I went with the Governor's party to the Tasman Island and Port Arthur, in the great steamer *Rotomahana,* for a day's excursion, to visit the now empty prisons of that old convict settlement. Eight hundred persons went at ten shillings a head, and most fell victims to sea-sickness; but we on the upper deck had a very good time, in spite of the high wind which always beats round those wonderful headlands. The basalt columns of Cape Raoul are more massive and fantastic than any I have yet seen in the world. The base of them is always white with breaking waves, and woe betide the ship which goes too near them! In the days when the poor convicts were kept at Port Arthur there were many months of the year when no hope of seeing a ship existed, and supplies became very scarce. The harbour itself was smooth as a lake, the banks covered with pretty bushes and trees.

Before I went to stay at Government House, the Head of the Gardens came and drove me up the Huon road to the shoulder of Mount Wellington; thence we walked to St. Crispin's Well, where there is a tablet to the memory of Mr. Crispin, a shoemaker, who grew rich and started the great waterworks of the city. Strangers and custom have gradually canonised him, and surely he had deserved the honour more than most saints! Four miles of walking took us to the lovely spot where the clear water bubbles out amongst the fern-trees and all kinds of greenery. After a rest we

plunged right into the thick of it, climbing under and over the stems and trunks of fallen trees, slippery with moss, in search for good specimens of the celery-topped pine, of which we found some sixty feet high. It was not in the least like a pine, excepting in its drooping lower branches and its straight stem: the leaves were all manner of strange shapes. We also saw fine specimens of sassafras (which yields an oil rivalling the real American sassafras in value), and the dark myrtle or beech of Tasmania. Quantities of the pretty pandanus-looking plant they call grass-trees or richea, really a sort of heath. The whole bunch looks like a cob of Indian corn, each corn like a grain of white boiled rice, which, again, when shed or pulled off, sets free the real flowers—a bunch of tiny yellow stamens, with the outer bracts scarlet. There is also an exquisite laurel, with large waxy white flowers. There were many gum-trees, some of them very big, but mostly peppermint- or "stringy-bark." The famous blue gum *(Eucalyptus globulus)* was rare even there: strange that this should be almost the only species known or grown in Europe.

Another day I scrambled up a staircase of fallen trees and tree-fern trunks, by the bed of a half-dry stream, for 1500 feet, till we reached the first ridge of the mountain, where an old convict and his wife lived summer and winter by boiling tea-kettles for visitors. After that I was led by Judge D. and his son to the foot of the basalt cliffs under the top, and was shown many pretty berries and flowers peculiar to the mountain. The Judge loved the place so much that he and his brother had bought the greater part of the mountain, to prevent its forest being destroyed and the flowers exterminated. It was a grand position up there—a perfect moraine of fallen stones, squared and cornered by volcanic action below, and above were gigantic walls and pillars, sharp-cornered and dry, without even the relief of plants among them; but all around were endless varieties of small shrubs, now loaded with beautiful berries, the flowers being over. Few capitals in the world have such a wild mountain-side near them.

Rainy weather came on, and I was glad to be in the beautiful rooms at Government House, my room looking over the blue bay with the great terrace of flowers in front. On that terrace was a fountain in which the L.s had kept a tame platypus for some time; but every living creature is ambitious of doing something beyond its powers, and that silly little beast wanted to climb up a stone wall, fell back and broke its spine in the attempt, and that was the end of it. Miss L. and myself were taken one day by the A.D.C. to an old barber's in Hobart, who collected and stuffed skins, etc., and he showed us all his treasures; the greatest being three little opossum-mice, the smallest of all marsupials, with prehensile tails—soft little balls of fluff with very big ears. They were only lively at night, but quite tame and easily managed in the day-time. The old man almost cried at parting with them, but at last I persuaded him to do so (for a con-si-de-ra-tion). The first night I had them I put the box containing them inside a basket, and they made such a scamper-ing that I could not sleep, and thought they were all over the room. I put them into a drawer the next morning half asleep, while I shook out the box, when the male mouse absolutely refused to be caught. If I opened the drawer he ran up the back of the chest into another, he had reduced me to despair, when I suddenly thought of a means of trapping him. I put the little box in which his wife and daughter were asleep into the drawer and left it for half an hour, and then, looking carefully in, I found him also fast asleep in the box, and so got them all three out safely. The fish at Hobart were wonderful. Captain H. had a trap from the end of the little pier, and used to bring up the most lovely specimens for Lady L. to paint every morning; but their colours faded quick-ly when exposed to the light. There was a grand ball during my visit, and a cotil-lon was danced for the entertainment of the French and Italian ships' officers then in the harbour, who put all their en-ergy into it. I went up the Derwent the

next day in the steamer to New Nor-folk. The river spread itself out like a series of lakes, with rocks closing it in where it narrowed, all arranged in hor-izontal strata like walls of gigantic ma-sonry. It ran through a rich bit of coun-try full of hops, and orchards loaded with fruit. The wheat harvest was going on much in the usual English way, with carts and stacks. Hedges of hawthorn loaded with red berries, sweet-brier, and blackberries,—all was too English,—it might have been a bit of Somersetshire, as I drove along the beautiful river-side for four miles to visit Mr. R., an English squire-farmer. His little house was smothered in flowers and fruit, the win-dows so darkened by them that inside one could hardly see to read. All hands were employed in picking boxes of plums and apples to send to Victoria and New Zealand, all unripe.

I was weak and good for nothing with a gumboil and swelled face, but was never allowed to rest for a moment. First I was carried off to see a black swan which could not be found; then to the salmon-hatching place, and other outdoor diversions. I was driven all over the country to see views; but ten Tartars and a drag-chain could not have made me sketch there, which, I fear, was a disappointment to my kind host. On Monday I was sent down to sleep at the inn, so as to catch the first steamer in the morning to Hobart, where I had or-dered a carriage to meet me and take me over the Huon road, which creeps round the shoulder of Mount Welling-ton, commanding lovely views of sea and islands. The forest scenery is of the grandest description, with undergrowth of tree-ferns and shrubs of many kinds, that called the Tasmanian lilac (*Prodan-tkera lasianthos*) being the most strik-ing. The other flowers were nearly over, and marvellous berries were ripening, like precious gems of every vivid colour.

I stopped at a nice little inn by the long bridge on the Huon river, and drove on again the next morning along its lake-like banks, past Franklin to Geevestown, where a whole family had settled and populated a district, estab-

lishing saw-mills and a tramway far into the noble forest they were gradually de-stroying. Mrs. G., in the absence of her husband, answered the telegram I had sent, and met me with some of the chil-dren and a luncheon-basket on a truck. They took me up some miles of beauti-ful valley, to the tree which had struck the Governor so much that he had begged it might be preserved, and he was going to have an inscription with its measurements put on it. It did not seem to me to be much larger than many others, certainly not nearly so large as the gums I had seen in Western Aus-tralia. They had cut a road up to its foot, and expected me to paint it there, with the sun in my eyes, and 5000 mosqui-toes in a highly irritable state round my head. But unless I put my head on the ground and looked straight up I could see nothing of the monster at such close quarters; no distant view could be got, and I again disgraced myself by doing nothing. Then I drove back to Franklin, where the good rector and his wife kept me, sending back for my portmanteau from the bridge inn. They took me for a ride the next day up the steep hills; then we tied the horses to a fence and walked four miles up a still more beau-tiful tramroad, and among bigger trees than those at the Geeves. We measured one tree in that valley seventy-six feet round at a yard above the ground, and we heard of a perfect monster we did not see. It was a most difficult thing to get accurate truth about those trees, or to see those which people talked of; they always melted away as we came near them.

The finest tree-ferns I had seen in Tasmania grew there; many of them were hung with clematis, like the Eng-lish one. The rector chopped about with his axe, made tea in a "billy," and was very happy, poor fellow. He seemed to have terrible work to extend and keep up the church. One of his outside dis-tricts was a ride of seventy miles, over an almost dead road. Once he had five bridges to mend or make to get home from it, and said his good horse saved his life when he could not keep awake on its back, and he fainted when he got home at last I asked if the people cared for him there; he said they were almost savages, but he thought they liked him better than they did at first. When he came, two years before, there had been neither church nor parson for thirty years, and the Roman Catholics and Dissenters had it all their own way. We met his chief rival—a most jolly old priest, who went everywhere on foot.

Franklin was a damp feverish swamp. The winters were very long, and strangers seldom came to cheer them. It had been an old convict-settlement, and the place and people had a bad name; wrongly, for they were a most sober, peaceable community. I asked if the people were better off than at home, and was told that out of a hundred cottages I should not find one without a piano! though the master was a mere labourer, and no instrument could be had for less than £30. Wages were very high, and the fruit-shops so abundant that a large profit could be made every year by the sale of the surplus fruit. I paid a visit to an old lady at Franklin who had two rival pets,—a cat and a cockatoo. When puss was petted or fed, cocky said, "Poor puss!" and rushed at her tail with his mouth open. The tail was full of knots in consequence; but puss had learned always to face cocky, and to keep her tail out of harm's way behind herself. It was a comical sight to see the two fencing with one another.

I had ordered a room, as I passed up the shoulder of Mount Wellington, at the Red House, and returned to it on my way back. It had been built by a man of taste, years ago, for the sake of the view. He died before it was finished, and it was now occupied by a widow with a large family of nice children, who made it delightful quarters to stay in. From the window I saw the town far below, with its lakelike river, and every variety of distant forest up to the white ghosts in front. Behind the house was the forest-covered mountain, and a pretty half-wild garden. I should have enjoyed ending my life there; it was all so sweet and full of peace. I received a letter here telling me (too late) how to find the remains of the famous tree called Lady Franklin. I had inquired for it at a cottage not two miles from the spot, and no one there knew anything about it. Little of it remains, but quite enough to show what it must once have been. I watched an opossum-rat in the road helping himself to the ants in an ants' nest; he was so busy that he took no notice of me, letting me stand close by for a long time.

Sixty hours after time my ship arrived, and I had to leave a large dinner-party at Government House to go on board, where, thanks to my kind friends, I found a cabin kept for me. It was frightfully cold, and I huddled myself up in my opossum rug and read Miss E.'s new novel and Disraeli's. My poor little mice were half frozen, and cold as apples; but I took them in my hands and rolled them about till they got life into them, when they began to yawn and stretch themselves again. Major D. and his wife persuaded me to let them take the poor little things on to Wellington by sea, where it would be warmer, to save myself the trouble of carrying them about overland. No wonder it was cold, with no land between us and the southern ice-cliffs! It was also foggy, and we could not get up to the bluff till past eight in the morning. But the mountains began to show before we landed, and the Southern Island of New Zealand looked fine in the distance: but for the cold I should have liked a month there. A little snow was nestling in the hollows of the rocks, and I felt it was useless for me to attempt it. The near shores were rough and rocky, covered with ti-trees, with many odd things amongst them of the dracsena kind, the oddest thing being the *Panax crassifolium.* In its young state it resembled the skeleton of a half-folded umbrella; some three or four years later, it would become a round-topped tree with fivefingered leaves. I saw also the "lawyer" creeper, *Rubus australis,* so full of thorns that no human being could make his way through the bush when tangled up with it.

The train had waited for us, and now took us slowly and with many stoppages over the rich marshy level ground to Invercargil. Masses of the native flax, with great black bunches of seed-pods on tall stems, and now and then a rag of red flower left on them, were all over the plain, as well as coarse grass like the tussock; and the views passing through the low boggy country were most picturesque, with rich browns and purples, streaks of water, and distant mountains, long-legged blue birds standing on pedestals of stakes in the foreground. But it was a bog, and no mistake, reminding me of the stories old Mr. C. had told of his arrival in it fifty years before, when he took three days in reaching Invercargil from the bluff, and nearly lost his life in the attempt. Now, it is done in one hour of easy railway travelling. Invercargil is a widely spreading place, with houses standing fifty yards apart, and has one of the cleanest and most comfortable hotels I was ever in. But the wind howled and the dust blew, and all was cold and dreary VOL. II N to me. I was glad to leave at seven the next morning for real country and new weeds. My train only went as far as Elbow, where I was turned out again for six hours. The air was thick with thistle-down, and the native weeds were being stifled by Scotland's royal flower. We passed over miles of grand scrub, every tree new to me (and no gums!), mostly of the " ti-tree " sort; perfect cushions of green velvet of different tints on queerly twisted trunks, whose branches sprang out at unnatural angles, giving a top-heavy look to the trees. They were all thickly padded underneath with bushes and creepers, and were a great contrast to the "touch-me-not" trees of Australia. Among them were great dracsenas with many heads, bearing a strong family likeness to those of Teneriffe. Even these were smothered with creeping-plants. Elbow has the great mountains all round its yellow plain, with a clear river running through, and quantities of the tall flax all over it. I settled myself to make a sketch in the glaring sunshine, and found it really hot. A woman told me that three days before the snow had come quite low down, but that few patches were left now. These mountains are 5000 to 8000 feet high. The flax-bushes are most beautiful, often a dozen tall brown stems of seed-pods to one plant, and when opened the black shiny seeds pour out in a string. They are most exquisitely packed in grooves in the pods. The remains of the flowers looked like scarlet fuchsias, and must have been most gorgeous when in perfect bloom. At four o'clock we again started through the wildest mountain country, all stones, with rabbits running over them up the steepest places in such numbers that the very stones seemed to be running too. They are becoming a real plague on the island. We descended by two zigzags to the edge of Lake Wakatipu, just as the sunset threw a great purple shadow slowly up to the top of its rocky walls.

A steamboat soon took us farther into the darkness, between high bare mountains reminding me of the Lecco end of Lake Como; but before real darkness came I saw some wonderful nooks and gullies in the steep precipices, filled with green scrub and dracsenas among the rocks, unlike anything I had seen before. Queenstown is on one of the few bits of flat in the whole of the wild lake, a kind of delta brought down by a small stream in flood-time. It is full of summer villas and hotels. Mine was a collection of the very smallest rooms possible: the first had absolutely refused to hold my easel with its three legs stretched out; the second just held it and the bed too.

The scenery was all bare and savage. Not a place to land on for miles after Queenstown, and no plants or trees to be got for foreground within three miles of walk, except a few lots of flax. My bones already began to ache with rheumatism, so I contented myself with finishing a sketch of the lake from my window on the ground-floor, with only the road between me and it. Every now and then it would lash itself up into a rage without the least warning, the great waves making as much noise as the sea, and sending breakers up against the little pier. The lake is said to be unfathomable, with fabulous undercurrents, so that things thrown in do not sink, but float about half-way down, and in calm weather can be seen in a state of per-petual motion. People come to Queenstown for consumption. The air was exquisitely pure and fresh; the inn well kept; my hostess, a model of energy and good method, had a gang of Chinamen to cook and do housemaids' work, with some nice girls as waiters, and was most anxious to make her guests feel at home.

I joined an excursion party in a steamer to the end of the lake on the 26th of February. It was a small boat, but quite full. A large club of Foresters in green, with a band of music, had come from Dunedin the night before, and were greatly enjoying themselves without getting drunk. There were some other odds and ends of travellers like myself. One young man came and introduced himself as the son of some people I had stayed with in Queensland. On every side I made and found friends. The clouds cleared off, and the weather was glorious, the whole scenery really magnificent, as we went near enough to the shore to see the curious plants in the little crannies. I saw young panax trees with leaves two feet long and yellow midribs. The cabbage-trees grew into grand branching masses like the drag-on-tree. It was funny going through all this magnificent scenery with such a crowd of second-class English people. They got so excited over the beautiful lake and the terrible band of music on board that they began dancing solemnly, and the band itself got some one to play on an accordion, and began dancing too: only the men by themselves, no women joined in. They told me that dancing was quite a passion with our countrymen in New Zealand. We were all landed on a lovely wooded island to dine, and I got a splendid view of Mount Earnshaw, a real snow-mountain 9000 feet or more above the sea, with a grand foreground of New Zealand plants. That island has been preserved, like some few other spots in that part of the world, for the sake of picnics! I wished there had been more of those places required; for saw-mills and fires as usual followed fast the introduction of white people into the land. The end of the lake is low, though backed by the highest mountains, whose other sides dip straight into the western sea. In their folds are those wonderful sounds or landlocked bays, in which the largest vessels could ride at anchor, though on their steep sides there is hardly a landing-place. The sun only looks into them for a few midday hours.

We picked up two wandering Englishmen in a boat, who were just returning from some glacier expedition on Mount Earnshaw, and I at once made friends. One of them, a Mr. M., aged seventy-four, reminded me of my father in his simple manner and power of enjoyment in little things. He had come out for health thirty years before, and had never returned; he knew every track in those hills, and almost every flower. The other was like many other alpine men—his face a deep red from sun and snow and natural warmth of colour. He wore spectacles, held his head on one side, and seemed to consider us all a "mob," as he sat and sulked in a corner; so I enjoyed waking him up, and making him talk, *nolens volens.* When I asked him what cloud he had dropped from, he looked astounded at my impudence, then found out I was an English lady, and became an English gentleman, full of agreeable talk. The whole mob were good-natured. They fastened the red-coated musicians into the little cabin, and made a terrible row trying to play their instruments. When at last they were let out, one of them asked, "Are we within sight of land yet?"—"Oh yes, on both sides" (within 50 yards)—"Then some one 'ang my 'at on a tree!"—there was not the slightest scrap of a bush within sight there, and it was impossible not to laugh.

I got very chilled when trying to paint, so went for a walk the next day up and down the edges of the cliffs for four miles and back. It was very beautiful, every crack having running water, and the scrub was full of interest to me. The only biggish trees were a kind of beech like that in Tasmania and Victoria. There were many berries, but no flowers; and I felt the happier for it, as the scenery itself was enough to study at once. There were plenty of veronica bushes, and fern everywhere instead of grass; the sheep were half buried in it. It looked a good deal like bracken, but was more graceful, with red stems. The hills were precipitous; even on the tops one could find no flowers, except sweet yellow musk, such as we grow in pots (an importation), and a few harebells. The wind was bitter, and the waves beat on the shore like the real sea. I felt I could never rough it in such a climate, and my aching limbs could not crawl fast enough to warm me. I sat and wondered if I should ever get home to England and see my gallery finished. Mr. Fergusson had written me that the shell was nearly ready, and I longed to be there without the trouble of going. But first I went up another hill to see Mr. and Mrs. M. in their pretty cottage and garden. They highly approved of my paintings of the lake, and said they were truer than any done before. Those nice people had been acclimatising English singingbirds and turning them out over the country; they generally did well, and were absurdly tame, following one about and seeming to listen to fresh English voices as something familiar, and missed by them there. Mr. M. said if I would only stay, he would arrange for me to go up into the mountains, and camp out in a hut made by the engineers of a new road over to the west coast, which was then planning; and he thought I might still find some of the alpine flowers out. They told me, too, how they had been once caught in the rains up at a high lake, and stayed till all provisions but three boxes of sardines were finished, when they were forced to leave by the only possible track not washed away, which took them three days. They lived on one box a day, no bread, no sugar, but a little tea, and they slept in their wet blankets. My bones ached at the thought of such an ordeal. The only flower on the hill above now was a white gentian growing in a cluster.

On the 1st of March I left Queenstown and its stony landscape, and returned in the little steamer to the head of the lake, through a storm of thistledown, looking like snowflakes, and all blowing towards the East; the surface of the water was white with them. The great lake had two large rivers running in at the far end from the snow mountains, and only one tiny stream running out of it at the other. Where did the rest go ? It seemed too cold for evaporation, and the dry rocky sides showed few signs of it. There was only an early steamer by which to catch a morning train once a week, so I slept at the little shore-hotel at Kingstown. It was overflowing with guests, and there was no one to carry the luggage from the boat, but two of the passengers disputed for the honour of carrying my bag, calling me by name, and saying they were so glad I thought their lake beautiful; and when I asked humbly if they could find me a room, the rough landlord said, "A room? You shall not only have a room, but a sitting-room too, all to yourself, Miss North." And when I said it was very good of him, he said, "Good? no more than my duty to give you the very best I have!" I could not make out that he had any reason for this kindness but the fame of the two sketches I had done of the lake. How I should have liked to have stayed, but for the cold, which ordered me on inexorably! It was a pretty spot, that one lonely hotel, and two years ago the good people had been very well off, with the post-office store and their hotel all flourishing; but one night's fire destroyed everything. Not even the children's clothes were saved, and now they were slowly recovering and rebuilding, and had time enough to do it in, not a creature coming near the place between the daily trains and steamers.

The next day's rail was slow and tiring; it took us through a rich country with plenty of corn, now cutting and carrying, and fields of coarse strong grass, with hedges of gorse and broom, no trees but the blue gum planted in rows, itself as much a foreigner in New Zealand as the two others! The travellers seemed either farmers or shopkeepers taking their holiday trips, but all were very civil; and when I went to sleep and nodded my spectacles off, they picked them up and stuck them on my nose again, which woke me up, and we had a good laugh together. We passed meadows dotted with a kind of grass, whose fibrous roots formed a pedestal all matted together above the ground, often some feet high, and looking like the grass-tree in the distance.

Dunedin is a well-situated town, with hills behind and bays in front; but the hotel I had been told to go to, in the suburb of Leith, was miserably depressing. Everything seemed poor. I tried to walk to real natural country, but only tired myself and my poor aching bones, and I was glad to get on again and further from cold. The railway carriages were crammed with most objectionable children. The views I had heard so much of I never saw, though I incessantly looked, and I was half dead and starved when we reached Christchurch and its well-regulated and extra-English hotel. The next day was Sunday, and it was marked by all the meals being crammed together, 10 A.M., 1, and 5 P.M., leaving sixteen hours to fast before another came; I was upset internally, and was very wretched for a week afterwards. My box, which I had left at the station of Invercargil to be forwarded on the day I landed, had never turned up or left Invercargil, and I was sick of everything belonging to that cold, heartless, stony island.

The sight of Judge I. and his wife warmed me; they were so thoroughly genial and alive. But though he was the Resident Judge, I had a long hunt before I found any one who knew where they lived! They knew everybody and everything, and drove me to the club to inquire for my cousin, John Enys, who came up just at that moment, swinging a pot of apricot jam in his hand, which he was going to take back as a treat for me, to celebrate my visit to his station. He took us to the museum, and showed us all the New Zealand stuffed birds, and its one native beast, a pig, also a rat which was generally supposed to have been imported. But the birds did their best to look like beasts, having next to no wings, the great moa skeletons looking like giraffes. John Enys had made a hobby of the museum from its first start, and spent all his holiday-time collecting for it. He brought a friend who had collected nearly all the nests and eggs of the country, and the two were most pleasant companions there. He took me four hours of rail westward the next morning, talking and joking with every one along the road, and seemed a general favourite. He had hired a horse and buggy, which met us at the end of the railway, and we drove over the dreary burnt-up hills to his house, which was called Castle Rock, after a pile of strange old rocks near; they looked like the remains of some fortified place. His own quarters were at the edge of a black beech forest, which gave a more cosy look to the spot, but they were a hard, cruel sort of trees, the very tallest not more than forty feet high, with leaves as small as the box, under which no green thing liked to live; their branches feathering to the ground like Cedars of Lebanon.

The house consisted of a few single-roomed huts joined together by a verandah. An old man did the cooking in another separate hut, into which we went when the meals were ready. We generally found him pouring portions out of a saucepan into our plates, which were arranged in a circle on the floor for the operation, after which he placed them before us, and went and sat on a stump till we had finished and fed the cats, when he and the shepherds came in and finished what was left. John had a cheerful little parlour full of curiosities all over the walls and tables, besides plenty of books and newspapers, and he was never dull. He corresponded with all the scientific people of those parts, and got into the wildest excitement over a new weed or moth. He sent a man up the hills some 2000 feet, and had some large specimens of the vegetable sheep brought down *(Raoulia)*—a mass of the tiniest daisy plants with their roots all tangled together, and generally wedged in between two rocks, leaving the surface of the colony like a gray velvet cushion: at a distance the shepherds themselves could not tell it from the sheep they had lost.

The garden was full of gooseberries and currants covered with ripe fruit. We rested a night, and then drove on so as not to waste the fine days, crossing miles of weary waste and some lovely tarns with reflections clear as in a looking-glass. It was all gray and stony and horrid, with patches of snow near the tops of the dreary bare hills. I was always suffering more or less, and could scarcely sit still. We had luncheon in a nice little inn, and then crossed and re-crossed the wide river-bed of almost dry stones, a hard pull for the horse. After that came a long mount through the dry beech-forest; till at the top we reached a completely different scene, and a vegetation which rewarded us for all our trouble. The most remarkable plant was a tree which looked something like a small-leaved dracsena, or screw-pine, but which was really a heath! All its under leaves were purple, and its stems bright salmon-colour; the flower was over, but the terminal spikes remained, and were also purple. The whole was one of the most curious growing things I had ever seen in any land. The great *Ranunculus Lyallii,* or shepherd's lily, was there in quantities, with leaves looking like those of the Indian bean; and the native holly of light blue-green and prickly scented leaves. Nearly all flowers were over, except those of the riband tree—a lovely bunch of white bells, with leaves of three different shapes and ages. The whole gorge was lined with small shrubs of every tint and shape. It was very narrow, and would have been perilous with any but quiet horses; but ours was most tractable. My cousin got quite excited over the different plants and the difference in them since he had been there ten days earlier with Professor Kirk. He found a bit of edelweiss very like the Swiss one, and a few remaining flowers on the kata—a parasite tree which had then quite coloured the hillsides with deep crimson. It seemed to delight in hanging at right angles from the rocks, and in the most inaccessible places. At the bottom of the pass, where two streams unite, we found a comfortable little wooden inn. I did my best to sketch in a wood carpeted with todeas and other ferns, in spite of a

tremendous gumboil and a swelled face, and a wind which whistled through the valley, making the whole house rattle.

John said we should soon get into a country of bare stones again if we went beyond this famous Otira Gorge; so, after two nights there we turned up the hill again, over the stony river-beds, through driving rain and hail and furious wind, and took refuge at Mr. B. 'sfarm or "station," as it was called. He was out when we came, but his two maidservants were delighted to welcome another woman, and were most hospitable. The shearing was only just over; about twenty men were on the premises, and three young gentlemen "helps," two of whom were ruthlessly turned out of the best room to make way for one woman. At dusk the master returned and echoed the welcome, and it was nice to have a roaring woodfire, a rocking-chair, and piles of old newspapers, as well as Scott, Burns, Hood, and, strange to say, Darwin's works to choose from. But Hood was the favourite author of my host, who repeated whole pages by heart in the broadest Scotch dialect. If we had put off a day longer we could not have passed the swollen river, which we left a mass of dry stones. All day and night it stormed; the mountains were wrapped in wonderful and constantly changing clouds. The men came in and shook themselves like big dogs before they entered the parlour, all dripping and half frozen. It must have been a dreary life they led, having little to do, except at a few times in the year. They left the sheep at other times to look after themselves. The winters were very long, and sometimes the snow drifted to such a depth that when the road was kept cut out, a man on horseback could not touch the top of the snow walls on each side. The sheep are often blocked up, and have been known to live without food for six or seven days. They will stand perfectly quiet, licking the snow to moisten their poor throats.

Mr. B. kept cows,—a great luxury for those parts,—and sent my cousin a potful of butter by every mail, while he supplied them in exchange with his surplus newspapers. When the rain had a little abated we drove back to Castle Rock Station, and the next morning found snow all over the near hills, and the ground white with frost all round. The mountains looked very important in their white coats, but the snow altered them less than most mountains, as they were always covered with enormous fields or drifts of shingle of a drab or dirty white colour. The place would be quite unbearable in its dreariness, but for the dark beech-woods at its back, which crept up the gullies to a certain height—dismal little trees of twenty feet high, shaven by the winds and trimmed by the sheep. Still, they were the only trees there, and we blessed them. The grasses were the chief feature of the country. They all grew in separate tufts, the toe-toe as high as the tussock, with noble bunches of high-stemmed yellow brush-like flowers; another was reddish purple, and another like ripe oats, but none were green. The whole country was yellow, brown, and white.

It was far too cold to sketch, but I enjoyed a day among my cousin's curiosities. His little room was crammed with them. He showed me several eggs of the kiwi; one sort was sky-blue, and nearly as big as the eggs of an emu. No wonder the bird was said to die after laying it. If it died, who sat on it? Had it a stepmother? We drove through torrents of rain to the station, and the mud splashed the very top of my hat; but we had four hours to dry in before the train started.

At Christchurch I stayed with Judge I. and his wife, and found the box, which had taken three weeks coming from Invercargil at the other end of the island. Luckily it had not been wanted. But rheumatism was getting more and more possession of me; and we crossed in the big ship *Rotomahana* to Wellington, the capital of New Zealand, where the wife of the Premier received me most kindly. Her husband was making a tour with the Governor, and I missed seeing him then, though I had the pleasure of a visit from him and Lady K. when they came to England. I was ill and miserable, though I tried to work still, going by railway three miles along

the shore, and then crawling to a garden (which had once been made by a man of taste, and now was used by a nurseryman). Here I got good studies of the nickau palm, the most southern of all palms. The garden had been originally made by cutting out clearings in the natural bush, and those palms were left standing as they were, with tree-ferns and many of the rarer native trees among them. The nickau is a very awkwardlooking plant, all the branches pointing straight upwards, with huge stiff leaf-stalks and sheaths; but the fruit is of the brightest scarlet, and its huge bunches, as well as the pearly white flowers, make the plant conspicuous amongst other green trees. The black tree-ferns are very handsome, with huge hairy black crooks, and the Norfolk Island and other araucarias were all ripening their cones there, showing how much milder the Northern Island was than the one I had just left.

Dr. H. gave me a delightful walk in the Botanical Garden. I saw one fern-tree forty feet high there; and he showed me the entrance to a tunnel made in a tree by some grub. He said that the other entrances were often stopped up with a bit of bark so cleverly that they could only be found by feeling for them with the tip of the finger. Dr. H. also showed me the curious Maori House in the museum, which is lit at night by magnesium-light; it looked most mysterious and awesome in the flickering brightness, with its myriads of huge eyes made of mother of pearl shining out of the dark wooden figures. But except when with him or with Mr. M. or their wives, I felt like a fish out of water in Wellington, all was so stiff and ugly. One had to drive some ten or twelve miles to get to a bit of unspoiled natural bush, and then one found the ground strewed with sandwich-papers and ginger-beer bottles.

I was quite glad when the Governor came, and I moved into his house and heard him abuse the island and all belonging to it with as much heartiness as I did. He said, justly, something must be wrong with a country which required so much laudation. Every one was assert-

ing its supreme beauty and superiority wherever I went. Every blade of grass was to be especially admired, and was different from anything anywhere else. I had expected Sir A. G. to be unapproachable, and found him the contrary. He had a cold, formal manner, but we got on well at once. He was most courteous, and showed me up to my room himself like a gentleman, as his wife was not yet arrived; and a jolly housekeeper came after him and said, "I am Mrs. H.," and gave me a nice hot bath, in which I fancied I soaked off a certain quantity of the puritanical atmosphere which had so oppressed me since I came to Wellington: it did me a world of good. The party in the house consisted of two very young AD.C.'s, a dull man who always agreed with His Excellency, and a Fiji prince with a wonderful hanging brow and big black eyes; he had been brought up amongst Europeans, and dressed and ate as neatly as possible, talking quite good English. The Governor did most of the talking, his pet subject being Fiji; he was always happy talking over that island. He was most kind to me, and when he found I really wished to take my rheumatic bones out of New Zealand, he did his best to get me a cabin to myself. So I left Wellington on the 27th of March, and reached Auckland on the 29th, stopping on the way at Taranaki, under the shade of Mount Egmont, a perfectly formed volcano of a steeper slope than any I had before seen.

Till I reached Auckland I did not know for certain if I should get a cabin; but when I found I had one to myself, and no chance in the next mail, I decided to go on in spite of longings to see the kauri forests. I was too helpless and full of pain to do that or anything else then. Auckland was filled with travellers. There was not a room to be had in any of the decent inns, so I had to stay all day in a noisy room with a bar on each side of me, and left the island with a bad taste in my mouth.

The *Zealandia* was not much better. I was put at table with a set of third-class colonists, who scrambled for the very indifferent food like pigs. The respectable portion of the passengers had embarked at Sydney, and filled up all the other tables. Those who joined at Auckland were looked on as interlopers, and it was some time before a creature spoke to me except the stewardess. One morning I could not open my cabin-door, and I called through the key-hole to ask my opposite neighbour to try. He was an officer returning from the war in Afghanistan, ordered by doctors to get as much sea-air as possible. He was quite surprised to find a genuine Eng-lishwoman there, and told me, "Now mind you sing out if I can do anything for you day or night, and it will give me a real pleasure to do it for you." It did me real good to hear his cheery songs and whistling; and after that I knew everybody. Two young Australian lads going to Oxford and Cambridge used to sit on the floor and tell me all about themselves, and I liked them better than any of the others. One passenger was the forerunner of a circus, always going a month ahead of it to make arrange-ments and write advertisements; and he had not seen the thing itself for three years. The Equator nearly cured my rheumatism, as I had expected, though I could not walk without difficulty for two months more.

1881.—We reached Honolulu on the 13th of April, and at six the next morn-ing I took a buggy and started up the hills before any one else appeared. I met many native ladies riding in their sensi-ble bloomer costumes, with wreaths of roses round their heads, all going at an easy canter, and looking entirely com-fortable on their horses. I went on till the hills got bare and uninteresting; and, after a stroll amongst the scrubby pan-danus bushes, I turned back and met the other passengers coming up. I bought a couple of the native wreaths, made of roses sewn on a foundation of fern leaves, which I hung in my cabin and pulled gradually to pieces as fodder for my little mice. I saw nothing new among the plants, but most of those common in India and Brazil were grow-ing in the gardens, as well as a few from Australia. The streets were full of Chi-namen, who kept most of the busy shops. The air was delicious, and I went to the hotel and got a good hot bath and cup of coffee, feeling in charity with all men, but not sufficiently charitable to oblige the steward by cramming others into my cabin. One of the fresh passen-gers was a young operatic singer with her old German tutor, who never let her out of his sight if he could help it. She sang two nights to us, with a powerful voice but little taste. It was lucky I re-sisted the temptation of stopping in the Sandwich Islands and going to Hilo to see the burning lake, as the two men who did stop were shut up in quarantine till the next month's steamer came again, and saw nothing. Smallpox was raging in the islands, and my driver said the present king was guilty of having in-troduced two great evils—that disease and the Chinamen—into his dominion.

San Francisco, where I landed on the 20th of April, was in a terrible whirl and noise, and the Palace Hotel, at thirty shillings a day, was quite perplexing in its vastness. I brought back my rheuma-tism by wandering about the windy streets. I found my banker existed no longer. A newspaper man showed me the shut-up house, and offered conde-scendingly to show me another, who he thought would do as well, conversing affably all the way. But I was sent on again to the Anglo-Californian, where they gave me money and a letter to Pro-fessor D., who they said would tell me all about the redwood forests. I hunted up his house, but found he was geolog-ical, not botanical, and was sent on to Dr. B. It is no easy thing finding hous-es in San Francisco. They seemed to have been dropped down promiscuous-ly, both stone houses and wooden ones, large and small. The one I wanted had a fence, but no visible gate or number. Inside the fence was a small morass, weeds, willows, and a tub of floating water-plants, which told me that it be-longed to a botanist. Dr. B. introduced me to a Bohemian woodmerchant, who told me the finest redwood sequoias were on his place near Guerneville, many of the trees 200 to 300 feet high; and he wrote me down such compli-cated directions for getting there, that I worked myself almost into a fever try-ing to make them out in the local Brad-shaw, and was relieved when the morn-ing came to find it raining hard, which put off the experiment for awhile.

I took the opportunity of being packed up to move myself to quieter and less expensive quarters. First I took a through ticket to New York for £30, with leave to take twenty years over my journey, if it pleased me. I had a good deal of conversation about it with a very intelligent gentleman, who gave me hints about things in my way which were to be seen dotted over the vast continent of North America. He also made me a present of a bottle of Dr. Hammond's rheumatic remedy, which he took himself in single teaspoonfuls, and which must be used with care, stop-ping every now and then, etc. I took one spoonful, then did the stopping part. It was easier to enter than to leave the vast Palace Hotel. First to get a white porter to carry my trunk to the street car (my big one was already on its way to Kansas)—none of the blacks would touch it;— then from the car to the ferry (no fly would condescend to take me half a mile under eight shillings); then to get another porter to carry my things on board the huge floating hotel. At last a charming Lancashire proprietor of flies turned up to take charge of me, and put me into the train, which went on a kind of viaduct over the water in front of Oaklands. After five stations he pulled me out and put me into his fly, which deposited me safely at Judd's capital hotel: a mixture of all that is good in German and American inn-keeping, with a pretty garden all round, excellent food, clean rooms, and ser-vants with absurdly friendly manners— all for ten shillings a day.

The days were quite cloudless, but the nights were cold; and I slept de-liciously under my 'possum rug. The country VOL. 11 0 about Oaklands was bare, but very green, the grass sprinkled with eschscholtzias of the deepest or-ange, nemophilas, blue and white lupins, white and lilac phlox, and many other flowers. Blue gum trees edged all the roadways, and were just then loaded with large white blossoms, besides the metallic green seed-vessels: the whole air was sweet with them. The place consisted of two miles of street, full of shops running parallel with the harbour, which is like a large lake. From that long street endless villas and gardens went straggling up into the low green hills behind. The roses and arums in the gardens were very pretty and luxuriant. There was a nice black servant belonging to an old sick lady in the hotel, who found out my mice directly I came in, and went round telling every one else about them, till I stopped her by saying that they would die if they were much disturbed, and it was to be a secret between her and me. After that she used to play pantomime whenever we met, expressing the profoundest mystery combined with mice.

There were some fifty tables in the dining-rooms, and a big man walked up and down, apparently for the purpose of preventing any one from going twice to the same table. He came and pressed one to try this and that, all the most complicated dishes of the long bill of fare. Everything was extra good, particularly the "ice creams." The small children, as usual in the United States, were wonders of solemn selfpossession. One girl of eight used to come in by herself, and, after a long consultation with the waiter, pick bits out of about twenty little dishes, and then retire with unbroken gravity. One black waiter brought me a ticket for a concert (fifty cents); it was got up by some people he knew to help a poor widow-lady back to New Zealand. He said he guessed I should not miss the money, and he should feel obliged if I would go. I said I could not go, but would buy a ticket. "Then you may as well give it me; I don't mind the music now and then, and I guess I'll just step in and help 'em on a bit," he said, not mentioning how he was to help them on; whether by the light of his countenance, or by assisting in the so-called music.

I was still rheumatic, and very lazy about starting for the redwoods, having to carry my things down "three blocks" to the steam-tram on the long causeway

at a quarter to six, without any breakfast, as that meal did not begin till six, and laws in that well-regulated house were unchangeable. But I left my opossum-mice to the care of the housekeeper, and departed. The bay was most lovely as the sun rose, driving off the smoke of the big city, and I felt a new creature when I got there. A few steps took me to the other ferry-boat, where I got a good cup of coffee and bread and butter, and was pressed to take eggs, fish, etc. When I asked if I might take it on deck to eat—" Oh dear yes; breakfast was not charged by the hour there, and there was no law against eating it where I liked." I blessed the free country, and rejoiced that I was no longer in dismal New Zealand. It was very cheerful on deck. The seals and sea-birds were taking their breakfast too, having a grand morning's wash and play, both on the rocks and in the sea round the boat. The hills were marvellously green, and sprinkled with live oaks. Getting into the train at St. Quintin, and passing the pretty suburb of San Rafael, with its gardens of figs, vines, and gorgeous flowers, we went through meadows blazing with patches of colour like the beds of annuals at home (only fifty times as large): nemophilas, lupins, eschscholtzias, deep blue larkspurs, pink mallows, sunflowers, etc. The country was as rich as it could be, full of inhabitants and neat houses.

I changed cars twice, but had not to wait for them. The last time I had a most amusing man for a companion, who had been to Norfolk, and had stayed three miles from Rougham, where there was a most primitive old lady whom he could not help astonishing. She asked him if he had ever met any dangerous Indians; and he told her how once he had thought it prudent to show a chief his arms,— a penknife and a corkscrew,—and told him how he had once killed a tiger with those dangerous implements, screwing the corkscrew into the beast's forehead to keep him quiet while he cut his throat with the knife; and the chief reasoned slowly that he must also have had an evil eye, or he could not have done it. "But did you really kill the tiger so?"

said the old lady, quite solemnly. "No, I never even saw a tiger: that was only a Yankee yarn," he said. "And don't you know it is very wicked to tell such lies? Remember what God did to Ananias and Sapphira," said the old lady, terribly shocked and in earnest. She had never spoken another word to him, he said.

We reached the redwood forests all of a sudden, and the railway followed the Russ river through them up to Guerneville, a pretty wooden village with a big saw-mill, all among the trees, or rather the stumps of them, from which it has acquired the common name of Stumptown. The noble trees were fast disappearing. Some of the finest had been left standing, but they could not live solitary, and a little wind soon blew them down. They had a peculiar way of shooting up from the roots round the stumps, which soon became hidden by a dense mass of greenery, forming natural arbours; and many of the large old trees were found growing in circles which had begun that way: a habit peculiar to that tree.

The little inn was capital; and all the gentlemen of the place dined in their shirt-sleeves, and were much interested in my work. They told me how to find the biggest trees, but every one was busy, and not a boy was willing to act as guide or to carry my easel. There was no difficulty in finding the trees; only in choosing which to paint, and how to get far enough away from such big objects as to see the whole of any one. Fifteen feet through, at a yard from the ground, and two hundred or nearly three hundred feet high, were the measurements of the largest. One had a room formed in its hollow trunk, and a ladder up to it. Great prayer-meetings had been held there year after year, and huts and benches had been placed all round it, to which people came frequently in summer for a week of picnics: a damp, swampy kind of spot, I thought Nearer the river it was prettier and more airy, and there I settled to sketch, in the shade of the young shootings from an old stump. There was an undergrowth of laurel and oak, and many pretty flowers:

pink sorrel, trillium, aquilegia, blue iris, and a deep pink rose. I got back to Oaklands after the supper hour (eight o'clock); but the porter brought me a large plate of crackers and butter, a tumblerful of the most adorable iced mixture, and a straw to suck it through.

A day or two after that, I started again with my luggage. I was two hours too early, and had to wait in that strange ferry-station a mile or so out at sea. The guard put me and my things into an empty carriage and locked me in, and when at last we had started and got to land again, we went for a whole day through a rich corn and grass land, getting warmer and warmer, every now and then passing gorgeous masses of wildflowers, till we reached the hot plain of Madera, where I had been told I should be dazzled by the flowers, and found them all dried up and turned into seed-pods and straw! Madera was the end of the new road to the Yosemite, and I met two fellow-passengers from the *Zealandia* returning from it, who persuaded me to go on there the next day. Coach-travelling was more than usually provoking at that season of flowers, as the coach never stopped in the spots where they grew. I saw at one place a great upright white datura growing amongst the rocks; at another place masses of "prickly elm," with wreaths of yellow flowers. All the flowers grew together in colonies of one species. One often saw only one mass, and no more. At the place where we dined they offered me a horned toad with a tail, which was perfectly harmless, and caught flies to eat. When there were no flies, he did not eat, and did just as well without, they said.

The people there were very quick to discover an Englishwoman, and when I offered fifty cents for my dinner, the girl said innocently, "What's that for? if I meant dinner it was a dollar!" I was not prepared for such double ways, so paid it, and my companions laughed at me, for they had only paid fifty cents. It was dark when our aching bones were taken down at Clark's. The old house I had been in before had been burnt down. A two-storeyed house had taken

its place, and the bills had grown longer; but it was most comfortable, and nice resting quarters. A road had been made for a coach and four to drive to the Mariposa Grove of big trees. One of them had had a great bit of its inside taken out, so that the coach and four could drive through it! I did not submit to such barbarism, but sat still and painted the snow-flower—a gorgeous parasite of the purest crimson and white tints, which grows at the roots of the sequoia, about 5000 or 6000 feet above the sea. I stopped at the first inn in the Yosemite valley, a homely quiet house, and wandered round it on foot for three days, making no expeditions, but enjoying the grandeur of everything in perfect quiet; and a nice old gentleman of Philadelphia, who had come in the coach with me, brought me wonderful flowers from the mountains above.

The first view of the valley struck me more crushingly even than the first time I saw it; and when I talked of walking back to paint the view I found it was seven miles off! It looked so near! The falls were all full of water; they had been dry when I saw them before. One evening I wandered on by the side of the river till I came to the camp of native Indians—miserable creatures with uncombed locks, and short pipes in their mouths. Those who still have sentimental ideas of the cruelty of white races in driving out the blacks have not even seen the little I have seen of them, or they would soon change their ideas. My old friend from Philadelphia rejoiced in the name of Smith. He was very good company when sitting on the verandah of an evening. He had travelled and read much; told me stories of the novelists he delighted in as a young man, and who were now all dead,—Dizzy, Bulwer, Scott, Lady Blessington,—also of his adventures in Yucatan and Mexico. His energy and love of all that was grand in nature reminded me of my old father. Every morning he rode up 3000 feet and back, and in the afternoon took a long walk, always bringing me back some treasures, with minute accounts of the places he got them from. I was quite sorry to say good-bye to him, and to

go back to Clark's, where I had another day of rest, painting the calochortus and cyclobothra, then back to Madera.

The day was most enjoyable: first through the huge trees, then over the lower hills amongst the oak-scrub and beautiful small pines, with long needles and large cones. The young oak shoots and leaves were of the most delicate rose-coloured velvet, shaded into white, and varied by green satin. We met tribes of hideous natives with their pots and pans, children, and horses, as well as squaws to do the carrying. I walked up and down the hills, and found many lovely bulbous plants, and at last the mariposa lily (calochortus), both pink and white varieties, shaped like the tigridia, and exquisitely marked. When we reached the plain a hurricane of wind met us. It was almost as much as the men could stand. I covered myself entirely with my opossum rug, and felt the wind even through that. We had ten miles of it, and arrived just as the train came up; but it wanted its supper as much as we did, and we had abundance of time and food. After that I packed myself into a comfortable new palace-car, to which no wind was admitted, and where I could have a good wash unhurried, and a good bed to rest my weary bones. I watched the hills and trees in the moonlight, far too tired to sleep, till sunrise, when we reached a high table-land dotted with a kind of dragon-tree and covered with aromatic shrubs, agaves, and yuccas, with rocky hills all round (reminding me of old Spain). Some aloes and yuccas were in flower. Now and then we passed a mass of purple or crimson flowers which puzzled me, but the train would not stop, till at 7.30 we halted at Los Angelos for breakfast.

The place did not attract me; and I was glad to get half an hour more rail to San Gabrielle, nearer the hills, where I had an hour to wait before the carriage came and brought me through three miles of gardens, both wild and tame, to Villa Sierra Madre. We passed enormous quantities of lemons, oranges, pomegranates, and vines. The waste ground was covered with a tangle of tall herbaceous plants: larkspurs, pentstemons, mimulus, salvias, and dozens of others. I picked twenty-five varieties in a very short space of time. The hotel was absolutely perfect quarters, built as an annexe to the pretty villa and farm of the owner of the land. It has already a great reputation as a winter resort for consumptive invalids from the States of America. The house is raised some hundred feet above the sea-level, on a spur of the sierra, and has a grand view over the rich plain beneath, and the sea and shore hills. It is surrounded by many acres of fruit-trees and garden-ground, with a large airy verandah in front, covered with creepers.

I reached this delightful place on the 9th of May (quite out of season), and found only one other guest there—an old quakeress, with a piteous cough and nearly blind; but she took a great fancy to me, and sat for hours watching me paint, saying she had enjoyed nothing so much for years. The last night I was there my father-mouse got out, and kept me awake all night. I had to shut all windows and doors, and to block up the fireplaces for fear of losing him. He ran to the very cornice of the ceiling in the moonlight. I watched him in all the highest corners of the room, rushing about like a wild thing, and I knew it was perfectly hopeless to think of catching him till the sleepy hours came at daylight. Then at last I found and captured him, with his head stuck into a hole, and all his body out, no doubt thinking that if he could not see me I could not see him. So I restored him to his sorrowing family, and departed from San Gabrielle, whose old convent was long an outside home of the Jesuit missionaries. It now stood atmost alone, with the railway-station near it. How the old fathers would have wondered at the noisy steaming thing which carried me on!—over dried-up plains, getting hotter and drier, and more and more flowerless. Often these plains were from two to three hundred feet below the level of the sea, and the still heat was very trying, the ground covered with dazzling sand, with a few scrubby trees loaded with mistletoe and cacti, some like pillar-posts thirty feet high, others branching like candelabra. One shrub *(Fmiquiera),* generally called the fishing-rod cactus,—like a bundle of spreading fishing-rods united at the base, and bearing a bunch of flame-coloured flowers at their tips,—was most striking. Great gourd-plants, too, were trailing over the sand, radiating like vegetable stars from a central stem; and many of the cacti had red or white flowers on them.

I had thought of stopping at Zuma, but the confusion and crowd in the unfinished station made me unwilling to leave comfortable quarters in the dark, so I went on through another night "on board," and the next morning arrived at a "Palace Hotel " most unlike the picture in the advertisements! Lots of loafers stood round the door, but the luggage was poked in at the bar-window. They tried to put me into a horrid halfroom, with divisions not much higher than myself, and a window looking on a white wall a yard or two off; but I resisted, and am doubtful if I bettered it. I had a view over the dust-and-rubbish-heap of the establishment, and over flat low town roofs to the queer marshy country and blue mountains beyond. My door opened straight into the court, so that I could have a draught, and as much rest as the flies permitted. The food was excellent, with great jugs of iced tea *ad libitum.*

I tried all day in vain to get a vehicle to take me to the hills, which I saw miles away; though they offered me a coach to go nine miles, returning in the middle of the night, crammed in with an unlimited allowance of miners, who did not confine themselves to iced tea. The machine had no springs, and my bones were bruised sufficiently already, so I took a stroll instead among the dirty roads and lanes round the town—so dirty that I wondered that the people had troubled themselves to cut the open drains on each side of them at all. I felt disinclined to stop at other old Spanish towns on that new line. At the same time the sunset tints on the strangely-moulded rocky mountains were superb: the purest blue shadows on the purest rose-colour, the nearer hills being fringed with giant cacti, looking in the distance like beds of asparagus which wanted cutting. It was too provoking not to be able to get to them. A strong person could have walked, even through the heat, but a rheumatic old woman could not till the sun went down, and then darkness came.

The next morning the train was four hours late, and no one was surprised. It took me across more hot sand-plains of cacti and euphorbias and true Spanish daggers, or yuccas, with great white fountains of flowers on their heads. At Denning the new line ended, and the Santa Fe began. It was a strange little "junction" station, made chiefly out of invalided railway-carriages, in the midst of the purest desert, surrounded by isolated groups of strange bare mountains, most gorgeous in their sunset tints. We had a capital dinner in a diningroom carriage fixed there; then I took my section of the newest and most luxurious of Pullman-cars, for three nights and days, from a fine gentleman in uniform, with a most efficient black sub under him. I was the only woman starting in it, with some very intelligent and agreeable diggers, who had been "prospecting" the metals in those strange mountains —the advanced posts of the southern end of the Rocky Mountains, round which we were making our way now to the northward again.

At eight o'clock the next morning we reached the junction with the short line of rail which leads to Santa Fe, the capital of New Mexico, and I have repented ever since of not having had the energy to explore it, but hope if I live to do so. Every year the journey will become easier, and the whole way to Old Mexico is now done by rail. The country had changed most completely. The mountains were covered with pines and cedars, and the ground with patches of lilac verbenas, which became blue as they faded, looking in the distance like water reflecting the sky. A delightful old lady came in there, wife of Paymaster-General Smith. He came to see her off, and we soon became real friends. She had been three years at Santa Fe, and described the climate and place in the most tempting colours. She said it was never without wild-flowers, with snow mountains within sight, and the most delightful drives all round the city. She had been all over the country, carried in an ambulance and living in tents, and entirely enjoyed it. She had also made an exquisite collection of old china in her wanderings, which she promised to show me, if I went to stay with her some day. At Rati there was an hotel where we had supper, which I marked to stay at when that "some day" came. It was at the foot of a pass, and at the entrance to a deep side-valley, near which I saw many curious flowers: patches of a small round cactus covered with orange and red-brown flowers, and pink and white ones also; azaleas, and iris. I am sure there must be endless flowers to be found there, especially in May and June.

After crossing the high spur of the Rocky Mountains we came down on vast and uninteresting plains, only just recovering from recent floods, with the carcases of drowned oxen scattered about, and so cold and damp that my new friend was glad to share my opossum rug. The stove was heated, and we slept the sleep of bad air for some hours without power of waking. Lupins, vetches, and Oenotheras were the only flowers I saw on that great green plain. The people on board were amusing. One most important person, with an order and a medal, read aloud to the others a speech he had written and was going to deliver to his constituents on "Commemoration Day"; and one Mexican lady went to bed for two days and nights with her hair frizzled out to the last degree of fashion, covered with embroideries, gold ornaments, and yellow beads, and had all her meals brought her by the black man. It seemed to me like lying in state alive. Mrs. Smith left the train at three in the morning, pressing me to come too, and pay a visit to her daughter and son-in-law at their country house. But that seemed to me too great a liberty to take, without ever having even seen them, though I believe they would not have thought it so. The dear old lady

took a fancy to me, as she said I was an example of what a woman could do in the world if she went quietly to work and was in earnest about it. She said American ladies were woefully helpless and tied to fashion; and I told her average Englishwomen were just as bad, the exceptions being too fond of words, not deeds. She said it was almost hopeless trying to improve the Mexican women. Even if they were sent to the States to be educated, they soon relapsed into the *dolce far niente* on their return, but they were very charming in manner and in looks.

I found the hotel in Kansas City so full that, after rechecking my trunk and having some breakfast, I went on again down the side of the great Missouri through a rich country. The Isabella vine was growing over everything, as well as the sumach in masses. There were crowds of people at all the stations, and busy life everywhere, the chief trade being oil (mineral), of which the whole country smells rather more than is agreeable. The trees were in their freshest spring dress of green: the most elegant wych-elms and willows, solid tulip-trees, exquisite cut-leaved maples, and oaks with leaves five inches long,— the boughs were quite weighed down by them,—hornbeam, ailanthus, hickory, and dog-wood — the latter in flower, but much smaller than the flowers in California. The robinia or locust trees were quite white with lovely blossoms, but they were said to be natives of Virginia. The sides of the rail were bordered by blue iris and tradescantia flowers.

St. Louis is a monstrous city, and its hotel is in character with it. The next morning I drove out to Mr. Shaw's garden, and fell in almost at once with the old gentleman himself, who greeted me like an old friend, and showed me all his chief botanical treasures. He said it did him good to find any one who knew his plants by sight, and could tell their names before they read the labels. His was a noble garden and park, full of houses, seats, and statues; it had also a museum, all made, endowed, and given to the public by this one old merchant,

who told me he came out many years before a poor boy from Sheffield. He was so happy talking about every plant that he forgot his breakfast, and I had to run away to prevent his being starved. Humboldt and Shakspeare were the two gods of the park, and the sculptor had put Mr. Shaw's jolly face to the figure of Falstaff on the pedestal of the latter.

The Mississippi did look big as I crossed its long bridge. I rather longed to spend five days and nights in going down to New Orleans to see the magnolia trees in bloom. I was told they quite poisoned the air with their scent, and made the ground dangerous to walk on, from the oiliness of their fallen petals and seeds. All the way to Cincinnati was parklike and wooded; the city looked grand on its hill in the sunset, over the great river Ohio. But big cities give small pleasure to such vegetable-lovers as myself, so I was "transferred" in an omnibus with four horses to another railway, where we had an hour to wash and feed comfortably, and then found a sleeping-car in a tunnel under the city.

I took "No. 10 lower," which was printed on a card I had secured by telegram while travelling on my way some hours before, and when fairly started the conductor came up eating a toothpick.—"Got into your right place at once?" —" It's a way I have," I said. —" Wall" (and he had to extract the toothpick to make the word big enough), "I guess you will be wanting to see the Ohio bridge at two o'clock in the morning, that's what you'll be wanting next?" I guessed I should, though I had never heard of it before; so at two I was awakened gently by my friend, with the toothpick still unfinished in his mouth, and made to come to the other side of the car and look at the great river, seven-eighths of a mile wide, and the hanging lights below, while we crossed on a bridge of iron lace-work, which seemed to be hung up to the stars above. The moon got up just too late. The whole was rather invisible, and decidedly chilly, and I was glad when it was over and I was permitted to go to bed again and not get up till eight; but as usual was awake with the sun, and found the train climbing a mountain pass, with pink azaleas and kalmias in bloom amidst the green underwood, with dark dog-roses and andromedas. How I longed to stop and pick them! But it was cold, and my fur rug most comfortable; and we did not stop till nine, when we found breakfast, with strawberries and cream, in a large open valley denuded of trees, at a big watering-place kind of hotel and garden. After leaving that we came to the beautiful summer river with its rapids, and a smooth canal running by its side on a raised bank, full of boats and barges. We crossed at Harper's Ferry by a curiously twisted bridge, and saw the ruined forts and walls which mark the place where so much fighting took place during the war. I did not wonder at each party being anxious to possess such a beautiful bit of country.

At Washington we were again transferred into a train ahead, which rushed on and deposited us in another pretty hotel in a garden, where we had an hour to spend, and a bad dinner, then were again picked up by the original Pullman car and the hero of the toothpick, who informed me "my mice had just waked up and inquired where I was." Those little beasts were a great delight to my fellow-traveilers, and helped to make me a popular character. The guards used to bring other guards to interview me about them, and they were pronounced most "cunning" by every one. (Cunning being a term used by Americans to signify smallness or prettiness, not craft.)

The Alldine Hotel at Philadelphia is perhaps one of the best in the world, and the most expensive also. All in keeping with the noble city, perhaps the finest in America. The parks and Zoological Gardens, the Palm-House, and the views from the high ground near them are delightful. I wandered about and enjoyed perfect idleness and solitude for two days, then went on to my friend Mrs. Botta's hospitable house in New York. The first morning she sent for a friend to come to breakfast, and take me out for a hunt after things I wanted. First we went up the "elevated" rail, one which leads from the sea into the coun-

try, over one of the principal streets, with iron lace-work resting on iron arches and pillars. Every kind of traffic goes on underneath, and the horses take no notice of it. Pretty little stations, with ornamental covered staircases up to them, also stand on pillars at every fourth "block," and one always finds two trains within sight on each line of rails. They follow one another every five minutes, sixpence being the fare from end to end. We left the rail at the other side of the great Central Park, and walked across some waste ground to the Natural History Museum, of which only the eighteenth part is finished.

We fell in with the Director, and "had a good time." The birds are exquisitely kept and arranged, and the whole building well lighted. We saw an interesting collection of things from Mexico, also a model of the curious Indian settlement near Puebla. I wanted to make out more about the strange plants of Arizona, particularly the *Fouquiera spkndens,* so we went on to Columbia College, and visited first its president, Dr. Bernard, in his den, talking with him through an ear-trumpet and tube: a girl was sitting in a corner doing telegraph work for him. Then we went to Dr. Newberry, who hunted over all his books, finally taking us to the herbarium, where we found not only engravings, but a dried flower. He took the greatest pains to help me, and his secretary, Mr. B., arranged to go on his half-holiday, Saturday, to hunt for flowers in the woods on Staten Island with me. The ferry and rail took me to his appointed station, where he met me in a buggy, with an old horse to drag it, and we spent a long day driving from wood to wood, and wandering about after cypripediums, magnolias, azaleas, kalmias, andromedas, and other nice things. The sarracenias and dionseas were also to be found in another part of the island, which was full of pretty villas and gardens belonging to the rich people of New York. Mr. Heald, the artist, took me for a flower-hunt on the other side of the city one day, and we got frightfully hot walking through the woods from noonday till four, like two old fools; but the masses

of pink azalea were worth some trouble to see. Solomon's seals, arums, and flowering ferns abounded there.

One evening there was a party to look at my Australian work, and I was treated like a lion, and interviewed in turn by everybody, till I got tired of perpetual roaring. Mr. Church heard one evening in an omnibus of my being in New York, and came off at once to see me about nine o'clock, making me promise to go home with him the next day to see his new house, and Mrs. Church, up the Hudson. He looked through all my paintings with real interest; which pleased me, for I still think him the greatest of living landscape-painters. But he was sadly altered and crippled by rheumatism, and could not use his right hand any more. I enjoyed much going up the big river again; it seemed far nobler than when I had seen it ten years before, perhaps because I came to it then after those huge Canadian rivers, in the cold autumn, and now all was warm and fresh, and the greens exquisitely vivid.

We mounted 700 feet above it by a new zigzag road through the forest, and came to the clearing on the top, in which was the picturesque Eastern-looking house with its Moorish arches and windows and coloured tiles, having a grand view of the winding Hudson beneath, and distant Catskill Mountains. Mrs. Church looked prettier than ever, though anxious about her husband, and she made a perfect centre to the curious Damascus hall with its high pointed arches, oriental divans, and central fountain. She had contrived to make the whole collection of curiosities look like the natural parts of a comfortable living-house: exquisite Persian rugs, bronzes, carvings, porcelain, etc. I had a Chinese bed which was a marvel of wood, horn, ivory, and even jade carvings, and its coverlet and pillows (by day) were made of the richest Japanese embroidery. They showed me three wonderful gray birds, with curiously metallic bell-like notes. It was difficult to believe birds could make such sounds. They had bought them in Mexico (from which country they had just returned).

Mr. Church was disappointed in the vegetation there, but wanted me to go to New Granada, where he said the spurs of the Andes were so high that each of the valleys between them had a different flora, that the people were kind and hospitable, and travelling not difficult. Mr. Church was going to paint some of his passages in arabesques of luminous paint. The passages had windows to light them by day, but no lamps; and he thought the phosphorus lines would be enough to show the way at night, and that the daylight admitted by the windows would prevent it from fading away.

On my return to New York, I went to stay again at Orange VOL. 11 p with Sydney Clack's master and his new wife. I found Clack himself married, with four girls, since I had seen him before, but he was still in the same situation, and he put me on board the *Germanic* on the 4th of June, which reached Liverpool on the 13th of June. The B. s also came across in the same ship, and the Hungarian prima donna of New York, Madame G., with her Italian husband. They were going to their farm at Bologna, to see their one baby, for six weeks only, and would then return to America for a professional tour and another opera season. Madame G. was a fine simplemannered woman, whom every one liked, and she had a grand way of singing which reminded me of Grisi. She gave us a concert one night for the benefit of the Sailors' Hospital.

In Queenstown harbour a card reached me from Mary E. to say she had tickets for Rubinstein's and Richter's two concerts on the 13th of June. The tide was low and delayed our landing, so that I only got home in time to go to the last; but it was a great enjoyment, as I saw many old friends in St. James's Hall that night, as well as hearing real music again.

My first thought after unpacking was of the building at Kew, and I did not long delay in going there. I found the building finished (as far as bare walls went) most satisfactorily, its lighting perfect. Mr. Fergusson kindly arranged about the decorating and painting of the

walls. After that I spent a year in fitting and framing, patching and sorting my pictures, and finally got it finished and opened to the public on the 7th of June 1882. I had much trouble but also much pleasure in the work. What need now is there to remember the former *1* Mr. Fergusson throughout was my best help and counsellor, and towards him I shall always feel the strongest gratitude.

I had intended putting an enlarged map of the world on the ceiling, coloured according to the geographical distribution of plants, in different shades of green and brown, the sea also shaded as it is in nature—clearest turquoise in the tropics, indigo in the middle seas, and green near the ice. I meant to add an index of fruits painted by myself, on the cornice, and twelve typical trees between the windows, but every one was against such an unconventional idea, except my old friend Mr. Fergusson, and he wanted some good geographer to make a model, and suggested consulting Francis Galton or Mr. Wallace. The first was most kind and helpful as usual, but covered the map he started on with level lines and curves from 500 to 10,000 feet, and that was of no use on so small a scale. Then I made a pilgrimage to see Mr. Wallace, and found him most delightful, and much interested in my plan. He recommended asking Mr. Trelawney Saunders to make my map, which he did,—a most exquisite piece of hand-shading, for which I paid £120,—but it was not in the least what I wanted, and did not give the limits of palms or fir-forests, so I resolved to give up my scheme, and to leave the ceiling for the present. I also got woods from all parts of the world to make a dado of. Only half of them came with names on them, and half were lost. It was a great difficulty to arrange them, but time mended all. The catalogue I wrote on cards, and stuck them under the paintings; and after I had put down all I knew, Mr. Hemsley corrected and added more information, which he did so thoroughly and carefully that I asked him to finish the whole, and to put his name to the publication.

Though the work gave me no little

trouble and fatigue, it brought me in contact with many interesting people, and sometimes mere strangers said things about it which gave me great pleasure. One day, when the door was accidentally left open, some ladies and a gentleman came in. He was rather cross at not finding Sir Joseph, whom he was seeking. He turned rather rudely to me, after getting gradually interested in the paintings—" It isn't true what they say about all these being painted by one woman, is it *1"* I said simply that I had done them all; on which he seized me by both hands and said, "You! then it is lucky for you that you did not live two hundred years ago, or you would have been burnt for a witch."

There also I first met Miss Gordon Cumming, who had so long haunted me (by name) in various corners of the world, and for whom I had often been taken. (We were both on a large scale, and both were sketchers.) I felt when I saw her that it was no small compliment to have been taken for her: she had a grand Scotch face and noble honest manner, with a deeptoned voice and sweet smile. She was a thorough lady: genial and warm-hearted, but so strong and resolute that it might be quite possible she had walked certain limp AngloIndians to death before now. Where she chose to lead they would follow unresistingly, as I did when she said she always went by the omnibus, it was so much cheaper than cabs, and she did not care what other people thought about it. So I was dragged over the muddy street and into a crowded omnibus, and then—she found it was a wrong one! I had a grand laugh at her, and treated her to a hansom next time. She took me to see her aunt, Mrs. C., a beautiful old Scotch lady, stone blind, yet seeming to see everything, all the family told her so exactly about everything. She felt over some Indian ornaments, and told me the patterns she preferred, just as if she saw them.

Miss Bird was a very different kind of woman from Miss Gordon Cumming. I had been told by a friend she stayed with in Ceylon, that she was so fragile and small that when he put up his hands to lift her down from a dog-cart they met in the middle as if he were lifting a bag loosely filled with fluff, and about as light! but I found instead a very solid and substantial little person, short but broad, very decided and measured in her way of talking, rather as if she were reciting from one of her books. I saw her first at a party, given by some relations of hers, who sent out cards—"to meet Mrs. Bishop *nie* Bird." I found her seated in the back draw ing-room in a big arm-chair, with gold-embroidered slippers, and a footstool to show them on, a petticoat all over gold and silver Japanese embroidered wheels, and a ribbon and order across her shoulders, given her by the King of the Sandwich Islands. She was being interviewed in regular Yankee fashion; and I was taken up to her the moment I came in. Miss Gordon Cumming put her great hand on my shoulder at the same time, on which Lady A. joined our three pairs of hands and blessed us—"three globe-trotteresses all at once!" It was too much for the two big ones; and we retreated as fast as we could, leaving Miss Bird unruffled and equal to the occasion. One story is told of her (of which I feel sure she is quite guiltless). She was asked if she would not like to go to New Guinea. She said, "Oh yes; but she was married now, and it was not the sort of place one could take a man to!"

Professor Asa Gray and his charming wife were staying at Kew when I first came home in 1881. He was working on the flora of the United States, and found more rest there and even greater facilities for his work in the herbarium than in his own country. He was most genial, and crammed with useful information, and had the rare art of adapting himself at once to any new acquaintance, seeming to know and enter into their particular hobbies. He set them galloping away easily on them, and showing themselves off to their best advantage, perfectly convinced that they were instructing Asa Gray, not Asa Gray them. His wife was very pretty and energetic, and left few of the sights of London unseen. She went up by railway every morning with a guide-book in her hand,

seeing all its antiquities systematically. One day I went with them both through Veitch's hot-houses, and we were shown all his wonderful hybrid orchids, with the parent plants, and the clever man who hybridised them. We saw also houses full of pitcher-plants, baby pitchers, not bigger than pins' heads, including the "*Nepenthes* Northiana," in search of which a traveller had been sent across the world to Borneo after seeing my painting at Kensington. But it will be difficult to imitate, in a cramping glass-house in foggy London, the abundance of air, though hot, of those limestone mountains.

One bright summer day I went down to Bromley Common to see my father's dear old friend, George Norman, then in his ninety-fourth year. His hair and beard were of the purest white, and he looked almost transparently thin and delicate; but he wandered from room to room, and talked with vivacity and interest of all the leading politics of the day. He had a reader who came for some hours every day, and thus kept himself acquainted with every article worth reading in the different reviews and papers, as well as with all the best new books. He talked to me of Green's *History of the English People,* of John Symonds's *Renaissance,* and other tough books (which some younger men think hard reading), as if they were novels. He sang me his favourite old Norwegian songs, and told the old stories in the Sussex dialect he always told me, and which his children and I always pretended to hear for the first time. I think he and his dear wife (my best aunt, though no real relation), surrounded by their children and grandchildren in that old house and garden, formed the happiest picture I can think of.

They drove me on to Down, the dear old man sitting with his back to the horses with that old-fashioned courtesy towards women, which is now nearly forgotten. Kentish lanes are full of beauty, with their high tangled hedges and fine oak trees. We skirted Hayes Common, and that grand park with the Roman camp in it which old Mr. Brassey is said to have bought and then

forgotten its possession for a whole year. When something reminded him of it, he said, "God bless my soul! I forgot all about it," went to see it, did not like it, and sold it again immediately. Down is about six miles from Bromley Common, a pretty village, and a most unpretentious old house with grass plot in front, and a gate upon the road. On the other side the rooms opened on a verandah covered with creepers, under which Mr. Darwin used to walk up and down, wrapped in the great boatman's cloak John Collier has put in his portrait. He seldom went further for exercise, and hardly ever went away from home: all his heart was there and in his work. No man ever had a more perfect home, wife, and children; they loved his work as he did, and shared it with him. He and Mr. Norman had been friends for many years, and it was pretty to see the greater man pet his old neighbour and humour him; for with all his great spirit he was very much of a spoilt child, and proud of his age. Of Charles Darwin's age I never had the smallest idea. He seemed no older than his children, so full of fun and freshness. He sat on the grass under a shady tree, and talked deliciously on every subject to us all for hours together, or turned over and over again the collection of Australian paintings I brought down for him to see, showing in a few words how much more he knew about the subjects than any one else, myself included, though I had seen them and he had not.

Mr. and Mrs. Vernon Lushington were staying there. She had the good art of making others shine. Every one wished to interest her, and to bring out that wondrous smile and look of sympathy on her beautiful face, and I felt that we owed much of the interesting talk of that day to her tact and power of fascination. She also played in her own peculiar way, as if the things she played had been written for her alone by Bach or Handel, while Mr. Darwin rested on the sofa, and made her repeat them over and over, with an enjoyment which was real. When I left he insisted on packing my sketches and putting them even into the carriage with his own hands. He was seventy-four: old enough to be courteous too. Less than eight months after that he died, working till the last among his family, living always the same peaceful life in that quiet house, away from all the petty jealousies and disputes of lesser scientific men.

Here follows a short note from Mr. Darwin, written just after this visit, showing his appreciation of my sister's work. The plant referred to is *Ilamilia eximia,* a native of the Middle Island of New Zealand, and allied to the *Gnaphaliums.* It is described on page 185.—Editor. *2d* August 1881. Down, Buckingham, Kent.

My Dear Miss North,—I am much obliged for the "Australian Sheep," which is very curious. If I had seen it from a yard's distance lying on a table, I would have wagered that it was a coral of the genus Porites.

I am so glad that I have seen your Australian pictures, and it was extremely kind of you to bring them here. To the present time I am often able to call up with considerable vividness scenes in various countries which I have seen, and it is no small pleasure; but my mind in this respect must be a mere barren waste compared with your mind.—I remain, dear Miss North, yours, truly obliged, Charles Darwin.

Another remarkable man I saw but once, but that once made a great impression on me—J. R. Green, author of the *History of* the *English People.* He was in a very far stage of consumption when I paid him a visit in Kensington Square. He could only speak in a whisper, but his talk was full of fire, ideas, and interest in the ideas of others; and his pretty, gentle wife sat by and treasured every word he spoke, till his coughing became violent; then she took us away, telling us how she was beginning to write quite easily with her left hand to his dictation, her right being paralysed after long years of incessant work. He dictated sometimes eleven hours in the day.

CHAPTER XIV SOUTH AFRICA

All the continents of the world had some sort of representation in my gallery except Africa, and I resolved to begin painting there without loss of time. In August 1882 I left Dartmouth in the *Grantully Castle,* a ship historically famed for having once been lent by its owner, Sir Donald Currie, to Mr. Gladstone, for a trip which restored the Prime Minister to health. It took me to the Cape in rather more than eighteen days—one of the shortest voyages ever made. The first and last days of the voyage were exceedingly cold— so cold that my fingers became almost too stiff to go on with the embroidery task I had set myself to do. I had traced the pattern from a carved wooden door in the museum at Lahore, and had it transferred on gold-coloured satin-cloth, hoping to finish one side of the *portihe* on my way to the Cape. But the ship went too quickly for me, and about half a foot of its length remained unworked when I landed—to the captain's great delight, who said he had beaten me in the race. We only stayed three hours at Madeira, and had fine weather all the way.

There was much lamentation on board when those going to Natal were told that they must not land, or they would be subject to quarantine. The pilot-boat brought out one letter only, and that was for myself; and as soon as the ship touched the shore at Cape Town, two friends met me, and put me and my boxes into a hansom-cab. One of them took me all the way out to Wynberg, seven and a half miles, round the western side of the Table Mountain, whose grand crags came down within a few hundred yards of the road, with groves of European fir-trees, oaks, and fruit-orchards, the ground under them covered with white arums, wherever the soil was moist. Near the road was a succession of pretty, unpretentious villas and cottages, in gardens more or less wild. Australian gums, wattles, and casuarinas were in full bloom, and perfectly at home there. On the sandy flats between the road and the sea were myriads of small flowers: oxalis of most dazzling pink; yellow, white, and lilac heaths, bulbs of endless variety, gazanias, and different mesembryanthemums. Mrs. Brounger, a most beautiful old lady with silver hair, gave me two rooms in her nice large old Dutch house. Her daughter, Mrs. Gamble, lived close by with her pretty children. Our meals were taken in either house alternately, both husbands being away at Government work.

Mrs. Gamble and I had many delightful drives with an old pony, which had a most remarkable talent for standing still. We used to drive him off the road into the thick bush and leave him there for hours, while we rambled about after flowers. The extraordinary novelty and variety of the different species struck me almost as much as it did at Albany in Western Australia, and there was a certain family likeness between them. But the proteas were the great wonder, and quite startled me at first. I had not formed an idea of their size and abundance: deep cups formed of waxy pointed bracts, some white, some red or pink, or tipped with colour, and fringed some with brown or black plush, others with black or white ostrich feathers. These gorgeous flower-bracts were bigger than the largest tulips, and filled with thickly packed flowers. One large variety seemed to carry its stamens outside. While painting it, I saw them begin to dance, and out came a big green beetle. I cut the flower open, and found an ants' nest. The energetic little creatures had pushed the stamens out to make room for their colony. I found all the other flowers of that kind possessed by ants, and in every nest a beetle. The young shoots generally sprang from below the flower-stalk of the protea, so that when the cone which succeeded it became ripe, it was protected and half hidden by three leafy branchlets.

Many of the species have their male flowers and cones on separate trees; like the silver tree, which only grows on the spurs of Table Mountain, where there are many groves of it, shining like real silver in the setting sunlight. It grows about twenty feet high, shaped like a fir-tree, with its flowers like balls of gold filigree at the ends of the branches. Every bit of it is lovely, but the most fascinating part is the cone, when it opens and the seeds come out with their four feathered wings, to which the seed hangs by a fine thread half an inch long.

Another species of protea resembles the waratah *(Grevillea)* of Australia. One of them is the "krippel boom," a thick bush with a rich yellow flower at the end of each leafy branch, on which the long-tailed honeysuckers delight to perch and take their suppers, plunging in their curved beaks, and tearing the flowers all to pieces in the process. The hills were covered with low bushes, heaths, sundews, geraniums, gladioluses, lobelias, salvias, babianas, and other bulbs, daisies growing into trees, purple broom, polygalas, tritomas, and crimson velvet hyobanche.

Many friends collected for me, and two baths stood in my painting-room full of wonders. The difficulty was to make up my mind what to do first. It was impossible to paint fast enough, but we can all work hard at what we like best. Miss Robinson, the Governor's daughter, called the first day after I arrived, in her riding-habit, at ten o'clock, and told me she had been dancing at one o'clock, up and off to the meet at three, had had a glorious run, and her fingers nearly pulled off her hands by her horse. She wanted me to move into Government House, but I knew when I was well off, and declined the honour. My quieter home suited my particular work best. Indeed, I only went three times into Cape Town during the whole of my stay in South Africa. The Botanic Gardens are fine, but people there were so very economical (owing probably to the many expenses of the late useless war) that they hardly allowed enough money to keep the plants watered, and Professor M'Owen, its agreeable director, was in despair about it. The museum is also an interesting collection. Mr. Trimen took me over it himself. He showed me water-birds with great red beaks, which can open oysters and eat them; also one which catches locusts on the wing, cutting off their legs and arms, dropping them as it flies, and swallowing their nutritious bodies. In the streets I saw baskets of penguins' eggs, which the Malays were buying and eating. The shells were a very blue white.

I had luncheon with the Governor, who offered to send me in a war-ship to seek the welwitschia. I did not feel sure he really meant it, and I made out that it would have to take me over a thousand miles and back in order to get to living specimens; even then there would be difficulties in going overland to find them. I thought it was asking too much of Government good-nature, but was sorry afterwards that I did not keep him to his word, as it was actually published in *Nature* that I had been so sent. Miss Duckett, who managed the great old Dutch farm of Groote Port in the absence of her brother in England, wrote and invited me to come and see her, and on the 7th of September I went by rail to Malmesbury.

The mountain looked glorious from the other side of the flats, all wrapped up in the morning mists, and the flats themselves were covered with gay masses of colour interspersed with patches of white sand. I had two changes of train, and found a covered country cart with four horses waiting at the end of the line, and a Boer to drive them, who only talked bad Dutch, and never took his pipe out of his mouth; but he was most willing to laugh at anything or nothing. A clever little boy of ten helped him, stopping him occasionally to run after and knock down young birds, which he put into the man's big pockets alive. He said he was going to put them in a cage. He also got a curious hanging nest of the yellow finch, and filled it with bluish eggs from other nests, which he meant to string and hang up to look pretty, he said. Whenever he liked he stopped, but I was not allowed to stop when I liked; and the new flowers which I saw and longed for were pooh-poohed! My driver was a true Boer.

The gazanias were marvellous, all turning their eyes to the sun. Looking west, all was blazing with gold and orange; looking east, I only saw the dull green backs. There were miles of the *Cryptostemma calendulacea,* which Australians call the African weed. Mesembryanthemums, portulacas, ixias and babianas were also in great quantities, and of every possible tint. One of the latter flowers surpassed any I have ever seen for richness, the deepest ultramarine blue with crimson centre, and growing so close to the white or salmontinted sand made it shine the more. Another was of a lovely claret colour, another pink or white. The vermilion and geranium-tinted sparaxis were most gaudy, and there were small white stars with rose-tinted backs to three of their petals, which only opened at sunset; these were most delicately fragrant: also small green and drab gladioluses. All these were growing on a high plain like the Wiltshire Downs or the country about Stonehenge, with great crops of corn, every now and then terribly bad roads, and a frightful wind.

We only passed two isolated farms all the twenty miles' drive to Groote Port, a most comfortable old place, with round gable-ends, and double flight of steps leading to the upper floor, where the living-rooms were. Miss D. had meant me to come a week later, as eight ladies were already staying on a visit, but they all said they did not mind it, and gave me their best room. She had put no date but Wednesday, and said the flowers would all be over if I put it off, so I gave up the work I was doing and came at once. She was a regular Queen Bess or Boadicea for ruling men, and had no small work to do on that farm. Every morning she gave out over 100 rations of bread, meat, spirit, etc. Every morning a sheep was killed, and every week a bullock. When she heard that smallpox had broken out in the mission-station three miles off, she established a strict quarantine, and asked a neighbouring doctor what he would vaccinate her people for. He said he could not do it for less than ten shillings each, so she had herself and her niece operated on, then ordered all her people to be collected in the barn, and herself vaccinated every man, woman, and child. I tell the tale as she told it, and the result: no one had the smallpox at Groote Port.

She had the queerest collection of servants there, and some little creatures to wait at the table who were black as coals, full of fun and games behind the door. They were great mimics, and took off all our peculiarities behind our backs. I caught one of them pretending to paint in a pair of straw spectacles, with a bit of white rag on its head like my cap, and cross-sticks for an easel, the others roaring with laughter. That same little imp, Topsy, wanted to know if the flowers I painted faded like other flowers when kept—an unconscious compliment which gained her an extra sixpence when I left. All sorts of races were there—Hottentots, Kafirs, Malays, natives of Namaqualand, and West Africans.

There were fifty ostriches stalking about. Once the old Irishman in charge of them took a holiday for a few days, and when he came back, "Old Cock" was missing, and discovered dead and broken all to bits in his struggles to get himself disentangled from an iron fence. The old man said: "Sure, he had killed himself in more ways than one.'' The ostriches are most attached couples, and seldom marry again if one of the pair dies. The cock and hen take turns at sitting on the eggs, but many wild eggs are brought in. These are hatched in an incubator in cotton-wool soaked in boiling water, and kept at over 100 degrees of warmth. They take about forty days' hatching. I was lucky enough to be in time to see the gradual entrance into life of the birds. First we heard them chirping inside, then the beak appeared, gradually the whole body worked its way out, the head and neck covered with the most beautiful brown plush, the eggshaped bodies with a sort of coarse black wool, neither fur nor feathers. The eyes and ears were perfectly active the moment they came out of the shell. The one I painted, half in and half out, turned its head to look at each person who spoke, and seemed to be attending to what we said. After a couple of days in flannel, it was put out in a little paddock, and began eating gravel and other hard morsels with great enjoyment. Their two big toes seem fitted into leather gloves many sizes too large.

The older ones were very amusing to watch, particularly when they first came out in the morning with mincing steps and much waltzing. They had a curious power of flattening themselves out on the ground, with necks and legs stretched out, so that they were quite invisible at a distance among the shrubby plants and dry grass.

The ladies staying at the farm were very Dutch-looking, but Miss D. had quite an English manner, with a gentle voice, notwithstanding her manly strength of character. Everything we ate was made on the farm, as well as a strong wine resembling Madeira. There was a grand vegetable and fruit garden hedged in by a tangle of aloes and geraniums, heliotrope and plumbago. There were two date-palms, pomegranates, loquats, cypresses, blue gums and wattles covered with their golden blossoms, a perfect wood of poplars loaded with the curious hanging nests of sociable finches, and masses of white arums below. Beyond that wood there was not a single tree for miles. One day we all went up to the top of the hill behind the house, 1000 feet of steep climb, where we got a lovely view of the distant sea, and Table Mountain beyond. I found at the top plenty of small starry flowers of various colours, and large yellow thistles, many lovely bulbs, including the pink and white *Hypoestcs stellata,* with eyes as changeable as the peacocks' feathers. One could not tell if they were blue or green, far less paint them.

We cooked kabobs, rice, and cakes, and drank strong coffee and wine, close to a muddy pool, which they called a spring. We waited there till the sun got low again. A willow-tree hung over the pool, covered with hanging nests. The pretty yellow builders were very busy over them, and were most entertaining to watch, as they swung their houses in the wind, turning and twisting themselves in and out in all manner of strange attitudes. The cock is said to build many nests before he finds wives to fill them; then the ladies often find fault with the architecture and pull it all to bits for the mere fun of rebuilding it.

One morning we started at seven, in a cart with six horses, Charles D. having come over from his farm (a few miles off) the night before to drive us, with his wife and baby and little black maid. We had a woolly-haired imp to open gates and sit under our feet, while the two pretty nieces rode on horseback. It was both windy and dusty as we floundered on over twenty miles of sand, only losing our way twice. We reached at last a lovely bay of sand and rocks, and a solitary old house and hut, where a large party of cousins were picnicking for a fortnight, running in and out of the sea in the most primitive manner. The house belonged to the family in general, and when no one was there it was locked up and left empty. Two old blacks inhabited the hut, and caught fish enough for all who might come. I wandered off by myself among the rocks and sea-flowers, and found abundance to entertain me. Small red-leaved aloes and dwarf euphorbia, wild olives and geraniums, brown and blue salvias, crassulas, and an endless variety of portulaca and ice-plants (quite exquisite when examined with my magnifying glass), lovely anemones and shells in the rock-pools, with big black birds stalking about on the sands. The family party were disappointed at not seeing me paint, but I was too tired to show off. However, I heard: "She just takes a flower and does it all at once in colours," etc. The hyobanche, both orange and crimson, were gorgeous, and reminded me of the Californian snow-flower. There were lovely balsams of all colours, blue lobelias with pink backs, and masses of large silvery everlastings. The *Monsonia* spectabilis was also a lovely flower, like a hibiscus, but with an elbow in its stalk a few inches below the flower-head, which was very remarkable. The droseras too were fine, with flowers of lilac and white as big as a sweet-brier rose: I was told of a scarlet variety, but never found it. On our return from this expedition we heard one of the valley ostriches had disappeared, no one could make out how. Miss D. said it was hatched from a wild egg, and was led away by its hereditary wandering instincts! They had just finished cutting the feathers of the old ones, pulling stockings over their snake-like heads during the process—and it was no easy matter to do it; but they cannot kick behind, only in front. I think they seemed all the merrier for losing their beautiful plumes, and waltzed round and round the next morning, flapping their wings, with as much grace as any Germans could do. I was never tired of watching these two-legged camels.

We had all been awakened that morning at five o'clock by a tremendous cracking of whips. Fifteen cousins in a waggon with eight horses came to take the girls off again for another picnic to the seaside. They afterwards rode home on two of the men's saddles, with the off stirrups brought over to put the right foot in. They said they cantered quite easily (with no pommels) over the twenty miles of sand. They had barely VOL. II Q time to pack up their dancing dresses before the great waggon arrived, picked them up, and took them on again to a ball at another relation's house some miles off, Miss Duckett sending on all our spare provisions to help the feast. The whole district was sprinkled with Ducketts or Cloetes, all cousins, and a most happy set of people. One day we had an hour's notice of sixteen coming to luncheon. All hands were called in to whip cream and make cakes, and everything was in apple-pie order when the hungry party arrived. They came in two waggons, each drawn by eight horses. One of the ladies wore a purple velvet dress; she and some of the others having the fair solid flesh and yellow hair Rubens loved to paint. They were all serene and happy, but not entertaining.

The rooms were always full of pretty flowers. There was a hanging basket suspended from the middle of the ceiling in the sitting-room, filled with arums, ferns, and hanging creepers. Brackets also hung on the walls for the same purpose. Every morning the girls brought in fresh wildflowers, often from considerable distances, going out on horseback to seek them before breakfast. Miss Duckett always found time to arrange them, in spite of the quantity she had to do. Her storeroom was a sight to see. They made their own candles out of the mutton fat, quantities of butter also, but had no market to sell it in. She salted it down, then when butter was scarce and dear in Cape Town, she washed the salt out again and sent it all in as fresh butter, getting a good price. The ostrich feathers, too, were worth sometimes as much as £8 for one good bird, and under £2 apiece for the others all round. She made raisins, as well as wine, and the most delicious grape-jam, with a little quince in it to give it a flavour.

At last the smoking Boer and his horrid boy came back for me, and stopped to rob nests as they did before, cramming the poor half-fledged birds into their pockets, then rolling or sitting on them and taking them out to see if their legs were broken. They demanded pay too, before I got out of the cart, like true Boers. The rail took me back as far as Stellenbosch, a fine old Dutch town in the midst of gardens hedged with pink and white roses, beautifully tidy, and surrounded by finely formed mountains. The town consists of streets of semi-detached one-storeyed houses, generally whitewashed, with quaint gable-ends, and half-doors suitable for gossip, a row of fine oak-trees between the pathways, and a run of clear water on each side of the road. As the trees meet in an arch overhead, it is dark and damp on dull days, but deliciously cool when the sun is hot. It is unlike anything else in Africa. The boarding-house in which I had a room, kept by a very old Dutch pair, was beautifully clean. After the fleas and muddle of the great farm it was a real rest, and I found the place so pretty during my walk before breakfast that I thought of staying a week, but changed my mind when the kind neighbours came to call on me, which they did in abundance, time being not much thought of in Stellenbosch.

One lady asked if my paintings were all "hand-work," or whether I used a machine! Education is the rage at Stellenbosch, and they had insisted on placing the station a mile off, for fear of disturbing the students! They learnt psalm-singing, if nothing else, and one heard it droning on in every direction (beginning soon after daylight). It was most doleful, and the key dropped full four tones before its last verse was over. I could not help thinking of the Rev. H. J., who warned me before starting that "Africa was a most untidy country, and I should find missionaries littered all over the place." The country round the town was very rich and well farmed; rose-hedges everywhere bordered the good roads, and wild pears, apples, umbrella-pines, and cypress-trees gave it quite an Italian look. The running river did my eyes good. Two nice young teachers from the German school also did me good by a visit just as I was going to bed. They knew all about me and my pictures. One had even been to Hastings, and it was a comfort to think the beautiful old town had some nice people in it who could appreciate the nature round, and did not think all but themselves were going to a bad place.

I breathed more easily when I escaped from that Calvinistic settlement, and the flowers seemed to get brighter and more abundant as I approached Table Mountain. On arriving at Mrs. B.'s I found her husband and son-in-law had just arrived before me, and the latter at once arranged to take me up the mountain. It was perfect weather for walking, the sun hot and bright, but quite cold for sitting still, and I longed for a fur-coat whilst painting in the house. A cart took us as far as the pass leading to Simon's Bay, between two spurs of the mountain topped with masses of the silver tree, whose golden flower-balls glittered in the morning light. Protea bushes and other low scrub grew near them, and the distant views of sea and hills were most exquisite, as we reached the shoulder of the mountain. After that we went up tolerably straight, finding a succession of lovely flowers: scarlet heath, white with brown centre, a kind of broom, polygala, lovely sundews, and many rush-like plants, tough and good to haul myself up by. Grand crags and rocks surrounded us as we reached the first great flat, then more rocks to climb, and the second flat was reached at about 3000 feet above the sea. In the middle was the series of springs or streams, in which the *Disa grandiflora* delights to dip its roots. It forms a thick edging to the water, and grows nowhere else in the world.1 In

February, when covered with its large scarlet butterfly flowers, it must be indeed a sight worth seeing, sharing its glories with the deep blue disas and gladioluses.

When I was there the plants were small and green, but 1 This is an error, as it has been found also on the Cedar Mountains in the Clanwilliam district, South Africa.—Ed. flowerless. Near them were tall reddish heaths and blue broom, tall masses of *Todea* africana, asphodels, tritomas, and watsonias, as well as tiny crimson rosettes of drosera and utricularia, not bigger than pins' heads, in the black bog-earth near the stream. Perhaps aesthetically it is fortunate that economy prevents the authorities of Cape Town from carrying out Mr. Gamble's scheme of irrigating it, and all the neighbouring country too, from a great tank on that flat; but it seems a terrible waste that all this pure water should run into the sea, while so many miles of thirsty country, with thousands of inhabitants, are dried up for want of it. We climbed still higher, but the clouds came down, and it was imprudent to go further where we might lose ourselves and could see nothing; so we hunted among the rocks under the clouds, and found the great *Protea cynaroides,* which has the biggest flower-head of all, larger than flowers of *Magnolia* grandiflora. It is somewhat like it in shape, only pink. The bush is the lowest of its tribe, only a couple of feet above the ground. Just then it had only its slender crimson buds on it, and those buds Mr. G. visited two successive months, but found them no bigger. We found one old mummied flower, with all the stamens gone, and a honeysucker's nest inside it. There were noble silver everlastings, and lobelias like gems.

We found some gorgeous caterpillars on the silver trees; they had every colour on their backs, put on pure, like gems, turquoise perhaps predominating. I took them, after painting their portraits, to Mr. Tryman at the museum, who said he did not think they had ever been painted before, and was glad to keep them: they reappeared as a large Atlas moth. He said the story of one

of these caterpillars boring holes in an orange and sucking out the juice was quite true. He had seen one of the same species bore through a peachskin. I asked him about birds fertilising the strelitzia, as was said, but he had not caught them in the act. The slightest touch to the end of its blue arrow (when ripe) jerks out the pistil and stamens, and might, I fancy, set the pollen flying. The frill which encloses them is wonderfully made. I dissected one of the great flower-heads, and found at least a dozen young flowers, with their gaudy bracts, tucked away in their honey-bed inside. Dr. Atherstone told me he had watched a tiny kingfisher with the same gaudy tints sitting on these flowers over a stream, watching for fish, and the fish took him for another strelitzia, and came up close to look, when he pounced down on the foolish things.

On the 10th of October I went by rail to Tulbagh. There had been heavy rains, and the country was fresh and green again. The mountains round the broad valley of Paarl are very grand, with perpendicular precipices and the boldest outlines. The ground near the river was covered with bulrushes, watsonias, and arums, cultivated in the same way as at Stellenbosch. Trollope says the High Street of Paarl is eight miles long: it is quite two miles, but every house stands in its own large garden, so that after all it is not a very large town. My window opened on a verandah shaded by large gum-trees, loaded with hanging nests made by a yellow finch which was perpetually building, chattering, and playing. There were some most untidy nests in the forks of the same trees, made by a smaller bird out of the pickings and stealings from those of the finches. Occasionally there was a row between the two colonies, but it seemed to me that the yellow birds delighted so much in the art of building that they were glad of an excuse to repair and begin over again.

The much-talked-of flowers were a disappointment. I was told it was a bad year, and what there were were over. I walked two miles over the dry flats to Dr. Balm's mission, and as it was on-

ly seven o'clock I went on towards the hills behind, but was seen and captured, and after some breakfast was given in charge to two wild converts, and taken to the Tigers' Kluft, where the skeletons of sheep and cows were even then occasionally found. I had a hard scramble, but only found a few bulbs, ixias, and babianas, and a tiny pink pelargonium. Then Miss Balm sent me back in her nice cart with two fine horses to pull it. I had one or two other hunts in different directions, and my quarters were so pleasant to work in that I stayed a fortnight. The place is pretty: all Dutch one-storeyed houses, with quaint gables, neat gardens, running water, trees in front, and a church or chapel for every three houses. All was Dutch, the poor doctor the only Englishman in the place. He had worked for years, till he could afford to marry the girl who had so long waited for him; then she came and died, leaving him a baby boy. He said life was too dreary to bear, and he talked of going to Madagascar—anywhere for a change. The inn was excellent, with many little niceties about it, such as embroidered pillow-cases which stamped patterns on one's cheeks at night.

I had a pleasant companion in the house—a pretty young woman with a curious Belgian husband in a black velvet coat, who was always receiving telegrams and going off in a hurry night and day, sometimes riding, sometimes in a waggon, sometimes by train. He had many subs under him—young gentlemen who also went off at a moment's notice. He gave himself great airs. I heard a fat old commercial gent reproaching him with having dropped the "de" before his name. He seldom stayed many hours at a time with his wife, but sent her innumerable telegrams, and they talked of Beaufort West as we talk of London. They were quite a puzzle to me. I asked the same fat commercial gent what he was, and he said, "Why, he buys sheeps and beefs for the butchers' company in Cape Town": that was the end of my romance! His wife said she had travelled much with him, and hardly knew what a home was, poor thing. She gave me a graphic account of the

Boers in the Transvaal. A sister of hers went there as governess once, to a family called "decent people." They were rich, and paid her highly, but there were only two beds in the house—one in the room given to her, and one which the parents had. The big girls and boys all slept in the passages on the floor, and quarrelled for the possession of a few mats and rugs. She wanted to go away at once, but they coaxed and bribed her to stay at least a month, were very kind and good-natured, and the girls and boys quick at learning, so she did stay three months, and thinks she improved their manners. After the few hours of lessons they used all of them to run into the stream together (tucking their clothes round their waists) for a wash. But in their way they were not bad people.

I paid six shillings a day at Tulbagh for my board and lodging; this included wine. An hour's more rail took me to the foot of the Mitchell's Pass, and a post-cart with four horses dragged me up it to Ceres, through the wildest scenery. Strangely twisted rocks were piled one on another, and I fancied, if one were moved, the whole would come down. Beautiful plants were growing amongst them, the most conspicuous being a purple-leaved cabbage with a huge yellow flower like sea-kale, crassulas and blue watsonias, and bushes covered with a yellow pea-flower set in green collars, which the natives make into tea. The most fantastic rocks are at the top of the pass, where they look as if they had been melted with heat and then dropped into ice-cold water.

We descended a few hundred feet into the plain of Ceres, a filled-up lake, surrounded by mountain-tops covered with fresh snow. The plain is twelve miles across, with several villages. The little town of Ceres, buried in its trees and gardens, looked like an island in the midst of the yellow flat, which was yellow with corn, patches of leucadendron, and burnt-up grass. It was a gay little town, full of shops and people, with delicious running water everywhere —a great contrast to the place I had left. The boarding-house I stayed at was Dutch,

and very dirty, unlike that at Tulbagh; but its situation at the end of the town was most delightful, as I could wander out on the flats without my hat, and find many flowers too.

The situation being so much higher, the season was later.

I was told it was not safe to wander in the pass alone, because of the "black people." I thought they meant people, but they meant baboons! And the young banker who was my fellow-boarder told me he was returning from a ball at a farm below the pass once with a friend, who had been doing the music on an accordion and had it in his hand, when a big baboon appeared close to them. His friend put down the instrument and flung stones at him, on which the creature dropped behind a rock, and the musician scrambled after. The baboon soon reappeared behind them in the road, picked up the accordion, and made away with it. Perfectly hopeless was the idea of following him over those loose rocks, but they saw him stop and examine the wonderful prize, and heard a hideous discord followed by a dismal howl, and that was the last ever seen or heard of the poor accordion.

My neighbours at Ceres were most kind. Mrs. C. had a nice open carriage, and gave me some delicious drives. Her husband brought me several plants from the Karroo; among others a euphorbia called the milk-plant, with fleshy green fingers and tiny yellow flowers on their ends. Its roots spread for yards, with cross-bars from which rose a parasitic flower called *Hydnara africana,* like a purple star, standing alone two or three inches above the ground. Its seed-vessel swells and swells and sinks underground, till the flower tumbles off leaving a ragged ring like the crown of a pomegranate, and the fruit is as big. The natives dig it up to roast and eat; it then tastes like the flesh of a cocoa-nut. I was full of work, and not over-gracious when the landlady's little girl came in with, "Please, ma wants you to do her a favour, and paint some flowers on her ostrich eggs!" She thought me very disagreeable when I said I had no time. After that I had to do my own house-

maiding. The cooking was even worse than the house-arrangements. They "curried" a whole uncut leg of mutton one day for dinner, and again a second time for supper, with neither rice nor "trimmings," only curry smeared over it.

The bulbous pelargoniums were very varied in colour, some green, some claret or black or brown. The roots of one were eaten by natives and called the Kaffir potato. The large mesembryanthemums were gorgeous, coming out pure white or yellow, but turning pink and lilac before they shrivelled up. The fruit was eaten and preserved in different ways; it tasted like a bad fig.

It became very cold at Ceres; the hills were white with snow. I saw the light through the chinks in my walls and ceiling, and the broken window give me neuralgia. In the dull weather, too, the verandah made my room terribly dark for painting. I pined for home, and resolved to give up going to Karroo Gate and return to Wynberg. As I was starting in the post-cart for the station, Mrs. M., the magistrate's wife, came up, and said she would go as far as the graveyard with me. Half-way I asked about Baines Kluft, and found it was not so far as I thought, so persuaded her to go with me, sending back word to her husband not to expect her till next day. It was a glorious day, and the snow-tops glittered against the deep blue sky; everything looked fresh after the rain. We got a fresh carriage at the station, and some bread and cheese. Mrs. M. borrowed a shawl, and we started, floundering through swamps, bogs, and swollen rivers for an hour and a half, till at last we reached the road over Baines Kluft, made many years ago. It was still a grand piece of work, well kept, and much used by trains of brand-new carts and waggons, going over to be sold at the diamond-fields, or to be bartered for oxen which the owners drove back on their return journey. Most of the flowers were over, but the wild scenery was worth the trouble of going.

We had heard that there was an hotel near the station at Wellington, but there was none. A good storekeeper let us sleep in a spare room near a "billiard saloon," and his sister fed us most kindly, and would take nothing for it. Such a nice woman, with sick children, and a lemur of Madagascar as a pet, a most fascinating little creature, excessively tame and sociable. It ran in and out of the house, and made tremendous jumps, sitting on its heels like an Arab, and folding its beautiful ringed tail round its neck when at rest. The brother who had sent it was so lonely when his white partner left him, that he used to go and sit under a tree and talk English to himself every day for a couple of hours, for fear of forgetting the language. I made a vow that night never to run away with other men's wives again! For the old lady gasped and choked in her sleep to such an extent that I began to fear I might find a dead magistrate's wife in the morning. I had a long walk after daylight, and found that Wellington is, like most of the towns in Cape Colony, a mile from the railway station. I went over a well-cultivated plain surrounded with hills, and saw many gigantic locusts, with yellow bodies, red legs, and blue and green wings, enjoying the crops.

At eleven I bade good-bye to the old lady, who said she had thoroughly enjoyed her holiday, and got into the train for Wynberg, finding Dr. G., the astronomer, as my companion in the carriage. He was one of the most agreeable men in South Africa, so I was lucky. His wife was a perpetual invalid and sufferer, since the year she spent in Ascension Island, of which she wrote such a charming description. I found much illness in my friend's household, and thought my room would be valuable, so after two days started again by rail over the same road I had passed before. But towards the end of the day I reached new ground at Worcester, an old Dutch town built on an exact square of ground, the green grass edging leaving off and the desert beginning in a perfectly straight line on each side, as if cut with a ruler and knife. I half repented of not having stopped to explore its monotonous old streets, still more so when we began to ascend by a crack in the hills

a steep winding pass like the Brenner, serpentining in and out of side-valleys. At the top we passed some grand purple-leaved aloes, with scarlet flowers, and little trees with gouty legs and bright green fleshy rosettes on the ends of their swollen branches, with long red flower-stems branching out at right angles. I longed for a mild accident to keep me there some hours.

At the station on the top of the pass was a baboon, which flung stones at any of the passengers who threw them at him, while another poor beast sat huddled up in a bit of rag, and when he was driven to retreat up his pole he carefully dragged his one treasure, the rag, with him. I slept at a railway-hotel at Montague Road, built by the Cape Government, which would have put three beds in each room, if Mr. B. had not resisted it, insisting on there being only one in each of the little cells. They had revenged themselves by cutting off a foot of length from them, and made them to fit bushmen (a race that don't require beds, even if any exist still). The next day's journey was entirely over the Karroo, covered with dusty shrubs not a foot high, with a few tiny flowers amongst them. After rain it becomes lovely and green (they say).

Beaufort West was the end of the railway, where I found a lively little town and a good hotel. I had a letter from Mr. Garcia, the magistrate, and expected to see some small Spaniard with a guitar, but was much relieved at the sight of a burly Englishman. He told me "he had been fortunate enough to secure an Englishman to drive me,—the son of a late clergyman, Mr. F.,—as those black fellows always drink." Soon afterwards I was accosted in a shop by the most disreputable-looking, bloated, blear-eyed old blackguard, smelling awfully of gin, and he told me he was the "gentleman" who was to drive me. I quite shied away, and when I confided my horror of him to another acquaintance there, he said, "Every one here drinks, but F. and a few others are not *always* drunk!" The next morning he was an hour late, and during the first stage before breakfast he took four doses of pure spirits, half a

teacupful each time, adding a few drops of water with great ceremony, to show how careful he was! He never seemed the worse! He emptied five bottles during the two days he drove me, telling me long stories about himself, and all to prove what a fine fellow Alex. F. was, talking always of himself in the third person, as if he were some one else.

I had to pay him £15 for those two days and back-fare. We went sixty miles a day with two horses over a good road, but it was all desert, covered with small scrub, strange dwarf euphorbias, and miniature plants, which after a day's rain were said to be covered with curious flowers and green leaves, as if by magic. Bleached skeletons, tall stalking-birds, and a few deer also, were seen occasionally to relieve the monotony, besides wonderful effects of mirage: lakes, islands, and even trees, though we passed none but a few mimosas in places which had once been damp, and saw no water till the end of our journey. We had a rest the first day at a lonely store— half hut, half tent—kept by a nice young Englishman only two years out, who had married his master's half-caste daughter, and never wanted work. He went about peddling: sold anything, and took anything in exchange. At night I slept in a nice German house,—a store and mill combined,—also solitary, and reached the railway at Aberdeen Road in the evening, to find the hotel taken up by some of Dr. Gill's party for watching the transit of Venus; but they were true gentlemen, and gave up the best room, where I slept soundly among astronomical instruments, and enjoyed hearing the tongues of freshly imported Englishmen again. A long day's rail took me to Port Elizabeth, through a perfectly new world of vegetation in Kafirland.

The hills on each side were crowded with aloes, the trunks six to ten feet high, mostly having single heads of spiked fleshy leaves on their tops. Some of them were broken into two or three heads, with red-hot-poker flowers; but the season was over, and I only saw one or two at a distance, which reminded me of the grass-trees of Australia in general form. When nearer they looked very different, having only a few leaves instead of thousands, all thick and fleshy, often tinted and mottled with red, forming exquisite curves. Gigantic bushes of prickly-pear cacti also grew like wild things (though not indigenous), covered with orange and lemon coloured flowers. As we got lower down the valley, there were masses of speckboorn *(Portulacaria afra)* with thick swollen stems and branches (like gutta-percha tubing badly put together), covered with small green fleshy leaves and tiny pink flowers. It is the pet food of elephants. Great cactus-like euphorbias, and quantities of one which resembles the candelabra of Teneriffe, this is said to be the cure for cancer, and is also used for stopping leaks in ships under salt water. There were many species of cotyledon and scrubby polygalas lilac with bloom, all tangled together by masses of ivy-leaved pelargonium. Nothing grew more than nine feet high.

Every now and then there was a clearing in which was a group of bee-hive-shaped huts covered with skins and bits of cloth dyed of a rich red colour, or topped with black burnt bush. Near them stalked the grandest figures in red drapery and feathers, like stage Mephistopheles, with women dressed to match, their arms and legs covered with metal rings. I had not expected to see such genuine savages so near civilisation. They seemed too good to be real. The women carried the children sitting astride on humps which they possessed naturally, and which ladies of Europe imitate artificially, without the excuse of their being useful as they are among the Kafirs. The children were also tied on with deep-red cloth. All this rich colour was produced by rubbing with a lump of rough iron. I saw one man, followed by his wives and children, all marching with superb dignity through the bush. They never even turned their heads as the train passed.

At last we descended from this wild country, and came to cultivation again, and to a river blue with large nymphseas standing well out of the water, their great saucer-leaves floating round them; miles of sandy flats, with low heaths

and pelargoniums of many colours, and lovely cotyledons in quantities, three or four bunches of their exquisite coral bells from one crimson stalk, sometimes salmon-tinted, sometimes bronze-coloured; but the latter grew on a larger bush. Port Elizabeth is far more like a capital than Cape Town: it is full of life and work, very clean and neat, with an excellent hotel called after my father's old leader, Lord Palmerston. Every one who could afford it lived on the hill above the town. Mr. N. called on me the evening I arrived—a most interesting man, and a great botanist. He brought two exquisite groundorchids in his hand, which gave me work for the two next days; but I managed to get up to his house at seven the next morning, where I found him hard at work in his shirt sleeves, watering his plants, and had a delightful hour with him in his garden and the neighbouring Botanic Gardens, which he had greatly helped to make. He seemed to know every flower of South Africa, and all about them, though he passed his days in his shop selling tea and sugar. He told me I was only wasting my time in the town, and ought to go at once to "Cadles "; so I did, driving over twenty-five miles across the "flats" to it. They were in themselves worth studying. The *Cyrtanthus obliquus* had a lovely bunch of drooping lilyheads, shaded from red and orange into green, with a sheaf of leaves each having one twist at the end. The coral heath and various crassulas, particularly the "rochea," were most gaudy. A lovely parasitic plant also grew there on the roots of the heath. It looked like a Chinese primula picked and stuck into the sand without any leaves, of the most delicate lilac with white throat, its petals fringed and scented. Long-tailed finches were fluttering over the low scrub, with gorgeous orange and red shoulder-knots, too much weighed down by their wedding finery to fly higher, and flapping their wings like kites; exquisite sun-birds, too, with bright canary-coloured breasts which collectors of stuffed birds never see, as the colour fades to white after death.

Cadles itself was perfect quarters: a

sort of farmhouse rather than a hotel, with the kindest of hosts and hostesses—the latter almost immovable from dropsy. She had half a dozen nieces or adopted daughters who did the work, looked after everything, and kept the place lively and in order. One felt more like a friend than a boarder. I had an upstairs room, opening on a verandah with a window at the other end, looking over the farm and offices across the kluft to the distant mountains to which it leads, and from whence the delicious water is brought to Port Elizabeth. All round the house is a sort of hilly tableland, covered with coarse grass, coloured with pink and white watsonias and other flowers. This tableland is cut up by great klufts or cracks, loaded with rich forest-trees, and tangled with creepers, wild vines with brown stalks and tendrils, plumbago, ivy-pelargonium, and various gourds: one they called "wild Chili " *(Gephalandra palmata),* with hanging egg-like fruits of scarlet or green, made the most exquisite festoons, but was poisonous. There were great candelabra-like euphorbias fifty feet high, and the calodendron or wild chestnut covered with large bunches of lilac flowers.

Huge baboons came out when one was not expecting them, and barked like dogs. I saw a pair of them one day sitting in a cornfield, munching handfuls, and spoiling much more. They let us come quite near, then decamped with an awkward rocking-horse kind of movement, reminding me of the old story of the dog whose tail was so tightly curled that it lifted his hind-legs off the ground. They were huge creatures, and did much mischief wherever they went. I was warned not to stray too far for fear of leopards. Only a few miles off a woman had heard a noise, set a trap, and caught a large leopard in it. Her husband was away, but she got his gun and shot it herself, and its skin was the great sight of the neighbourhood.

Just over my balcony window was the nest of a big blackbird with brown wings and most sociable ways. He was for ever chattering and whistling to his wife, and had many notes in his voice. I think his wife was a vixen, and nagged at him in return. The cat had a great mind to have the young birds, but whenever she came and fixed her big eyes on the nest, the cock came down and fluttered helplessly about at the other end of the verandah, so diverting her attention. They told me puss would have had the worst of it in a fight, his beak and claws were so strong. From my other window I used to watch the great teams of oxen harnessed in the morning. They arranged themselves like a regiment of soldiers in line, keeping their heads close in regular order, so that the man had no difficulty in linking them together with the ropes. The two wheelers always took the end place as a matter of course; the others might go as they liked, but the two strongest were proud of the honour of going next the cart, which right the others never disputed. Sixteen was the usual number of animals harnessed to an ox-waggon. Out of that same back window I watched the two boys one evening sitting on the ground with a lantern between them, playing with two young owls, and a grave-looking cat beside them, VOL. 11 R wondering if she ought to have wings, or if they ought to have four paws—which was wrong?

I had been long seeking a good specimen of the *Protea cynaroides,* the biggest of all its race. I saw the plant on the Cape Table Mountain, but searched in vain for a flower. I had mentioned this to a friend I was lunching with at Port Elizabeth. He rubbed his head for a moment, then said: "I know where it is!" rushed into a neighbour's house a few doors off, and brought me out a magnificent flower. I almost cried with joy at getting it at last, I had missed it so often; took it with me to Cadles, and painted it there. The bracts were like pink satin, tinted at the base with green, and a perfect pyramid of yellow flowers rose in the centre. While I was eagerly at work over this gorgeous flower, my landlord brought me a lory or touraco, with a lovely red beak and eyelid, and its green wings lined with that deep magenta colour which has made this bird famous; for it washes out in soap and

water, and, what is still more strange, the bird is said to have the power of re-colouring it. The colour when washed out has been analysed and found to contain much copper. I was dumbfounded when the bird was brought me to paint, as I could not give up the protea, so made a compromise, and managed to show only its head and part of the famous wing, the rest of the bird being hidden by the flower and leaves.

It was hard work to paint all the beautiful things they brought me at Cadles. One day one of the pretty nieces brought up a Kafir baby, stark-naked and supernaturally solemn, of a dry gingerbread consistency and colour, not polished like nigger babies. They rub powdered earth, not oil, over them, and make it take the place of clothing even in the coldest weather. The elder ones are perpetually dancing and laughing; I never saw them unhappy. All the service of the house was done by Kafir women under the young ladies, and very well done too. The food was most abundant and good. On Saturday Mr. H. telegraphed to know if I were still there, and came over and spent his Sunday in taking me to the head of Van Staaden's Gorge.

They gave me a perfect pony from Basutoland, a strong roan, which treated me as if I were no weight at all, and both walked and cantered to perfection. My companion led the way on an animal he knew well, which stood stock-still whenever he got off to hunt flowers, till he was ready to get up again. It needed no tying up or leading. I suspect the horse knew Mr. H.'s ways even better than Mr. H. knew its own. He was more off than on his horse, going into ecstasies over a dozen tiny flowers on our way over the heathy flats. We saw acres of the *Lanaria plumosa,* white and woolly, with a touch of violet on its six slender petals, and green lily leaves. Then we crossed a deep and very steep kluft through the rather deep stream, and up the almost perpendicular bank, hanging to our horses' manes, through bushes covered with white woolly balls, and the bright scarlet antholyza, known at the Cape as Aunt Elizas. We soon

reached the hills, and the aqueduct leading one way to the gorge and the other to Port Elizabeth, whose streets are bordered by delicious running water, and every garden has its fountain. Few towns are better supplied, thanks to Mr. G. The gorge was very narrow, and bordered by reddish cliffs, through which ran the clearest of rivers, with deep pools amid masses of ferns, pelargoniums, watsonias, blue hyacinths, yellow and white daisy-trees, everlastings, polygalas, and tall heaths. Under them we found precious parasites (harveya), white, pink, and scarlet, while above, in rocky cracks, hung euphorbias and zamias, or Kafir bread-trees. At the head of the gorge we came to a waterfall and a reservoir.

Just where the water bubbled out purest and freshest were quantities of a small pink and white disa and lovely droseras. We returned over the windy downs on the other side of the hills amidst acres of protea bushes of different sorts, and huge everlasting-plants standing a yard or two above the ground, with white velvety leaves round a thick stalk, surmounted by a cauliflower head of white petals and yellow stamens. These looked like tombstones at a distance. A gentleman who had been also to the gorge cut one of the great things down, and carried it home over his shoulder for me to paint, for which I was grateful, for it was no small weight. One of the proteas had a deep dahlia-carmine centre and pink bracts edged with white ostrich feathers, the leaves exquisitely tinted with lilac, like the bloom on plums. After leaving those downs, we came to a marshy hollow, and saw the *Sparaxis pendula* for the first time. Its almost invisible stalks stood four or five feet high, waving in the wind. These were weighed down by strings of lovely pink bells, with yellow calyx, and buds; they followed the winding marsh, and looked like a pink snake in the distance, making me scream with joy when I first saw them. "I was sure you would do that," said my guide contentedly. As we rounded the mountain he showed me a blue-green patch on the top of it, looking like a swede-turnip field in Norfolk, and said it was a mass of agapanthus! It was a day of days!

Mr. H. often came over, and his enthusiasm as a flowerhunter was quite equalled by his genial good-nature. The young people of the house used to send him many wildgoose journeys in search of impossible plants, and made up strange flowers to puzzle him. Sunday was a great day at Cadles; as many as forty sometimes came out to dine and sleep there, and were stowed away without any confusion or discomfort, but they never encroached on our comfortable upper floor, which was occupied by one or two invalids and myself. The pretty nieces sang and played and danced and looked as if they had nothing to do. The native Kafirs, who had been there all their lives, lounged about with pipes always in their mouths, in all manner of strange and picturesque attitudes, at the doors of their huts. No one seemed to work, yet everything was well done. Dutch servants and Christians are said to be very different, and to make the worst servants. One of them was going to Natal as a cook once: when asked if she did not think her friends might object to her going so far, she said, "No one minded; she had had a husband once, but the Lord had been kind enough to take him."

The family at Cadles were not at all pious, but one of their Kafirs was; he used to preach, and was the only one who stole. When accused one day of taking a leg of mutton, he pulled a Bible out of his pocket, and said, "How could I steal with this blessed book in my pocket?" At last I made up my mind to tear myself away from that charming place, and found it not so easy to accomplish. I missed one chance of a return carriage through my deafness, then had to share one with people who could not get up in the morning. To fill up the time after packing, I read the poem of "Sigurd" by W. Morris, and really enjoyed it. It was lent me by a very interesting invalid, who was dying slowly of chronic bronchitis. I drove over the hot flats, now dried up. There were few flowers, and the hotel was full for

a cricket match, so I availed myself of Mrs. S.'s kind permission to go to her nice house on the hill. When I asked the Malay cabman what he would charge to take me down to the railway (about 200 yards) at seven the next morning, he said fifteen shillings! I laughed, and he said ten. I left him and got one for seven. The hour was too early for the hard-worked Malay!

I spent the afternoon in the Botanic Garden, then went on to Mr. H., whom I found as usual watering his plants in his shirt-sleeves, a little daughter pumping for him; so she got a rest, and I all the names I wanted from Mr. H. as we sat on the verandah with a pile of books round us. His energy was wonderful. One of the flowers he spoke of I could not quite make out; so he was off like a shot to the Botanical and brought back a leaf, while his big fine-gentlemen sons lolled about on easy-chairs, too lazy even to get up when I said good-bye. The house was perfect too; much of it was built with his own hands. He had established a Natural History Club, of which he was president, and had made it quite a fashionable pursuit in Port Elizabeth. He had built a tank for water under a small wattle-tree in his garden, and described to me how a yellow finch came and built nine hanging nests on it without stopping, and without any wife to put in them. Then he looked about, dressed himself up in fine feathers, and brought first one wife, and then another. Other cocks came and did likewise, till there were twenty-five nests all hanging from that small tree. Mr. H. fed and petted all the birds which came to his garden till they were quite tame, and all his plants had histories.

The railway took me through the Adda Bush: a flat, swampy locality, full of spekboom trees, which are said to tempt the elephants down close to civilisation, and herds of them are still found there. Some twenty miles of dense tangle prevents mankind from interfering with the poor beasts, and the climate suits them better than it does their enemies. It was a great relief to begin ascending, and the road became very steep and wonderfully made. The views got wider and

wider, over bare hills covered with coarse yellow grass, sprinkled with pink watsonias, with green trees only in the cracks, of which the aloes, euphorbias, and aralias towered above the rest, some of the aloes splitting into branches like the dome-palm or dracaena, with slender curved stems. At the top of the pass we came to groups of the oldenburghia, a most striking shrub which grows only on these hills, and on the very tops of them: its stalks and young leaves are of the purest white velvet, the older leaves lined with the same, but the upper sides resemble the leaves of the great magnolia. The flowers are like artichoke flowers, purple, with white calyx, stalks, and buds, growing in a noble bunch. The whole bush is under six feet high.

The hills became very bare as we descended to Grahamstown, which is built in a perfect hole; but it was pretty inside, with many nice people in comfortable houses with lovely gardens. Its Botanical Garden was particularly well kept, full of interesting plants, the wild hillside and rocks coming down into it at the back. Mr. H. had given me an introduction to Mrs. G., the wife of a watchmaker there who had built a curious house with a tall tower, and had seven sons all fond of natural collections of different sorts. These young men brought me constant relays of beautiful flowers. I stayed in a quiet room at the railway-hotel, where I could work well with a good light, and seldom went out except for drives with Mrs. A., a wonderful old lady of over eighty. She had two spirited Basuto horses, bright chestnut with white specks, which always stood on their hind-legs before they started, and began kicking if they stood still for more than three minutes. Once off, they were quiet as lambs. Her husband, Dr. A., was the one man of the place, and full of information. He also collected for me, sometimes riding thirty miles before breakfast to get a flower; he was the most active man I ever met. His garden, which he planted forty years before, was well worth coming across the world to see, and full of strange plants, mostly native. The *Strelitzia augusta* was in full flower, as were many varieties of aloes. The biggest of all aloes had been called after his relative, Mrs. Baines. I had heard her name ever since I entered South Africa as the great authority on all sorts of natural history, and was delighted when she walked into my room one day and said she had come from the country on purpose to see me. She showed me some of her own paintings, stippled on white paper, with a line of neutral tint round the edges to raise them (done much in the way old Anne North did her flowers in the year I was born). She had painted many of the stapelias, and brought me two to do—brown and yellow stars with a most evil smell. They attract flies, which try to get at the nectar, and thereby fertilise the flowers, then are rewarded by being themselves caught by their legs, and probably have their lives sucked out of them.1 Their efforts were frantic and most futile to get free from the tormentors.

"Fly can't come," the little coolie housemaid remarked. I never was bothered with flies in the room till the stapelia attracted them in; and after a time they found out its craftiness and avoided it, taking instead to my poor nose and spectacles for a promenade. That same little coolie girl was most graceful and bewitching, with a Hindu mark on her forehead, gold nose-ring, and bangles. I suggested after a day or two that she might make the bed. "You wantee bed made?" It was quite a new idea to her; so she walked over the top of it with her pretty bare feet, then beckoned me to take hold on the other side, and we smoothed and put the things back again (without any shaking or bother), and she jumped over it again laughing. Every day after we repeated the ceremony; it made no extra dust in the room, but I doubt if my English Emily would approve of the method!

Mr. G. brought me a lovely tiny yellow *Limnanthemum Thunbergii,* all over hairs. The flower and bunch of tiny buds all grew from the spring of the one leaf-stalk, from which also the roots descended. I kept it in a soap-dish full of water, and every day a fresh flower opened. "He no wakee yet," said my little maid, when she brought me my morning coffee too early for it. But all people in Grahamstown were not made in the same mould, and I was much bored by stupid visitors whose time was of no consequence. One day when I had missed the breakfast, and came in hungry and glad to get a cup of cold tea and bread and butter, three girls forced themselves into my room, with a crowd of others behind them, and began asking me stupid questions till I fairly lost my temper. "Was I not afraid of spoiling my 1 Mr. Hanbury (at Mortola) once told me that in his garden the flies actually laid their eggs in these evil-smelling flowers, taking them for carrion.—Ed. eyes? I ought to save them." I asked her in return what eyes were made for, and did she think it would be any use to leave them behind me ‰ Like her beloved diamonds or gold, what good would it do to save them *1* She thought me mad, and they all fled, and at last I got my breakfast. I liked the old people best, and went to see an old missionary's wife of over eighty, who told me of the dreadful days of the Kafir War, when she had had three times to fly into the bush with her baby in her arms, leaving her burning house behind her. She called it a wise dispensation of Providence, and I did not contradict her; but she seemed none the worse, and was a sweet, placid old lady.

Another lady sent me a moth-eaten specimen of a bluebird, with long red legs, toes, and beak, to paint. She said it only went to one spot in the colony once in every seven years, a habit which sounded peculiar! It was very ugly, but rather like a bird of New Zealand, and its toes almost long enough to walk over water-weeds. I spent Christmas Day at Grahamstown at a picnic with the A. s—a very solemn feast, at which the daughter's time was chiefly taken up with packing and unpacking provisions, plates, cups, etc. The drives over the bare hills were every now and then rewarded by the sight of a great lonely lily, or the huge pink king of all onions, the *Buphane toxicaria,* all alone without any leaves. I never would pick them, it was so beautiful in them to adorn such dismal plains. The Kafirs poison their arrows with this plant.

All trees have been burnt on those hills during the different wars; even the cracks near Grahamstown are bare, so we had to go a considerable way to find a picturesque spot for our picnic, and found when we reached it that others had taken possession before us of all the sheltered nooks. Great waggons and fires were near; horses were drinking in the clear stream; it was gay with brightly dressed Coolie and Malay women and children; parties of Europeans also, who cheered the popular doctor when they saw him. It was such a rare sight to see him taking a holiday, and was intended as a special honour to me. I got a sketch with four different kinds of euphorbia and aloes in it, jasmine, the orange tecoma, and the long-tubed gardenia. The Kafir plum and blackberries, with orange fruit, were there too in quantities. Among a party of roadmakers up another kluft I was accosted by a man who said he had seen me on Lake Wakatipu in New Zealand.

On the 6th of January 1883 I started (with Mrs. B.) in a private carriage for a six hours' jolt-jolt to Port Alfred. We crossed low hills covered with dwarf scrub and euphorbias, or bare as the Sussex Downs, Kafir huts occasionally on their tops, with patches of Indian corn and scrub in the hollows. The scarlet clusters of upright fuchsia flowers of the Boer boontges *Scholia speciosa),* a very knotty, shabby tree with dark foliage, was the most conspicuous thing, with two other species of the same, and the dwarf erythrina. We also saw some trap-door spiders' nests made on the flat ground; not in banks, as I had met with them elsewhere. Our stupid driver put us down at the wrong hotel, from which we had to walk down the hill to the Kowie River to be ferried across, then had a hot mile's walk across the wet marsh and up the opposite hill to the other, where rooms had been taken for us, carrying all our luggage ourselves in the hottest hours of a hot day! Fortunately we found friends to help us and to show us the way. Dr. Becker had come to meet me, meaning me to stay at his nice place up the river with his wife; but as usual a companion (when I do have one) spoils all those nice arrangements, and he could not find room for two. Even when we reached the hotel there was no way of putting us both up, except by sharing a bed or sleeping, one of us, on two chairs (which my friend did). The situation of the hotel was pretty, with thick scrub round it on three sides, and a view over it to the white sandhills at the edge of the sea. There was a hedge round the garden of deepblue ipomcea, which was said to be indigenous higher up the coast; but I never found it.

Ten minutes' walk through the woods or over the marsh below took us to the sandhills, where different people were camping with their waggons during the summer months for sea-bathing. They were not tidy in their ways, but the sand was always drifting and giving a fresh surface, so they could not do much harm to the place. At the end of the river a pier was being slowly made by convicts, and a railway to meet it from Grahamstown will in course of time make the pretty place a cheaper and easier resort for its dried-up inhabitants. Mrs. T, the wife of its engineer, took us in her boat a few miles up the river, where I drew some old zamias and strelitzias hanging over the water. Then we went to see Dr. Becker, whose house stood high over the great river just at its bend, with lovely views both ways. He had had the good taste to leave the giant euphorbia and other native trees. He had also a collection of stapelias and other small prickly plants; some of them were almost invisible without a magnifying glass, but most interesting. The wild birds too he fed on the verandah, and he had an aviary full of curious ones, some of them from Madagascar, and a wonderful collection of insects. I was amused by hearing a difference of opinion about one on Mrs. B.'s part (a most obstinate old lady). She left the room muttering, "That's not a beetle; I know it's not a beetle!" and Mrs. Becker turned to me: "As if the doctor did not know one when he saw it. Why, even at school he used to be called Beetle Becker."

I had another pull up the river with a picnic party, and wasted a whole day in an uninteresting spot, cooking muttonchops, etc., near a deserted mill. Late in the afternoon we pushed up a creek among shallows and rocks, till we could go no farther, then walked on, and found some date-palms in full flower, also blue nymphseas, and bulrushes weighted with nests of the gorgeous black-velvet finches, with red or gold backs. We saw also lories, hoopoes, shrikes, and herons. The river was lovely as we came down at sunset, the euphorbiatrees standing out like white skeletons against the bush, with clusters of pinkish aloe-tops like rosettes among them. Every now and then there was a brilliant coral rochea, or crassula, near the water's edge, which showed itself half a mile off amid the dark rocks and foliage. Mrs. B. only stayed two days, but her sister and her husband, a brother of Dr. A.'s, came and drove me back in their carriage, which I much enjoyed. We made two days' journey of the twenty-eight miles, and stopped every five minutes. The whole way was pretty, and quite different from the road by which I went to the Kowie— one part especially, where there was a kluft full of wild datetrees bordering the stream and rocky banks; the place bristled with aloes and euphorbias. A kind of asphodel was growing up from the ground like a spear stuck in by its handle-end, and no leaves. We found aloes with salmoncoloured bells, most metallic green buds, and blotched leaves, also a giant asclepiad called pachycarpus.

Dr. A. had asked me to stay in his house on my return, but all his rooms were so darkened with vegetation that I despaired of finding one I could see to paint in. At last I was taken across a sort of drawbridge to an attic or wide verandah, dark with a solid mass of creepers, bougainvillea, banksia-roses, etc. It was full of old boxes of rubbish, and some crazy steps led into another attic with a small room at either end, one of them given up entirely to a colony of bees, which had built in a corner and resisted intruders; the other belonged to a

son, who was on the opposite side of the colony. There I settled myself, digging out a hole in the bougainvilleas, which let in a blaze of rosy light through their flowery wreaths. It took me some time to make the opening sufficiently large to get natural-coloured light enough to paint by. One side of the room was separated from the verandah by broken green house-sashes, one of them off its hinges. The roof itself was all of a slant, books, hats, pipes, and various treasures of men in delightful disorder, but it was deliciously quiet and out of the way. I bolted myself in at night, and shared the whole storey with the bees and an occasional rat, bird, or lizard, and through my hole in the bougainvillea I looked on wonderful groups of aloes of many species, and other rare things collected by the Doctor in his long African life.

The first night, I confess, some of the noises were startling. The gum-trees overhead continually dropped their nuts, which went patter, patter, patter over the zinc roof. There were also strange creakings and moanings from the branches of creepers. Lizards and rats were perpetually on the move, but when once I knew what they were they no longer disturbed me. The doctor brought me a strange euphorbia from the Karroo, shaped like a melon, with tiny yellow flowers on long stalks down its ribs, and marked with red stripes as if done with a paint-brush between them. It was a most odd plant, but the sheep will eat it when all else is dried up, as they do the "milk plant." I painted also a very curious caterpillar which pretended to be a snake when frightened, drawing in its small head and neck till the third joint looked like a snake's head, a sham eye of black with a green rim just in the right place. I found these same creatures both brown and dark green (perhaps they had the power of changing colour like chameleons). They were over three inches long when stretched, and coiled themselves like snakes if touched.

I had determined to go overland to St. John's, and the Governor, to whom I wrote, kindly telegraphed to the different magistrates to be good to me if I came in their way. One friend in Grahamstown (who had had an exhibition of my paintings in her house while I was at the Kowie) told me it was dangerous, and some people had lately been washed away when trying to cross the rivers; but the doctor said it was not necessary to cross them at flood-time, and I might as well go. He went to Cape Town to his Parliamentary duties, and the sunshine went with him. My bower was soaked with wet. There was a perpetual succession of dawdling, dull society, and I fled down to pack at Mr. S.'s comfortable house at Port Elizabeth, whence I sent my paintings home. I found my store-box so battered by its solitary voyage, that it had to be emptied and mended; but workmen were clever and active in Port Elizabeth, and a day did it all. I slept at Coerney in the Adda Bush, where there was a nice little hotel, full of children out for the holidays. They followed me about, collecting odd flowers for me; they had no idea of being in the way, and were not. Elephants and buffaloes were both in that bush, but we saw none. A tortoise I saw walking about on the tips of his toes, and the children put little loads on his back, which he did not in the least mind, though he objected to them on his nose. The landlord of the Tuerberg came to see what I was doing, and asked "what I did with them paintings." I said I sent them to Kew. "Oh, I know, that's where they sell things by auction," he said. (He was a Boer!)

The plants seemed all fleshy or thorny at Coerney, but there were some pretty bulbs, one of them flowering pure white in the morning, and changing through pink to crimson at night. Mrs. A. sent for me to sleep again on my way through Grahamstown. The post-cart was to start at eight. The time came, and I myself hauled down my things over the drawbridge, where I found the poor old lady with a heap of ill-tied loose parcels for me to take as "provisions." When at last I got a man to carry my trunk, and rushed off, I was called back to be told I ought to make the man carry my bag also. I did swear then! I was overtaken by her husband, dress-

ing as he went, and told I had lots of time; and so I had, for the post-cart did not start till long past the hour. It was a two-wheeled vehicle, stuffed full of letter-bags. The driver sat himself down on the bit of board which was resting on the back lumps, and kicked out a hole for my feet to go into, as children make nests in haycocks; so I was not uncomfortable, and when all was full four schoolboys and their luggage were thrown in on the top, with extra long legs and arms like baboons, and about as sensible, and we had a long day of battering and bruising one another. I only saw two flowers I coveted, but could not stop to get them in H.M.'s post-cart. One was a dwarf aloe, with long mottled side-leaves, and spike of lilac bells, the other a noble magenta ipomcea with dark eye, growing on a shrub a foot high (not creeping, like most of its tribe), its stalks and tendrils hairy. It grew near the Fish River, and I have since heard that it grows nowhere else.

As we crept up one long hill the driver showed me a baboon, sitting on the top of a tree, keeping watch to give warning to the whole tribe, which I saw below in the valley. He said they always did that. I saw also quantities of shrikes—a bird of the most brilliant metallic peacock-blue colour, with yellow eyes. It is a cruel bird, and spits its game on the long thorns of the acacias and aloes, as the butcher-bird does. Scarlet pelargoniums peeped out here and there among the plumbago and sweet white jasmine. We reached Beaufort at four; but I had two big lumps on my spine, and a scarlet face, and was little inclined to seek society or give letters of introduction in the little dull town. The weekly cart started at five the next morning, so I set out without even getting a cup of coffee. My driver was as black as a coal, with a long white ostrich feather in his hat, and I had the cart to myself all the way: a great luxury. The road along the Kat River was very pretty; but Balfour, where I meant to stop, looked dressy, and in a hole, so I went higher and was left at "Therous."

The air was delicious, but it was like a dozen low alps I know in Switzerland:

bare alps, with no shade except in the deep klufts. Even there the trees seemed round-headed and commonplace, with not even euphorbias to mark the continent. It was a solitary house kept by pious temperance people, very clean, and the food particularly good; but I found no new flowers to tempt me to linger a week, and felt I should go mad before it was over. The flowery season was past. I toiled twice to the top of the pass and back in vain, to find nothing worth painting. My only companion was a poor Englishman in consumption. He had been sent out a year before as a last chance, and had got much better at Grahamstown. Then he was advised to complete the cure by travelling and seeing the country in an ox-waggon. The second day of cart-jolting broke some blood-vessel, and there he was stranded, and scarcely able to crawl. I am happy to say I met him afterwards on the ship which brought me home, and know that he got back to his family in Wales safely.

Some of the dripping rocks higher up the mountain were pretty, covered with streptocarpus, small pink lilies, campanulas, ferns, and balsam. They were impossible to bring home, they were so delicate. The asparagus was also lovely, but not equal to that which I had seen at the Kowie, where there were many sorts in flower at the very top, tritomas and agapanthus lilies in quantity. The purple *Sparaxis* pendula is the pride of the Katberg, but that too was over. The top is flat and table-like, resting on precipitous walls from 100 to 500 feet high. Trains of waggons were moving on in the early morning and late evening, resting always during the heat of the day, with fourteen or sixteen beasts in each. The loads were enormous, all going towards the diamond-fields, the mainspring of all trade in South Africa. Strange that those glittering little stones should govern half a continent! The carriage came at last, and four bullocks dragged me up the hills. The views were certainly fine, but, as Mr. Lear wrote, "Cumberland is nearer and prettier," and there was nothing in it characteristic of Africa. The road was very bad, but

I had a capital Kafir to drive me, and before the after-glow had faded out of the sky we had got over all difficulties, down to the plain, and reached a decent inn before dark. The next morning I reached Queenstown by breakfast-time.

The only remarkable plants we passed were large red lilies, coming straight out of the ground without leaves, and often a foot or eighteen inches across: a perfect ball of carmine stalks and flowers, the latter with thin, poor petals, but making quite a patch of colour on the green plain, from their abundance and size. Stunted mimosa or acacia trees were dotted about, and beautifully-formed hills filled the distance, the highest one 6000 feet above the sea. My room at the inn had the full sun on it, and was like an oven. Dr. B. gave me one of the tuberous roots of the dwarf erythrina, which he said is most useful in surgery for making cork-legs, etc., being all a light pith. It was a dreary country, and I was glad to escape and to have an airy saloon-carriage all to myself in the train to King William's Town. It is a very uninteresting country to pass through, with the exception of a few klufts with groups of zamias in them and tree-ferns. I had telegraphed to a friend, who met me on arriving. In the Botanical Garden we saw the poor director, who had reached the dismal stage of the usual disease (every one was in the same stage of it thereabouts). They settled that I must go to see the Perie forest, and stay with a family there, whose father was a sawyer, and had a second mill at East London, while his son managed the one in the forest.

It rained all night, but my friend was clear to start, so off we went, he riding, I driving a country cart over the most awful roads. We lost our way, and went short cuts. Once when it seemed too bad for wheels to pass, I got out and fell in the mud; after that I slipped on some steppingstones and got soaked in the river from head to foot, in which state I arrived at the house. I had to change every

Vol. 11 s thing at once. The good Frau was very hospitable, and gave me her parlour, making me up a bed with a small sofa and a chair; and there I stayed four days, for the rains came on with a vengeance. Mrs. C. got home next day somehow, and sent a carriage back for me. The driver said I must not wait a minute, or the river would be impassable. Mrs. S. said, "Don't go, it is dangerous," and sent the man off, who found that it was! He had to invent a new way of getting home over the tops of the hills, so I settled myself to paint Kafir-plums in the "parlour." It was also the dairy, with a strong smell of buttermilk, and the children used to find their way in at odd hours, day and night, to drag their fingers round the creampans and suck them. The stores were also kept in the chimney of my room, and there was a hurdy-gurdy with twelve tunes, and a musical snuff-box, which were generally going both at once in it. There were nine children, who spoke English and DutchKafir, and had neither pins nor hooks and eyes to their dresses, and little respect for ordinary decencies of life. The mother was a grand woman, with golden hair, a German by birth. I never saw her without her baby, which was generally feeding in the manner intended by nature. She gave me all the best she had, including the one washingbasin and bit of soap. We all lived on brown bread and butter, with now and then a scone or pancake for variety, with tea and coffee, milk and brown sugar, pumpkins and potatoes. The scenery was pretty, with the real forest broken by grassy slopes, clearings, and many streams, too full to cross just then.

At last the rain ceased, the sun shone, and the good Frau took me and three children three miles through the forest in her ox-waggon to the saw-mill. I enjoyed it much, and felt far safer in that long wood-waggon than in a cart with horses. The long stretch of the machine broke the jolting. The two Kafirs who drove us ran backwards and forwards, and climbed over the beasts, managing to keep the huge machine from accident, over the narrow ditch they called a road, and up and down the steepest pitches to the streams, while we had to look sharp to prevent our hats being torn

off by the brambles over our heads. We stopped near the saw-mill, and stayed all day in the cool forest, where I got sketches of the great yellow-wood trees, covered with lianes and other creepers. The Kafir boom, or large erythrina, was a tall tree, with great thorns or knobs over its stems. The eldest son and his partner lived in a hut near the mill, and were delighted to see "mother and baby." All the men who worked there sent down to her for the "grub"; that is, flour, butter, sugar, and a bottle of rum every week. They kept fowls, and had a bit of garden to grow mealies and vegetables in, leaving enough of their wages over to buy tobacco and ornaments. One man had been sending for "grub" and working for some one else, so the Frau went to his hut and told him to "clear out, or she would set fire to the hut." The woman was in bed, and did not seem to mind it. She was a lazy creature, who never did anything else. I saw her children outside torturing a cat. They put her under a bit of zinc roofing, and danced on the top of her: "sweet nature of the untaught savage!" As it was again fine, and no cart appeared, we stopped a wood-waggon and engaged it to take me and one of the girls who was returning to school to King.

We jolted merrily along with six fine bullocks, sitting on the floor of the long springless cart, till we reached the top of the hill, and saw the promised carriage going on rapidly by another road, and Mr. C. jogging after it. They turned and looked at us, but went on; so did we, and we were not overtaken till we reached the half-way house. The cart was driven by the same man who had come after me in the storm, and I soon found out he was the famous driver, Mr. Hewitson, of whom I had heard so much. He showed me the height the river had risen in the late rains, and that it would have been certain death to have attempted to cross the river then. We picked up a nice young Englishwoman and her child, who were going with him to Mutata to join her husband, and he persuaded me to go at the same time and on to St. John's. I felt confidence in the man, and agreed to his very high price. He offered to give me quarters in his own comfortable house, instead of my going back to the wretched inn; so I went, and his good wife had all my clothes washed. One of his daughters drove me out shopping in her nice pony-carriage, and I felt I was with civilised beings again: it was so comfortable. Directly I came, two huge water-melons were cut and eaten with cakes and good tea, and then, luxury of luxuries, a hot bath!

Mr. Hewitson was a grand man, six feet two, and broad in proportion, and was always cheery. Every one seemed to like him, and no one was jealous of him. Of course he had many other trades besides driving his four horses. He had lately contracted to put up some hundreds of miles of telegraph posts. He liked the hard, out-of-doors work, and asked a good price for it too; but did it so thoroughly well, and was such a good fellow, that he always got what he asked. I grudged it less, knowing the man he was, and how nice were his wife and family. We started at three in the afternoon, the girls standing on the wheel to kiss their father before he drove off; then we went straight up the down-like hills, reaching the little inn at Key Road station about sunset. It was just the place I had been longing to find to stay at. The landlord had been a magistrate in the Transvaal in the very thick of the war. He had had to escape for his life after fighting the Boers. They offered to give him some employment, but he could not turn his coat so quickly, and after almost starving and waiting in vain for his own country to do anything for him, he took that little inn. His poor wife's eyes filled with tears as she told me of all their troubles, and I should have been glad to have stopped, for her sake, but could not change plans then. Our fellow-travellers came by train during the night, and we left at daybreak. My companions were: charming little Dolly of three years old, always singing to herself, and laughing, and her mother, who had been a hospital nurse in England, and was now going to join her husband, a sergeantmajor of C.M.R. at Mutata. We had a long day, and finished

it by descending the steep road to Key Bridge, a terrible hole, where nobody could sleep. But I found many interesting plants: a large-flowered pink pelargonium with bulbous roots and yellow buds (I lost it and never got another), a white hibiscus with crimson eye, and a large magenta ipomcea among the grass—all else was dried up. At moonlight I saw a pretty scene—a party of Kafirs camping round a fire under the trees, half of them only clothed in their barbaric ornaments. The next night brought us to better quarters on the top of a hill, where a white party had collected to arrange some races, and we were all crowded up again. At another house, where we had breakfast, the owner was out. The place was possessed by a number of pets, swarming with fleas, but most entertaining—one monkey particularly, who grudged the dogs every morsel of food they got. Once it stood on its hind legs and opened the big dog's mouth with both its paws, staring down its throat with a despairing expression at not having a third paw to pull out the choice morsel it saw there. The big dog looked perfectly helpless and resigned in its hands. We saw a group of moorhens, with long gray legs and bodies, and a perfect crown of brown feathers round their heads. Long-tailed finches were fluttering about over the tall grass, with gorgeous shoulder-knots. Fine aloes and big lilies marked the Baslin River. It had rained the day before, and one could not help remembering the stories told of its floods.

Mr. H. offered to send for the boat if I feared to cross with him; but I said at once that if he could, we could, and we found it was just practicable, no more. The river was divided by an island into two branches, and there was a considerable rush of water on either side, and not many inches to spare between the top of the water and our feet. On the other side was a tidy inn, where people sometimes have to wait for many days before they can cross. We stayed all through the hot hours, and I caught some pretty butterflies in the bush on the river banks. Higher up grow the tallest aloes known.

One called after Mrs. Raines was measured by her brother, who said it was seventy feet high. We climbed still higher over the bare hills, and in one wild spot we came on a party of natives celebrating the majority of some of their boys. These heroes were painted white, and hung with petticoats made of grasses, with long feathers on their heads. They were dancing to a crowd of savage spectators, after which they would be kept on that hillside for three months in solitude, then have another feast, when an animal of every sort would be killed, including a small boy (if this can be done without being found out—and if so, how does any one know it is done f) When all the ceremonies are over, a red blanket is given to each, after which they are allowed to marry.

The whole country was covered with groups of native huts or kraals, crowning the tops of all the hills. Few white men lived on that road. More bare hills took us to Mutata: quite a typical town of South Africa, all zinc and canvas, with hardly a tree, but an unfinished brick cathedral! Nearly every shelter was full; but I got a room to myself, which was a treat, and the long-wished-for bath, and before I was out of it heard that Major E. was waiting to see me—a fine courteous old soldier, who had married a young wife, and had several small babies to give him an interest in life. He had a picturesque home, made out of five Kafir huts linked together, and a pretty garden of roses. A moorhen was standing on one leg on the top of one of the huts, with a noble crown of feathers round its head. It was very tame. When it saw its master coming it would prance up to him, flapping its wings, and when within touching distance would whirl round suddenly and retire again.

The next morning I started off alone with my driver into Pondoland. The Major promised me two mounted police, but only one overtook us, some miles away; the other could not find a horse. The road went up and down over the tops of beehive hills all day; they were so steep that we should have upset if we had not gone over the very tops.

They were green, and there were fine bits of forest in the klufts between them, tangled with creepers and parasites like the woods of Borneo. I caught a few butterflies, and a great many grass-ticks, which were as venomous and abundant as the carapatas of Brazil. The Pondo natives are well worth the journey to see. They train their hair into a kind of felt cap round the tops of their heads, stiffened with glue and grease, and finished with a round ring, highly polished. This one hair-dressing lasts a lifetime, and their bald heads stick up in the middle of it. They wear the bones of fish or birds stuck through their ears. Others dress their hair in ridges like ploughed fields, the furrows sometimes going lengthways, sometimes across the head, but always solidly matted. My good driver always stopped when we met any of these gentlemen and had a talk with them, in order that I might have time to see and even sketch them. Once we saw a warrior having a war-dance all by himself on the top of a hill. His attitudes were marvellous! After throwing himself backward so far that he would have fallen but for the counter-balance of his long weighted spear and shield, held out at some length in front, he would make great springs forward, or crouch on the ground like a leopard preparing to spring. I have since heard that they were fighting at the time in that neighbourhood, and he was probably making signals to the next hill-top. They were a strange people. They had vast flocks and herds. The women must not touch a cow, or even look at it or its milk, unless the men give it to them. When Mr. H. asked one to give him some sour milk to drink, he was told, "The man was out, and she could get none." They have their heads daubed over with red clay, and their hair twisted into stiff corkscrew ringlets. Both men and women paint their faces a bright yellow when in full dress.

We had to drive three miles out of the way to get to a farmhouse kept by two ex-soldiers. The house did them credit: it was clean, and in a lovely situation surrounded by green meadows. It rained in the night, and we lingered till eight o'clock, hoping that the day would improve. I walked much of the way, and got well soaked in the long grass. Once we got half a village to hang on behind the carriage as a drag: the steepness of the road was quite frightful. The scenery got more and more magnificent as we neared St. John's River, and came down a "good road," which seemed to me much like the bed of the stream. Just as we reached it, we met four gentlemen riding, who stopped us; and Mr. 0. , the Resident, said I must come at once to his house at the mouth of the river; so I was put into a boat, and said good-bye to Mr. H. I enjoyed the grand scene, all glittering in the sunset lights, and the rowers in front of me performing the most fantastic gymnastics between each stroke: putting a hand behind their backs, or throwing it out straight before them, or the back of it to their foreheads, singing at the same time a wild sort of chant. Quantities of Kafir-finch nests hung between the bulrushes, and toucans and kingfishers darted about among them.

As it got dark the great gates on either side the river looked prodigious, with their rocky crowns, three hundred feet of sheer granite precipice a thousand feet or more above the water, the intervening slope being covered with unbroken forest down to the river's edge; only on one side was it practicable to walk, and there much blasting had been required to make a tolerable riding road. At the end between the two cliffs was the sea, with its double line of breakers over the bar, which only permitted vessels to cross at the very highest tides. My host had ridden on before to warn his wife of the invasion, and said it was lucky I had not come a day sooner, as the last baby was only a fortnight old; but she was most kind, and gave me her husband's study for my bedroom—a native hut, with the extra luxury of a calico lining to its ceiling, which prevented the scorpions from falling on the top of my head. It formed one of a circle of round huts, surrounding a gay garden of verbenas, petunias, fuchsias, roses, and other European cultivated flowers, and was always full of still gayer but-terflies, but with wings so battered they were hardly worth catching. The grand cliffs looked down on it, and on the other side of my hut were the rolling waves and golden sand, only separated by a narrow belt of milk-trees, with ferns, lilies, and a sort of dracaena under them, tangled with convolvuluses.

It was very peaceful to wake the next morning amid all this, and to be in no hurry. They were late people at the Residence, and I had a walk all over the place before I saw any signs of breakfast. Then came family prayers, with the baby in the arms of an extraordinary old wandering madwoman, and black servants who did not understand English. The resident magistrate was a curious mixture. He had tried many trades: sailor, doctor, lawyer, and parson. I suspect the bishop's adopted daughter had something to do with these changes. She nursed him through a fever, he married her, and all his dreams of converting the heathen departed. He was now administrator of Pondoland, and had strong convictions that white and black could not live together, and that the latter must go sooner or later, if the other comes. I cannot believe in any one with reason and experience of the races thinking otherwise, except, perhaps, in the extreme tropics, where the black native has the best of it, and will perhaps survive the whites. He had plenty to do, for the different tribes were always at war, and he was constantly riding off for many days at a time, trying to patch up peace among them. He took me and his little boy up the river one day for two miles, close under the opposite bank. Some of the trees were almost lying on the water. Two Kafir plants I drew in that position, with lianes hanging from them, and monkeys to please the child. We heard the leopards and baboons disputing and discussing our characters in the forests above, but the great beasts seldom showed themselves below, and did not like human society. Toucans also showed their great beaks in the tree-branches.

Mr. 0. had a garden some two miles up the path-side of the river, where he grew Indian corn and every kind of vegetable, and flowers in abundance. Here he spent all his spare time at work. There was a "rain tree" there, under which the ground was always wet for ten months in the year. This is caused by an insect which bleeds the leaves (some say). Others say the stalks and leaves collect dew and distribute it again. St. John's settlement was only three years old, and the growth of the trees and fruits planted there since was something extraordinary; but it was a damp, hot climate between those hills, and the natives had the good sense to avoid it, and to live on the high table-tops above. Mr. 0., though he had given up parsonic duties, still dressed in that style, and looked particularly clerical on Sunday, when all the family went in state to church (under the trees), and the 100 soldiers were marched there with drums and fifes playing, *nolens volens.* Few of the other white people went, and every one carried his own chair, but did not put it where he liked; for Mr. 0. complained that his official dignity put him just into the sun, and out of the shade, and he had to submit, without his hat, to danger of a sunstroke for an hour and a quarter, and also to the prosing of a High-Church chaplain, who only got a weekly opportunity of speaking to his fellow-creatures, and enjoyed it. They used all to come home exhausted. A cathedral was building, and there were grand discussions about its decorations, the private chapel for the bishop, etc., a never-ending subject.

Another subject of conversation was the wreck on the sands, whether or not it could be got off; all the spare population were perpetually working at it. Once it was got almost into the river, then the ropes broke, and it drifted back again. The old madwoman had announced that God Almighty put it there, and however much men tried they could not get it away; and to her great delight it was not got away except in bits, broken up to sell as old iron, though the poor people worked day and night at it. I waited in vain for the chance of going on to Natal overland; it always got more and more improbable: 120 miles through a country where the tribes were actually fight-

ing. So I painted more flowers. A loranthus (tree-parasite, called by Anglonatives "honeysuckle ") was very interesting. When I touched the end of the bud, if ripe, it suddenly burst, and the petals sprang backwards, while the pistil in the middle, which was curved like the spring of a watch, was jerked out a yard or more. A tree called the "wild pear" was just then in full bloom, and very conspicuous in the landscape, with its fine white flowers.

Mr. 0. went off on an expedition to try and make peace up the country, and came back after a week of storms and rain, riding down that narrow path by the river at night, in pitch darkness. He seemed to have quite a charmed life, and to delight in danger and fatigue. How it did rain! The river roared like thunder, almost drowning the noise of the rolling waves. It came down grandly into the sea, without any delta or marsh, pure and clear till the salt waves met it: but for that immovable bar the largest ships could find a safe harbour at St. John's, but no boat ever entered it while I remained, except the monthly steamer— a wretchedly small boat with no cabin or comforts of any kind. Letters came once a week in a post-cart from Mutata to the station four miles up the river, and thence on foot; and telegrams were continually going and coming, carried by tall men in blankets, with bones eight inches long stuck through their ears, all the way to Mutata. Many of these wild people used to come to "the study" as usual, and were much surprised to find me in possession. The forests were so full of grass-ticks that, after no little suffering from them, I generally walked on the golden sands at the edge of the sea by preference. They were covered by a perfect network of *Ipmnam pes-capm,* with millions of seeds and lovely pink flowers, the long trailing branches often twelve to twenty feet in length, radiating from the central root like a huge green octopus. There was also a handsome pinkflowered bean spreading itself in the same fashion on the sand. At the end of the sands the cliffs rose 300 feet, with the signal-station at the top, and views over grassy

downs, far away down the coast as well as back to the river, with its great gates 1300 feet high. Below that hill I found beds of dwarf hibiscus, with a white flower and claret-coloured eye, and masses of blue agapanthus and tritoma.

At the camp were one hundred picked men of the reserve, who were steadily drinking themselves to death. Work, play, punishments, and rewards had all been tried in vain by their despairing commander. He himself spent his leisure time gardening, and gave the men bits of land and every encouragement to work too, but few of them took to it. There were two lieutenants and a doctor who used to play at lawn-tennis on the sea-sand at low tide. Insect life was very abundant at St. John's. Gorgeous butterflies abounded; small lizards ran over the walls and jumped on the tables, making long springs, with their tails held well off the ground. Puss thought the latter a very choice morsel, and would give them three taps with her paw, upon which they dropped it, and she swallowed the still wriggling dainty. Scorpions were also common. They sting sharply, but not dangerously. I was warned always to look into my sponge before washing my face. The poor horses were much tortured by grass-ticks, and were painted over with tar before they were turned out to grass, as they sometimes died from the inflammation caused by the ticks. There were many stories of snakes, but I did not see any alive. They were said to come in pairs (as in Jamaica), and if one were killed the partner would come to the place where it died tolook for it. Mr. 0. told me also of a female snake which laid two eggs after death. Sometimes we had a perfect plague of big moths at dinnertime, requiring real force to drive them away from the food. When I tried to move one which had poked its proboscis into a bottle and was sucking up the wine, it turned suddenly round quite fiercely at me. It was a beautiful creature, with feathery legs, and a proboscis as long as itself. One strange insect had a neck like a cannon, quite straight, and as long as all the rest of his body.

Bishop Callaway arrived while I was

there. Mrs. O. was his adopted daughter, and, like every one else, was devoted to him. He was very big and merry, had begun life as a London physician, and gave up a good practice to come out as a missionary with Colenso; but he was very High-Church, and so they separated. He was some twenty-five years doing good work amongst the natives: doctoring them, translating their curious fables into English, and the Bible into Zulu, making friends of the people, and setting them a good example, with his good old Quakeress wife. Then they turned him into a bishop (losing a good missionary), and a partial stroke of paralysis and want of sight made him still more helpless. He was a man of the world, interested in everything that was going on; and the banishment at St. John's he did not enjoy. The subjects of talk there were very limited. The Eesident talked of his own various experiences; Mrs. O. talked of her babies; and Captain Sprigg of Oliver Cromwell and Simon de Montfort (his two pet heroes) for hours together. Most of the negotiations with the Pondo chief seemed made through his white secretary, who, like John Dunn, had any number of black wives, and used to supply Mrs. O. with daughters for servants in return for their education. What that was, I never quite made out. They were all said to have different mothers, but were nice good-tempered girls, and very happy always. There was another family of boys, who, I fancy, worked on the same sort of terms. The eldest was a policeman, and got £5 a month; and he was engaged to the eldest "Mary." I wonder how many other wives he would aspire to. To have less than two was vulgar. No Pondo who was anybody would show such poverty.

My hut was water-tight, and very comfortable, except for the abundant mosquitoes (who bit by day instead of by night there), and the rats woke one up at night, often close to one's head. One night there was a terrible noise; something hard was banging about, knocking the metal bath and wooden boxes all round. I saw something long in the moonlight moving over the floor.

Flying to the door, I set it wide open. All was still outside. I sprang on my bed, lit my candle, and poked at the thing with a long Kafir spear, hoping it would go out. It rushed under my bed, and I saw it was a rat, only a rat, jumping frantically, which quieted my worst fears; so I put out my light again and slept. In the morning I found a horrid trap had been set (unknown to me). The poor thing's leg had been broken by it, and he had escaped on three. Some days after there was a fearful smell. We could find the dead body nowhere, so I had to go into the sitting-room-hut till the ants had cleared it away.

The ants were very busy there, but the ichneumons were even more interesting. The bishop called me one day to follow one, a large blue insect with long yellow legs, which took up a caterpillar two inches long, and seemed to ride him like a hobby-horse, holding him tight with knees and elbows, and using its own feet to trot along with him, keeping the long grub quite clear of the ground till they reached the top of the insect's nest, when it put down its burthen and began clearing the earth away, scraping with its fore-feet, and kicking out the earth like a dog with its hind feet, going back now and then to take measurements of the grub, which it brought close to the edge, and finally pulled in. Then it crept out, and began covering it up in layers, trampling each down, till the hole was full, when it put dead leaves over the mouth to hide it all up, then flew away. The clever creature had first stung the grub and reduced it to a half-dead state, laying its eggs in the body, which was still warm enough to hatch them, after which the young things would eat their way out, growing fat on the body of their foster-mother. We also examined several hanging nests in the roofs of the huts, made by various species of the same insect, and also supplied with gamelarders for the young. We found the bodies of spiders in some cells; in others only the fat young creature after he had eaten the spiders.

The bishop told me many interesting stories of his African life. Once a snake

of eight feet in length was found coiled away in his study, and one of the men said he had seen it climbing up behind the books three days before, and though he was shaking with fright, he did not say anything, as he supposed it was one of Dr. Callaway's friends who was too big to put in a bottle. They believed in transmigration of souls there. The bishop also told me several stories of people who had been partially paralysed by a very poisonous snake, the tuamba, which merely raised its head and looked at them, then glided away satisfied. Both he and Mr. O. said they had known people who had lost all power for two or three days afterwards, and for the time were unable to move from the spot. In Natal I was told by young S. that he himself had been mesmerised in this way for a time, as a boy, but soon recovered. He had had a wonderful old mastiff which the natives treated with profound respect. He used to curl himself up in unexpected places amidst the coarse grass near the path to his house, and when the Zulus came strutting up in all their war-paint a sudden growl would bring them down to their usual frog-like position of humility. Then they would make the dog long speeches, addressing him as "noble chief, brave warrior," etc., to which he replied by a series of suppressed growls, till his master came to relieve guard.

While I was there the doctor received a letter from one of his converts: "Dear and Reverend Sir—I am sorry to tell you I got in a great passion yesterday, and I kicked my wife very much. Will you please to pray to God to forgive me, and not make me do so any more." It was not a bad example of what Chinamen think bishops are: "Letter A, No. 1, Praying Men." The doctor observed he did not wonder at the man kicking such a drunken old hag. He thought he should have done the same under the same circumstances. His own wife was most gentle, but absolutely stone-deaf, and seldom spoke.

There were plenty of wild bees in the woods, and when the natives wanted honey they put a stick into the hole first; if the bees came out, they knew all was safe, if not, they knew a snake lived also there. The bees were accustomed to him, and took the stick for another snake. There was a swarm near us, and the first morning they came into the dining-room and were very disagreeable; but after that they knew us all, and allowed us to have a share of the food. Once we spent a day on the other side of the river, close to the sea's edge. The rocks on that side went down to the waves, with lovely pools and aquariums amongst them, and were fringed above with *StrelUzia augusta* and aloe-trees, besides various fleshy plants, mesembryanthemum and portulaca. It was far the most beautiful side, but, though so near, very difficult to get at. There was a spring a little higher up, to which we used to send for drinking-water.

When at last it was decided that the overland journey was impossible, and that I must go by sea, the steamer did not come! and I thought I never should get away, but another fortnight brought a large steamer, the *Lady Wood,* often talked of but never seen before at St. John's. On the 11th of April she took me over the bar easily, all the population, as usual, collecting on the shore to watch the feat. We started at three in the afternoon, and kept close to the coast, passing curious rocky cliffs full of caves, with waterfalls falling over them, and blow-holes, while enormous porpoises played round us. At one place the sailors pulled up thirty large fish shaped like mackerel, as fast as they could throw in their bait of red rag. The ship was crowded with excursionists from Natal, and I thought myself lucky to get the captain's cabin, next the engine. His dog shared it with me; but it was hot! Before I took possession we had a kind of supper-tea spread on the hatchway. At nine the next morning we entered the harbour of Durban, and a good-natured young man brought my things and myself by the tram to the Marine Hotel there, where I found a nice airy room, and friendly cats in collars, which walked in and out of the window, and generally slept there, but did not object to my intrusion. They were quieter than rats in traps! Strange

to say, there were no mosquitoes, though the front of the house looked straight down on the shallow muddy bay, only covered with water at high tide. It was surrounded by low wooded banks, dotted with houses, and a group of low stunted date-palms and pandanus formed the foreground.

In the evening Mr. A, Donald Currie's agent, drove me up the hill to dine and sleep at his house, as his wife was going away the next day. They lived close to the Botanical Gardens. Their house was quite hidden by the bright blue VOL. n T ipomcea, generally called " morning glory." I never saw it more lovely. The hedges all over that hill were hung with other ipomoeas, bignonias, tecomas, thunbergias, and a lovely white creeper from Barbados. I saw also an exquisite hibiscus growing tall, like a hollyhock, with a deep blue eye. In the gardens I found splendid zamias of all sorts, and stangerias which came from St. John's. Their leaves are so like large fern-fronds that they have deceived botanists, as they did me at first. Colonel B. was known everywhere as Colonel Butterfly. He had done good service in the war, commanding the volunteers, and had been photographed with his net in many groups of them: never without his net, an appendage to which the poor Empress Eugenie objected not unnaturally, when it appeared conspicuously in front of a view he presented to her of her son's grave.

He gave me some curious insects, and the flowers they haunted: a yellow mantis on a yellow everlasting, and a pinkish one on a pink everlasting flower. Mrs. S. showed me the most minute pencil-drawings of orchids by her late husband, and a wonderful flower he had discovered, called the *Ceropegia Sandersonii,* a creeping asclepias, with white and green cornucopia flowers, covered by umbrellas.

Then I took the coast railway due north to Verulam, passing five round-topped euphorbia trees, and then rich crops of sugar and corn, cultivated by most picturesque coolies from India, all over bangles and gay garments. These people did so well and ate so little that

colonists said they were the curse of the country. They were bound over to work for five years for their employers; after that they might work for themselves. They bought land, cultivated gardens, and even employed Kafirs to work for them, so making labour dearer than ever. They and the flowers made the country look very gay along the coast railway. After that, I drove seven miles farther through pretty country up to Tongate, to stay with Mr. and Mrs. S. Their house had never been finished, but was already rendered dangerous by white ants, which were eating all of it that the damp had left. It stood on the top of a hill with a lovely garden, and distant views all round. Cotton, with pink, white, and yellow flowers; sugar, coffee, and fruittrees were there in quantities, all in good order. The youngest son only was at home, and was his father's right hand in everything. He used to play the cornet and piano in all spare moments. The father was a gigantic old man in gold spectacles, and a stupendous hat like a target. He reminded me of a typical Tory squire at home, perfectly unreasonable in his dogmas, but quite ready to laugh at his own unreason. He used to walk about with his arm resting on the arm of his clever little wife, she in a straight waterproof cloak, looking like a figure out of a Noah's ark. She was always most earnest about everything she did, and spent hours trying to puzzle out the names of every little weed. She sang also, with an old voice, but much taste, and tried to paint in oils, while I was there, but didn't like it. She had already made a valuable collection of water-colour studies of the flowers of Natal.

The cotton-harvest was going on, and a curious crowd of Zulu men and women were at work over it. They were a most merry race: in the evening guavas were thrown to them, and they had a grand scramble; afterwards rewarding us by performing some demoniacal dances, "hul-huling" all the time to fill the place of music. The one in front led, outdoing the others by his outlandish gymnastics. Ted told me of two large birds which went to the same nest year after year, adding a storey each year, till it became a huge mass as big as a haycock! Snakes were abundant there, and boas which devoured chickens two at a time, leaving another pair all squeezed and slimy to come back to. If a snake were killed, his partner came the next day to seek him. One day we went to the seaside, over a terrific road, and found a large English party, living between a two-roomed Kafir house and a tent. The children found treasures of shells and seaweed, and led a most happy life. There were forests of the *Sl-relitzia augusta,* with its orange seeds ripening; madder and sarsaparilla were growing there too, and all manner of fleshy plants, besides variously tinted convolvuluses.

Mr. and Mrs. S. gave me terrible accounts of the mismanagement of everything during the war. Their house was only forty miles from the Tugela, and once it was reported that the Zulus had crossed the river, and were on their way up towards them. The village about a mile off was soon empty. Lord Chelmsford stuck up a printed notice in Verulam, that his troops were going to fortify themselves, and that all ablebodied men must arm, and defend their families and property as they thought best! A useful set of soldiers they were! But the natives round Tongate turned themselves into scouts, and said if the others were coming on, they would know in abundant time for the S.s family to fly; and the daughter was actually married in the midst of it all. When Zulus do invade a country, they always send a party the day before to clear the road, killing every live thing on their way, and then waiting till the main body comes up. Lord Chelmsford was warned by John Dunn and others of the traps which were being made for him, and of the danger of dawdling in the way he did, but treated the advice with contempt. Dunn's moralities were not good, but he knew the natives thoroughly, and how best to treat and govern the people he elected to live among. People who knew him say he was an educated, thoughtful gentleman (apart from his savage life).

My friends were on the best of terms

with all their dark neighbours, who were the merriest savages I ever saw. While I was there, they had about fifty women picking cotton, who were all over the place, chattering, dancing, singing, and imitating the calls of wild animals and birds. Like them, they could be tame or savage, according to the way they were treated; but their brains are not organised to take in and understand questions of politics and theology, which even white men differ on. Two nice girls, the daughters of one of the oldest American missionaries, rode over some twenty miles to stay for a few nights. One of their men had been building " Catch-why-ho's " (way of pronouncing it) new kraal, and had long talks with the master himself, who declared our Queen to be the most beautiful woman in the whole world. He had brought back cart-loads of boots, and said that though he gave up all other clothes, he would stick to them and to the chimney-pot hat!

The garden at Tongate was most lovely. There were masses of the Mexican *Dahlia imperialis,* taller than myself, like miniature pagodas of great white bells. The erythrina tree, called "Kafir boom," was just covering its bare branches with the brightest scarlet flowers, much resembling one of the Brazilian varieties, and a great white-flowering ipomcea with long white stalks and upright waxy buds was festooned over it. The seed had been brought from Barbados without a name, but probably came originally from the East Indies. The aristolochias also were luxuriant, and loaded with strings of huge pitcherflowers. The papaw trees were enormous, and their fruit particularly delicious and ripe: bananas were in perfection.

A most enthusiastic botanist came to see me, and said I must go with him to see a group of aloe trees forty feet high, the only ones left in that country; so I went to Verulam to stay a couple of nights, and he drove me over. He was a butcher by profession, but had bought considerable property, and started a large sugar-mill. Near this we found the noble group of trees on the

bank of the river. The trunks measured two feet through at a yard above the ground, and rose to perhaps twenty feet of stately gray stem, then split into forks, which re-split into numberless pairs of great leaf-bunches, bearing three to five spikes of scarlet flowers, like red-hot pokers, in July, when they might be seen forty miles off. They were the sole remains of forests which had disappeared in that part of Africa, perhaps for centuries, and even those three trees have been cut down since I was there; so I have been told. Mr. H. sat and watched me at work, much pleased to see his dear aloes at last done justice to. He said not even Mrs. S. had been to see them, and when he wrote a description of them to Kew, they had coolly asked him to cut one down and send them a "section" for the museum!

In his garden at Verulam he had many beautiful things, and I made one study of the flower and seeds of an East Indian cycad. After leaving the tangled rim of forest country near the sea, the railway mounted the hills, with views of table mountains rising one over another, and the sea beyond them. It was quite cold on the summit, where I spent the night at a capital railway hotel, 3000 feet above the sea, surrounded by endless miles of rank grass or maize fields, with no flowers but a few prince's feathers, brought by the Indian coolies and sown with their millet, as in the Himalaya. I saw zamias and tree-ferns in the cracks of the mountains here and there.

An archdeacon met me at the Maritzburg station the next day, and put me into the bishop's carriage, which took me to a house where I found his youngest daughter at luncheon. She had a hectic flush and a hard cough, and said it was the first visit she had paid since her return from England. An old gentleman who came in, she told me, was one of their worst enemies. He seemed perfectly civil, but the whole family had isolated themselves by their Zuluism. We did not pass a tree after leaving Maritzburg, crossing a dreary waste of long yellow grass or ripe corn till we came in sight of Bishopstowe, with its many-gabled house and gum-trees, like an oasis in the desert. It stood on the top of a small hill, and every tree there was planted by Dr. Colenso. Under the verandah covered with creepers he stood to receive me, giving me his arm with as much courtesy as if I had been a princess. It seemed quite a dream of old days to meet such a thorough gentleman again, and difficult to understand how one so genial and gentle could have made himself so hated by the majority of the country. His conversation was delightful, but he gave me the impression of being both weak and vain, and very susceptible to flattery. His two elder daughters seemed to manage him. They were perfectly devoted to him, and to Zuluism! which governed everything. The dear natives were incapable of harm, the whites incapable of good. They would, I believe, have heard cheerfully that all the whites had been "eaten up " and Cetewayo proclaimed king of Natal. His portrait was all over the house, and they mentioned him in a hushed voice, as a kind of holy martyr, and had hardly a good word for any white man, except Colonel Durnford, whose life poor Frances wrote. I found her sadly in want of sympathy, and almost reduced to despair and hatred of Zuluism, though she was the authoress of the book about them, and hated the Government more. I did my best to disentangle her artistic difficulties, and give her courage to go on painting from nature. The companionship of sweet flowers would have done her more good than sickly sentimental phantoms of high art, such as she was attempting, under the influence and spirit of Burne Jones's school in England.

The only natural thing in the house was the poor old mother, very delicate and feminine. She seemed delighted to get a new listener from the outer world, and to tell me stories of her youth. She did not worry herself about Zuluism, and it was a relief for me also to escape the family mania. I was taken to see the printing-press, which was continually contradicting every fact stated by the Government or officials, who in their turn contradicted every fact published by it. Messengers were continually arriving with fresh lies (I believe) from "the king," over which the bishop and his daughters passed all their time. It would have driven me mad to stay long in such a strained atmosphere. The king had sent them a dog to take care of; some Englishman had given it to his majesty, and it was said to be worth £60, but could not bear coloured people. It seemed in a consumption when it first came, and was not much better since. It looked entirely disgusted with South Africa. Dr. Colenso had a fat retriever which never left him. He used to talk with him during the meals, and the dog seemed to understand all he said. He had also a pet lemur from Madagascar, which generally lived with the cows, but spent the hot hours of the day in a guava-tree, eating and spoiling the fruit, till it was time to go and fetch its friends home to be milked, after which it cuddled itself up close to me for the night. It hated dogs, and bit his majesty's pet as soon as it arrived, which did not add to the poor creature's love of South Africa. It also hated Zulus. Cats, rabbits, and a crane wandered about the pretty garden all sociably together, and never strayed further, as they found (like myself) that there was no place to stray to when once they left the oasis. All round was a pathless desert of long burnt-up grass, inhabited only by grass-ticks. There was a wind too, and it was cold, and the cold produced its usual effect on me, so I fled.

I found there was no way of getting either to Zanzibar or Mauritius for six weeks, when a ship was going to the latter place, touching at Madagascar; but I was ill and homesick, and decided to go home and take a rest, so left in the *Melrose* on the 22d of May; had another talk with my botanical friend at Port Elizabeth, two days with the Gambles in their new house among the silvertrees at Wynberg, and reached home on the 17th of June 1883. The ship which I had once thought of waiting for in Natal was never allowed to land its passengers at Tamatave, and was crowded with refugees from there, so that it was fortunate I did not go by her. The three months at home were delightful, and gave me fresh strength and courage for the task I had still set myself to do.

Mr. Fergusson had already planned another room at Kew, promising that it should be finished by the time I returned from my next expedition, and when I left England on the 24th of September the walls were already up. Meanwhile I enjoyed seeing old and new friends again, and reading the books I had longed for when out of their reach in Africa. Among the most distinguished of my new friends was Professor Owen, who asked me to dine with him in his cottage at Richmond one Sunday, and told me much that was new to me about the countries I had lately seen. His friend Dr. Richardson, the famous temperance apostle, was also there. He had lately had a legacy left him, by some sarcastic friend, of some famous old port wine. The Professor tried hard to make out where he had buried it, in order that he might go and dig it up and transfer it to his cellar some dark night, for he did not object to such medicines.

He was eighty-two then, and his sister, who lived with him, was much older, and stone-deaf. He took me over the new Natural History Museum, which he had begun, and which Dr. Flower is now arranging in a way that will in time make it the very best in the world.

Before starting on another long journey, I went out to see my sister and her family at Davos, stopping on the way to pay a long-promised visit to my old friend Madame Sainton, who had bought an old country house seven miles from Boulogne. The chateau had been merely a high-roofed tower then of considerable age, the lower storey, a pretty octagon room with windows looking both ways, fitted with tasteful carving and gilding in the old French style. She had added a dining and billiard room on either side, and bedrooms over all. Every year they spent their summers there, taking out merry parties of pupils to make holiday and study music. The grounds were pretty, adjoining a real forest.

Harvest was going on, aud fruit was being picked in the pretty orchard country. On the other side of the house farms and villages peeped out amongst the trees. My old friend looked serenely happy there, though she was always more or less invalided, and unable to take more exercise than strolling out to see her one darling boy painting a large picture of some peasants sitting on the ground before him, while a small boy held a shaky umbrella over his head. The young artist began with daylight, and seldom moved till noonday. It was grand to see how his parents admired him: his mother quietly purring over him, his father, with all the impulsive gesticulations of Toulouse, bounding about like an indiarubber ball, and talking incessantly, dressed in brown velvet and a wideawake. One day we walked two miles through the fields to pay a visit at a neighbour's house. They were all sitting in an arbour, smoking and drinking tiny cups of strong coffee, liqueur, and soda water. There were three old ladies: one fashionable one from the town, in a front and ringlets, the other two in white caps, knitting, many children running in and out, all very homely and happy. We also went into the pretty little church and paid a visit to the young cure, in a model cottage buried in pear-trees, all loaded with fruit. How different it all was from England, though only that narrow channel separated us!

Sixteen hours of rail took me to Basle. The next day I was at Davos Platz, in the comfortable new house my brotherin-law had built there. The ceilings and all fittings were of different species of pine, arranged in patterns, with the knots brought together in the centres. The sitting-rooms were also wainscoted up to a certain height with the same. My sister had a grand collection of carnations of various tints, which she treated like pet children, taking them indoors during the winter, and covering them up through a summer snowstorm with flannels and blankets. She watered them morning and evening with all kinds of tonics, and above all let them hang their heads in a natural manner, instead of tying them to stakes as gardeners do at home; and these flowers thrive in the pure air and bright sunshine as much as the invalids do. But the occupation of living for health which went on all around was most depressing. My brother-in-law alone seemed to thrive there, and could work his brains incessantly, getting ill whenever he came to the lower world. To me the cold was hateful, and I soon came home again, by way of Amsterdam and its exhibition, but saw so little of Holland that I will write nothing of it here.

CHAPTER XV SEYCHELLES ISLANDS—1883

On the 27th of September 1883 I left Marseilles in the Natal. Four most remarkable donkeys were my fellow-passengers, on their way to New Caledonia *to* found a race of noble quadrupeds as yet unknown in those distant islands. One of them had long drooping ears, with a lank silky mane. It was jet black, and a monstrous beast: no reasonable ass could believe it to be of the same species as himself. The others were monstrous too, but they had fuzzy wigs, more like ordinary donkeys. People wanted me to take their portraits, but one hasty visit to their end of the ship was as much as I could endure, and I pitied the poor French soldiers who spent their days there among the hencoops and fleas. The captain took the S. s and myself on shore at Aden in his boat, and we took the usual drive over the wild rocky road to the tanks and back. As we crept up to the fort, we could see more than two miles of camels loaded with water and grass, in an almost unbroken string, winding their way upwards from the country. These animals were perpetually going and returning along the same road to the distant wells. The famous tanks still refused to hold water, in spite of thousands of pounds spent on them; but they had succeeded in making a garden there, and caperplants festooned the rocks round them.

On the 13th of October I landed in Mahe at daybreak. The lovely bay is surrounded by islands, Mah6 encircling two sides of it, the mountains rising nearly 3000 feet above it. The cocoanuts mounted higher than I ever saw them do before, rich green fruit and spice trees linking them to the natural forests above. On the top of all are fine granite cliffs, not in the long lines of St. John's, but broken up and scattered amongst the green. The little town with its trees and gardens is squeezed into a narrow valley, so that only the houses along the sea's edge were seen as we approached it over the long pier. On each side was a wide stretch of black mud and sand, covered with exquisite turquoise crabs with red legs, so beautiful that I dropped my bag and screamed with wonder at them, to the amazement of my porters, who said coolly they were not good to eat! An avenue of tall sangu, dragon, and melia trees bordered the road up to Government House, a pretty low bungalow. Hanging baskets made of fern-stems ornamented the verandah, and a tolerable specimen of the "coco de mer" with its first nut upon it, was planted in front.

The tree was about forty-eight years old, and the biggest in Mahe, where none grew wild. Vanilla was growing up it, and elsewhere about the garden in thick masses, covered with its sweet flowers and bunches of pods. Barringtonia, terminalia, and other large Indian trees were planted for shade close to the house. A hill with a burying-ground came down close to it on one side, and the town, with its closely-packed houses, choked it up on the other.

Mr. and Mrs. B. received me most kindly, making me feel at home, and I walked across the low pass to the other side of the island that same afternoon. It was exceedingly beautiful. Nutmegs, cinnamon, and cloves were all growing luxuriantly, but the people are too lazy even to pick them, and I crushed under my feet the purple fruit of the latter, which had been allowed to go to seed and fall from the trees, no one troubling to collect the buds at their proper season. The trees of both cloves and cinnamon were from twelve to twenty feet high, and every leaf and twig was sweet, the young leaves of the most delicate pink colour. Every little hollow was filled with vanilla gardens. That plant being trained on espaliers like old-fashioned apple trees, the lazy people could attend more easily to its culture, and they soon realised a good return for the money spent upon it.

Walking was said to be impossible, so my two first expeditions were made with four bearers and a chair. They charged fifteen shillings for the day; but as I found that I walked on my own feet most of the time, and the men were greatly in my way, I never had them again. With two exceptions, the roads were all like the beds of streams, and were literally stream-beds, except in extra fine weather. The first expedition was made with Mr. E. (in search of a cocoa-nut with six heads), over the shoulder of the island and along its south shore, up and down from one sandy bay to another. These are separated by rocks all worn and furrowed by water, and piled up in heaps on their coral foundations. Great twisted cashew trees were wedged in amongst them, spreading their long arms over the sand. Their fruits were a far brighter scarlet than those I had seen in India. All the common Indian trees seemed to grow more luxuriantly in Seychelles than they did at home. The breadfruit trees were loaded with fruit, and so were the cocoa-nuts, oil-making being the principal occupation of the islands. The tree we went to seek was a very ugly deformity, but a good excuse for a delightful walk. We returned round the east coast, passing a grove of the blue fanpalms of Mauritius on the way, and making a short cut across a bay, through the shallow water, and over the wet sand among shells, corals, and blue crabs, a world of wonders; but all the inhabitants seemed on the verge of starvation, and living on credit.

The other chair expedition was made with the overseer of forests, who took me up the one good road which led to the heights, where the few country-houses of Mahe were placed, before which the natural forests were already beginning to disappear. There, for the first time, I saw the noble wildpalms and the pandanus trees, the "vacca marron" being the most remarkable of these, topped as it is with a green dome of screw-pine branches, beneath which numbers of straight aerial roots descend, many of them reaching to the ground, and forming a tower of scaffolding among which the original trunk is often lost. The whole looks like a skeleton lighthouse with a green roof. Another pandanus grows only in wet places, and is of great height, with a single trunk rising from stilted roots, then splitting into three branches, which again each split into three, bearing enormous heads of drooping dracaena-like leaves. The fruits and flowers of all these varieties were much alike. I was so busy trying to paint these wonderful things that I gave offence to some friends of my guide, who wanted me to breakfast with them; so I had to climb up their hill to make peace afterwards. The man was nearly black, and had married a pretty Frenchwoman. They lived in a neat little round house of two rooms made of wood and matting, perched on the very point of a conical hill, with an exquisite view over the bay and island of St. Anna. The lady had most fascinating manners, and a much-flounced amber satin skirt trailing on the ground, with a clean white linen jacket above it. It was one of the wonders of the Seychelles how that gorgeous lady persuaded herself to marry that dark gentleman. He showed me his garden: Liberian coffee, as well as Mocha, lemons, oranges, and every kind of tropical fruit, and a penful of tortoises, which all turned towards him when he called them by name, flinging in grass and weeds for them to eat.

Many people kept them as pets. It was considered a rich kind of thing to do in the Seychelles, as keeping deer is in England. One family I heard of always named a young tortoise at the same time as a new baby, keeping it till the child grew up and married, when it was killed and eaten at the wedding-feast. In one place I saw about thirty, which were twenty-two years old, and about two feet in length. They grew fast up to that time, then seemed to stand still for centuries. Like the double cocoa-nut trees, they were all descended from those brought from the island of Aldabra, where alone the great tortoise is still wild. General Gordon[1] brought over two large ones, which were still in the grounds of Government House, and laid eggs regularly. These were covered up, and took six months hatching. There was a regular preserve of turtles in Mahe, where one was killed every week, and did duty as "meat."

On the 22d of October I started in the little Government sailing boat for Praslin, and after three or four hours without wind got slowly over the twenty-five miles of sea, and landed at midnight in the lovely moonlight in Dr. H.'s little boat, two hospitable dogs licking my face and hands as I jumped on the sands, and nearly knocking me down. Johnnie B., a nice boy of thirteen, had been sent over to take care of me; and we had a real good time in Praslin with the H.s in their nice new house. It was not a hundred yards from the sea, but was shaded by tall mango and other trees; only through their branches could one get a peep of its blue water, which at noonday was as deep in colour as a sapphire. Half an hour's row across took one to the island of Curieuse, the only other island where the "coco de mer" grows wild.

To see and paint that was the great object of my visit; so the next morning after my arrival Mr. H. took me round the east side of Praslin in his boat. Four capital sailors rowed us. The head man, Emile, was a native of Madagascar, with a fine forehead and straight nose; the others were Seychelles Africans, all merry and strong, and on the best of terms with the energetic young Englishman. We passed close along the shore among beautiful boulders of salmon-coloured granite, 1 It was General Gordon to whom the ingenious theory occurred, that the "coco de mer" or large double cocoa-nut of the Seychelles was the original Tree of the Knowledge of Good and Evil.—Ed. grooved and split into fantastic shapes by heat or ice. Many of the little islands had waving casuarinas on their tops, while bright green large-leaved "jakamaka" bordered the sands of Praslin, varied by patches of cocoa-nut and breadfruit.

Above were the deep purple-red, stony-topped hills, with forests between, the famous coco de mer palms shining like golden stars among them. The waves were so high as we reached the southeast angle of Praslin that we had a few anxious moments in our little boat, and decided that it was not safe to go the usual way over the breakers at low tide; we must go out to sea, and round some of the other islands. So out we went, up and down through a great Pacific swell. At last we put up a sail and ran into the valley of the coco de mer: a valley as big as old Hastings, quite filled with the huge straight stems and golden shiny stars of the giant palm: it seemed almost too good to believe that I had really reached it. There was a thick undergrowth, and we had not started till late, so that I could only make one hasty sketch of a tree in full fruit: twenty-five full-sized nuts, and quantities of imperfect ones, like gigantic mahogany acorns. The outer shell was green and heart-shaped; only the inner shell was double, and full of white jelly, enough to fill the largest soup-tureen. The male tree grows taller than the fruhVbearing one, sometimes reaching 100 feet; its inflorescence is often a yard long. The huge fan-leaves of both trees are stiff and shiny, and of a very golden green, different from all other palms (except the cocoanut) in colour. I saw many wild palms in the underwood, with lilac stems armed with circles of orange thorns, having edges of the same colour to their young leaves. One was cut down, and the young stem chopped in four bits to carry away on a man's head, the pith making a good salad when sliced like cucumber. We had sent the boat round and walked up the valley, in which were more than a thousand of the giant-palms; but we could not stop, and I never was able to get there again. We walked across the island to the VOL. 11 u north shore, the last part of the road being through miles of cocoa-nut plantations, where we saw some few birds, including "whydah-birds" with long tails, also a red fondia with its brown wives. The Creoles had driven nearly all birds away, and they had taken refuge on an outside island called Marianne, from whence the doctor had lately imported some of different sorts to Praslin, much to the disgust of the natives. A pair of merles had built their nest close to his house and laid eggs in it, and tiny sugar-birds were hard at work at a dangling fragile pouch of cotton from the bombaxtrees near, close to the verandah where I worked, hanging it on a drooping leaf-stalk of the *Spandias cytherea,* a tree like a very spreading ash. There were also two martens, much like the mainah-birds of India, with yellow beaks and feet. They were most impudent, and would come and perch on the chairs of the verandah, chase the cocks and hens, and defy the dogs, whistling most pertinaciously, and calling "Toby, Toby, Toby!" till the dog ran half mad.

The island of Curieuse was only half an hour's row from our shore. One poor old Englishman lived there, having married its heiress. He lived in an old house which had never been altered for two generations, and was picturesquely dilapidated. A long double avenue of large lilies or crinums bordered the road approaching it from the shore for a good hundred yards. These flowers stand five feet high, bending their great crimson and white petals towards the light, cocoa-nuts and mangoes arching overhead. Near the house were groups of huts, wedged between boulders, and thatched with the great fan leaves of the coco de mer, the stalks forming ornamental points at the corners, and finishing the roof into a curve like the gates of a Japanese temple.

There were many of these trees on the island of Curieuse, and a path was cut to one of the biggest, with a pile of boulders behind it, on which I climbed, and perched myself on the top; my friends building up a footstool for me from a lower rock just out of reach. I rested my painting-board on one of the great fan leaves, and drew the whole mass of fruit and buds in perfect security, though the slightest slip or cramp would have put an end both to the sketch and to me. Bright green lizards were darting about all the time, over both the subject and the sketch, making the nuts and leaves look dull by contrast. There were twenty-five nuts on that tree, and countless imperfect ones. After descending safely from the boulders, we returned to the shore through some swampy ground tangled with *Ipomcea honornox,* catching a few crabs by the way: big black fellows, with huge front claws with which they stopped up their entrance-doors; but the black people elude these in the cleverest manner possible, sliding in their hands close to the roof of the hole and seizing the creatures by the back—they never get pinched. 1

Before I began my sketch we had seen bits of stale fish pegged into the sand with sticks where the water was not more than a foot deep, and soon the watchers saw tracks under the sand leading up to the bait. Mr. and Mrs. Shellfish seldom came above the level, but pushed up the sand as they followed their noses to the dainty bits, and were thus easily tracked and caught. I found a pail full of beauties awaiting me, not dead, but walking about with their curious fleshy bodies covering half their shells, like jackets, many of them of bright colours trimmed with chenille fringe or ermine. We found lovely harps, as well as cowries, olives, and poached eggs, all taken possession of without the slightest ceremony by soldier-crabs, like the whelks at home. We took them home to bury in an ants' nest for some weeks, when they would be cleaned of the fish, and only require sweetening in the sun before packing off home. I used to take off shoes and stockings and paddle about on the lovely sands among the rocks. But corals are very cutting to unhardened feet, and the pinna shells turn up their knife-like edges and wound strangers desperately, so that the thing is not quite such pure enjoyment as one fancied it to be at a distance. Johnnie used to go with me, and when he saw a shell-fish worth collecting he would pick it up with two of his toes and give it to me instead of wetting his sleeves by putting in his hands. He was semi-amphibious, and talked English as if it were a foreign language.

At Curieuse there was a lepers' camp.

There were not many there then, as they are no longer compelled to go. They seemed contented and happy, though fearfully diseased. One woman had neither fingers nor toes, but could do sewing and thread her needle. In old days, when the place was crowded, they were buried without coffins. They had such a horror of this that their one idea in coming to the island was to make enough money to buy one, and they worked and begged till they had succeeded in their object; after that they lived on contentedly, keeping the treasure close to their bedside in case it should be wanted.

Manioc roots and rice with some cocoa-nuts form the chief food of all people on these islands, but when they choose they can catch plenty of fish. There is an endless variety, and they seem all good food to the blacks. By scraping up the sand just above the receding tide, or even under the water, great quantities of pretty bivalve molluscs could be procured, which made an excellent soup. *We* also made curry of the long arms of the octopus, which tasted like prawns, and looked very tempting, each joint being curved and notched like a segment of a gothic pillar. Isinglass was also made from a green sponge. Breadfruit, boiled or roasted, was our substitute for bread, and made a pudding also with cocoa-nut milk: it was good every way.

The valley behind the house was full of "latamir" palms; the most useful of all perhaps, for in those islands the houses are all thatched with them, though the roof-ridge is finished with the bigger fans of the coco de mer. Over those palms, and over the boulders, were twined long green snakelike leafless stems of the *Vanilla Phatonopsis,* the hanging ends turning up with two slender leaves just before the bunch of buds and lovely white flowers. Another beautiful orchid (Angrcecum *eburneum*) grew on the hills of Mahe, and these two were the only really beautiful native flowers I saw in the islands, all the rest being more or less foreigners, chiefly from the East or West Indies and Madagascar.

On the shore the great "jakamaka" trees were very fine; their trunks lying on the sand, their great branches sprawling over it toward the sea, were covered with polished green leaves, like the india-rubber; but unlike those figs, they had huge bunches of pure white flowers and stalks, with a pink ball half hidden among their golden stamens. Some flowers had green or yellow balls; I fancied perhaps they were the male bells. These trees were very sweetscented, and the delight of bees. Being a species of gamboge, called *Calophyllum inaphjllum* by botanists, they are full of precious oil and gum, which only wants the energy to use. The "bademien" or terminalia was also loaded with great bunches of deep-red pods containing eatable almonds. At He Aride I saw one of these trees, which had rooted itself up and lay on its side. It was the one big green tree on that scorching island, and all the population were seeking shade under it.

The whole island had been bought for £120 by some rich Creole of Praslin, and he kept people there to grow bananas and other tropical fruits on the one bit of flat ground which was to be found in front of the red-hot rocks and boulders, on which one could not rest one's hand at noonday. There was no water, only that which filtered through the sand into wells from the sea, and the low bushes near the rocks were covered with small terns *Sterna veloz)* with white heads, so tame that they let one take them off their nests without attempting to escape. Cruel little Johnnie collected some dozen, and tied them in a bunch by their feet, dying and dead, to send to his mother by the next boat. The owner of the island was making quite a fortune by selling them in Mahe to make pigeon-pies (very fishy). It was not easy to land on Aride, but a pirogue was sent over the wonderful opal sea to us. We got into it and waited, then went in with a rush on the top of the wave. Mrs. H. had her pet dog Toby in her arms, furious to get at a big dog on shore which had declared war, till Toby landed, when it hauled down its colours and became a lamb; after that

Toby reigned there as supreme as he did on his own island.

I went to Aride principally to seek Dr. Wright's gardenia, and found a perfect little tree, shaped like a sugar-loaf, ten feet high, having only fruit on it— no flowers. But I found also a lovely sarcostemma like the Indian "soma," full of sweet flowers, with yards of leafless green stems. The pines and bananas were enormous, and the shores were studded with lovely shells, with which we loaded all our pockets, and went back much heavier than we came, passing close to Boobie Island, a pile of rocks white with seagull dung.

Another day I went with the doctor to La Digue, a large fertile island containing six hundred people, who possessed grand cocoa-nuts and consequent riches. Many boats were anchored there, which took the oil to Mahe; but water was scarce, and the manager told me food was also. He looked half starved. We reached the island through a gap in the coral rocks, so narrow that they might have been touched on each side with our hands. In bad weather it is impossible to land, and it is never easy. A former doctor was drowned in the process. The colours were marvellous on these clear seas, and that day while the doctor was paying some extra professional visit in another clear bay, I stayed still in the boat and looked down through the water at gorgeous flowerbeds of coral, with blue and gold fish darting over them—things so lovely that I hardly believed them real. It was pleasant work rowing amongst those islands. Our men were very merry, talking, laughing and singing all the way. Emile, the head-man, had a grand profile, and was a native of Madagascar; two others were natives of Seychelles, and one was a pure African. Apart from him, the other two would have been called black; near him they looked pale. These sailors were amphibious, and entirely devoid of fear at sea; they would always go the most difficult way if it were the shortest. Dr. Hoad told me Emile was not always amiable. Once he had imprudently tried to pass through a dangerous passage among the rocks and surf, and the boat was turned right over. The doctor found himself swimming in pitch darkness among the sharks, and heard Emile fighting with the others as to whose fault it was, never thinking a moment of helping the lost doctor, who fortunately was able to swim half a mile to the shore.

We occasionally caught odd fish while waiting for the doctor. One was a pilot-fish, with a flat cohesive jaw, which stuck to the shark, and got the benefit of his fishing. Another had a long whip tail, and once they speared a hawk's-head turtle or "carre" which a shark was trying to get into his mouth: a rather large morsel, as it was over three feet long. I bought it of the sailors for £2: 10s., the value of the tortoiseshell back. Catching them is the principal aim of sailors in those islands, and they divide the profits made by each boat, one man often making ten pounds in a season. The one I bought was found to be full of eggs, which were collected in a pail, buried in the sand near the house, and kept till they hatched, after which they were kept another six weeks with difficulty, as they have an inclination to run into the sea as soon as they leave their shells, and would be quickly gobbled up if they did. They are fed on fish, and some of the natives keep them till their shells become saleable; but to do this is more trouble than they are worth.

Mrs. H. had many pets, and much poultry. The hencoops were made of single fans of the coco de mer tied just under the stalk end, standing up like tents. A stupid goose spoilt all her eggs but one, and would have trampled the poor little gosling to death if it had not been taken away from her and put under a hen, after which all the other geese seemed to think they had a mission to kill that hen. They passed the night close to her, and followed the little yellow fluffy thing about wherever it went, bowing to it, and making a terrible noise; but it seemed to have no natural affection for grand relations, and stuck close to its good foster-mother. Dr. Hoad had a flying-fox for a pet before I came, which used to climb up him and nestle against his face like a cat, then

hook itself on his chair, and hang itself topsy-turvy to be fed; it would not swallow upright. It seemed to have attached itself to him alone, and did not care for his wife or any one else. I tasted the flesh several times, but it was too gamey for my liking.

There were many French Creole families scattered over the island, who possessed considerable property, but lived generally on borrowed money, and were a wretched race in every way. Leprosy was scattered thickly among them, and they were almost entirely without education. They showed their family pride (as at Mahe) by keeping preserves of tortoises, and the Hoads had lately been at a wedding-feast at which one was roasted whole in its own shell, and was the principal dish. There were thirty other dishes all on the table at once, and it was the custom to take something of each. It was thought quite uncivil to pay short visits: word ought to be sent the day before that you were coming, then they would all have their best clothes on,—men, women, and children,—and all sit in a circle round the generally-shut-up reception-room, fanning themselves, and saying, "Quel chaleur!" at intervals, "Jamais! Jamais! Epouvantable!" the words before and behind lost in the heat. Then vermouth would be handed round more than once, and all the women took large glasses of it, which increased their fervour about the heat, while the creaking cocoa-nut mill played its dolorous accompaniment outside. The only thing which rouses those gentlemen and ladies is that music ceasing, when they go and scream at the black people and bullocks, and set it going again.

At one house there was a French manager. He had been a fan-painter at home, and he and his mother seemed made of different materials from those around them, including his poor low-spirited Creole wife. He was intelligent, active, and already tired of his position, his mother thoroughly disgusted with it, and she confided to me how *triste* it was there, and how much she objected to her son having married into a *famille noire.* The place they lived in had once been

the creation of some man of taste. There were many beautiful shrubs and flowers growing round it, tangled with weeds and wild things, and a grand grove of the Madagascar palm, whose leaves have been passed off as feathers of the gigantic roc (according to Colonel Yule). Some of the trees were loaded with long pendent branches of fruit, resembling those of the sago palm, great bunches one over the other, the whole being from four to six feet long, and half hidden by a wrapping like brown paper.

One morning the manager took me a two hours' climb and scramble up to another valley full of coco de mer palms (far larger than any I had seen before), as well as other giant palms, pandani with stilted roots, and magnificent ferns. We had to cut our way, and I sat down and slid over slippery rocks, and dropped into foot-holes cut for me on palmbranches or anything else that came handy. In those forests there were so many thorns on the tree-stems that one had little power of holding on by one's hands, and it was no easy matter getting down an almost perpendicular bit of forestcovered hillside; but when it was done I was well rewarded.

After crossing the stream to the other side, a waterfall fell fifty feet over a wall of rock hung with ferns, into a pool among the boulders, half hidden by foam and steam. Above and all round were huge coco de mer trees, loaded with full-grown nuts or long sweet male flowers (those trees being always much taller than the fruit-bearing ones); masses of flagellaria or creeping bamboo hooking itself over them by the ends of its leaves (like the *Gloriosa superba),* with a grass-like flower and yellow berries. After sketching as well as circumstances and impatient guides would permit, we climbed up the other side, and passed under one tree hung with thirty perfect nuts: one a triple nut, and very few of the usual imperfect ones. Small purple orchids were growing among the ferns on the ground. It was a rich treat to see all this, and very tantalising to have to leave it so soon, and to come out into the hideous clearing, with plants of cacao, coffee, and manioc dotted over it. Crowning a hill in the midst was the hut of a sub-manager, perfectly shadeless; but its owner said it was often bitterly cold at night, and he was glad to go to bed when it got dark, and to heap all the things he had on the top of him to keep from freezing. He was a sociable character. Having no human friends, he kept cats. He never killed the kittens, so had enough of them. He gave us a capital breakfast of curry, fish, eggs, and manioc, which takes the place of bread in the Seychelles, one plant often yielding twenty-five roots as big as ordinary field carrots: they had here none of the poisonous juice the Brazilian species have, which must be pressed out before the root is fit to eat. The usual way of preparing it was by boiling; but they also made the same cakes they called cassava in the West Indies. Chocolate, cloves, and cinnamon were growing on those hills, and vanilla below in the hollows, as well as miles of cocoanuts on the shore.

The doctor had promised to pick me up in his boat on his return from La Digue, about four o'clock, but it was past ten before he came. We were just giving him up, after straining our eyes for hours, looking into the dark night. I could see the outlines of the other islands he had to pass through when I shaded my eyes, but never saw the boat till it grounded close to me, and never heard his shell blown. Landing is always a little difficult in the Seychelles, except at extreme high tide, owing to the coral shelf which surrounds the islands. One has either to be carried on a man's shoulder, or dragged over the sand in a tiny canoe, which is more agreeable. It was no easy matter to get away from Praslin. Many boats went and came, but they were full of dried fish and natives (equally unpleasant at close quarters), and except during exceptional winds rowing-boats took eleven hours, sailing-boats any time. But at last Mr. B. sent me one of the Government whale-boats, and I had a most agreeable row over in eleven hours with Johnnie B., and a kind welcome at Government House; but it was not comfortable quarters for long. The place

was just under the old burying-ground, close to the dirty town; so, as Mrs. B. wanted a dry room for the baby, I packed up, gave up mine at once, and went off to Mrs. E. She had turned her nice dining-room into a room for me, which was delightful, opening on the wide verandah, with the glorious view over the bay and grand mountains beyond, and their ever-changing clouds and shadows: great nodding scarlet hibiscus bells as foreground.

I had perfect peace. Mr. E. was at his office all day; his wife, a real sweet English lady, for my companion, with her model servant Madalina, and her two boys. Instead of drains, I had the scent of forty feet of stephanotis in flower along the rail of the verandah, mixed with *Roupdlia grata* and jasmine. Cocoa-nut trees hung over and framed the different views, the island of St. Anne's making one perfect picture in itself. Seven other islands came into view from my window, as well as the lovely coast of Mahe itself, with its purple granite rocks above and the exquisitely coloured sea below. The house, raised on terraces above the road, was the very last on the north side of the bay, and the hill rose so steeply that I wondered the whole did not slip into the sea with a splash. Steep steps led from the back of the house to the kitchen-hut and home of the family who had formed the household for years. They were quite black, and the father was Pion in Mr. E.'s office (the Treasury); the wife did cook and housemaid's work, the boys all the rest, laughing all the time, as if it were a joke. Till the rains became too violent, the backverandah was turned into a dining-room; it was surrounded by pots made out of fern-stems, and filled with caladiums and ferns, shaded by scarlet hibiscus.

A crowd of cocks and hens collected at every meal to be fed, two especial favourites perching on the box of rice in Mr. E.'s hand, when he used to pull the cock's beard and stroke them both. Four wild doves also used to come and feed on the verandah, so impudent that they never moved away when the dog Snap walked through them. We had the

most delicious fruit in abundance. Sixteen large pines could be bought for sixpence, the mangoes were as good as any in India, and papaws most excellent, also melons. The wild raspberries were brought down from the hills in baskets made of banana-leaves, shaped like boats; the fruit were not good raw, but slightly stewed, and then left to cool, they were delicious for the next day, when we ate them with cream. Some black people kept four cows close to us, so we always had plenty of milk and cream. Beyond the house was a path along the lovely coast for some miles. I generally went for a walk along it before breakfast, diverging up to the hills at different points. The road in the morning was always full of black people coming and going to market in their clean dresses, carrying fruits and flowers, and chattering merrily. They all said *bonjour,* and I said it also so often that I caught myself once saying it mechanically to an old hen and chickens which I nearly walked over. Most of the trees along the coast were foreign, as well as the flowers: hibiscus, convolvulus, allamanda, etc. The Madagascar "ordeal-plant" was loaded with white waxy flowers; noble pink and white crinums grew like weeds along the coast, as well as caladiums of different sorts; and poincianas dropped their scarlet stars in heaps on the ground.

Centipedes are the only evil things in the island. They live in the hollow between the wood and the palm or pandanus stalks which line the walls of houses, and come out when the evenings are damp. They are three to five inches long, and their bite at the time is like touching a red-hot poker, but it goes off without leaving any permanent hurt. Our dog Snap always gave notice when he saw one, but took care not to get within dangerous reach of it. He had a great talent for finding the eggs of strange hens, and would stand and bark till the boy came and took them. He also knew all our own poultry, and would not permit any neighbour's cocks and hens to come even into the garden without a good chase after them. A shilling was the usual price for a duck or chicken fit for the table, three pennies bought fish enough for the whole family for a day, a rupee bought a sucking pig, and vegetables cost next to nothing.

I had the offer of one house on the hill above, belonging to a Mrs. Chocolade, a very black lady, who introduced herself during one of my walks as being just like me: she loved *la tranquilliU* and lived all alone; she could let me a little house which would just suit me. It consisted of one good wooden room with a window on each side, resting on a rock and three legs of masonry, having a space below unenclosed, in which the last inhabitant apparently did his cooking, judging by the heap of black wood-ashes. It was thatched with palm-leaves, all clean and new, with a grand view; the only drawback was, no water; but for that I would have taken it, and got Madame Chocolade to do for me. I had a good walk with her, and she introduced me to her friends on other hills, screaming at the top of her voice, "This is a real Englishwoman!" She said they all liked English, and hated French, appealing to her friends for confirmation of the sentiment in the same tone, which they gave with a chorus of approving grunts, till the rocks echoed again. Some of the blacks worked hard. I saw a woman wading along in the shallow water one day, fishing with both hands and feet at the same time. She was picking up shell-fish with her toes, using one hand to bait her hook with them, or putting them into the basket on her head, while she held the rod in the other. Another day I saw eight men dragging a net in great excitement round three fountains of silver smelts, flashing in and out of the water at the edge of the sands; a man walked in front of each end of the net, splashing the water back to make the circle larger, and they filled sacks full of the fish, as well as a canoe.

I seldom went into the town, through its gossiping streets of idle people or past the poisonous stretch of black mud. We heard from Mr. E. enough of the scandal, and of the one subject, quarantine, and whether it was, or was not, smallpox which caused it. Our doctors said it was not smallpox. Mauritius said

it was. They sent two doctors (Creoles), one after another, to make it so, and Dr. B. found one isolated case which he said was that disease, but no other. He was a curious character, who tried to please both parties. He had been in the Seychelles twenty-five years, and knew more of its natural history than any one else I met there. He and his Greek wife were very kind and hospitable in their offers to me. I went one day to their house, and painted their parrots, which came originally from Silhouette: queer, misshapen birds, with enormous beaks and patches of red and yellow badly put on, one of them having a black ring round its neck. Both were quite helplessly bullied by common pigeons, which came and ate up their food, while they jabbered in a melancholy way, and submitted. They had absolutely no tops to their heads, which perhaps accounted for their stupidity. They had a stand on the back verandah, where they slept and were fed. They were not tied up, but went and stole their own fruit off the neighbouring trees.

The doctor had also a wild dog as a pet. It had great tusks which stood up outside its upper lips like a wild boar, and a thick mane like a lion, being otherwise a smooth-skinned dog. Dr. and Mrs. Brooks lived on the other side of the town. Still farther off lived the health-officer, Dr. Sepper. The Creole party accused him of letting in the man from Zanzibar who brought the disease they called smallpox, and persecuted him for it (they even brought an action of manslaughter against him for those who had since died of it). They said he should not play cricket; they stole the ball, and while I was there did many other absurd things to show their hatred of him.

At Christmas and New Year the whole population got mad drunk. All the black and brown people began by going from house to house, wishing *banana* or *bonne annee,* and in return got a glass of rum, or money to buy it. At night we heard singing and raving all round; it was like the island of lunatics, and we barred all the windows well before going to bed: to sleep was impos-

sible. Mrs. S. asked the Judge and the O.s to dinner on New Year's night. The Judge (or some one for him) sent word that he was too drunk to come, and poor Mrs. O. said she feared it would be impossible to get her husband sober enough to walk there. The Judge afterwards had to put off the sessions for three days, because he was too drunk to hold them! There was only one man in Mah6 who did not drink: the American consul—a queer, wooden old bachelor, who was allowed £300 a year by the United States for doing nothing there, and who filled up his time by retailing gossip in a true Yankee drawl, with a thin seasoning of native humour and never a smile. He had a habit of giving Christmas boxes to his friends every year,—soap, towels, scent, notepaper, etc.,—but said that this year he had ordered them to be sent out from the States, and the Messagerie had taken them on with the plum-puddings to Australia; so his friends got none, the one mail refusing to leave or take cargo.

Rice and other provisions necessary to the people became so dear that they were half starving, and there seemed little chance of my getting away, and no chance of getting on to Mauritius. I walked up one morning, with Snap, to breakfast at Mr. W.'s, some 2000 feet above the sea. The first ascent up the red hill was as steep as any I have ever been over, and must be dangerous when wet; but after that it was all lovely, crossing several streams, and through exquisite forest scenery, where the *Angrcecum dmrneum* was growing in abundance among lovely ferns and boulder-stones. At one part the road went over one huge unbroken rock for 200 feet or more, and passed under quite a grove of tanghinia trees, whose white waxy flowers strewed the ground underneath, looking like narcissus. The berries were not in season, but are said to be purple like plums: one is enough to kill twenty people. Beyond them, I reached the original forest, full of wonderful palms and pandanus, with the great white stems of dead capucin and sideroxylon trees standing high above the rest, and soon reached the col or watershed, whence

I descended again before reaching the hill on which the mission-schools were placed. The whole walk only took me two hours and a half, and I returned home at 2.30.

I afterwards stayed three weeks with Mr. and Mrs. W. He had begun life as a blacksmith in Somersetshire, but fancied he had a "call," and came out to be cured of the idea. After five years of perfect loneliness in Mahe, they had now two fair little children of their own and sixty black ones to look after. The schools were originally intended for the children of slaves, but now that none existed others were taken: I could not make out by what rule. They all seemed very happy there, and did not puzzle their brains with too much learning. Report said they were famous thieves when they went down into the lower world, but that lower world had also a great reputation for untruth. I found them quite good-natured and honest when among them. Psalm-singing seemed their chief study; morning, noon, and night it went on, and I rejoiced in being blest with only one ear that could hear. The situation of Venns Town is one of the most magnificent in the world, and the silence of the forest around was only broken by the children's happy voices.

From that flat-topped, isolated hill, one saw a long stretch of wild mountain coast, and many islands, some 2000 feet below, across which long-tailed boatswain-birds were always flying; behind it, the highest peak of Mahe frowned down on us, often inky-black under the storm-clouds. They were gathering round it when I came up on the 7th of January, and for a whole fortnight the rains came down day and night, showing me wonderful cloud-effects, dark as slate, with the dead white capucin trees sticking through like pins in a pincushion. There were few living specimens of any age, but those were noble ones, the young leaves a foot in length, looking like green satin lined with brown velvet, and growing in terminal bunches at the ends of the woody branches. They seemed to me much like the gutta-percha trees of Borneo, but I could make out nothing certain of the flowers, and was told "it had no flower," or a "red flower," or a "white one," each statement most positive, from those who lived actually under the trees! The nuts every one knew, and collected them as curiosities. Flowers were sent afterwards to England, and Sir J. Hooker declared it a new genus, and named it *Northea seychellana,* after me. Under the capucins were abundance of tree-ferns; noble palms with pink young leaves, salmoncoloured fading ones, and orange and scarlet fruits, some drooping and some standing erect, high above the leaves; tall stiff trees of *IFormia ferruginea,* with white flowers and brown furry buds, whose young leaves of the deepest carmine tints are nearly as long as those of the capucin. These are most remarkable for the joined petioles to the leaves, forming cups in which I always found a reservoir of water in the early morning to nourish the young succulent leaves. The more mature and woody ones did not require them, and they were dispensed with. VOL. 11 X

Many other trees were there, whose names no one knew, with unobtrusive white flowers, scarcely any coloured, one of the few exceptions being a colea, whose yellow trumpetflowers grew straight out of its trunk and woody branches. Under them were great starry leaves belonging to evil-smelling brown arums, and an endless variety of ferns, including the great bird's-nest. One day we had a fine morning. Mr. W. sent boys out to cut a way, and we scrambled up and down valleys of boulders, through the wet forests, and up to the top of the Nun's Nose Mountain. The hanging roots of the pandanus were a great help in pulling ourselves up the walls of mud and granite; but the palms and many other growing things were so full of long thorns that my hands were bleeding and torn before we reached the top. Just round the summit we found the pitcher-plants festooned and trailing over the shrubs; but a dozen feet below this there was not one. The stems were crimson, and as thick as my finger, and the habit so different that a London nurseryman would possibly have given it a different name from the dense mat which covered the top of the mountain. But I traced some of these stems and found they joined the others, and that they had only "adapted themselves to circumstances." The top of the mountain consisted of one smooth granite boulder covered with carpets of nepenthes and creeping grass. The nepenthes was matted together, and could be lifted up by the yard without coming to any root-hold, every lid of its pitchers the brightest crimson, like a green carpet with red dots, as I looked down on it; and hundreds of male flowers stood up from it. Among them I found some of the missing female flowers, which every one in the Seychelles said were as yet unknown. Near the edge of the summit were fine tufts of brown flowering grass, as high as pampas grass, and quantities of the lovely *Angrcecwm eburneum.* I saw one of these exquisite orchids perched on a root in a stream looking at its face in the water, surrounded by pink begonia and maidenhair fern.

We got soaked before our return, and the schoolgirls who had been washing in one of the valleys, and had left their clothes to dry on the rocks while they returned to breakfast, found them afterwards 500 feet lower on the rocks! The man who went down to the post after provisions had to go two miles round to avoid the swollen streams. It was a sight worth seeing in itself, this rain in the mountains; but when it did cease for half an hour the ground was so steep that I could always get out and make studies of trees, and so managed to finish some paintings. The various kinds of pandanus were even more wonderful than the palms. At last the sun showed itself again, and we walked down the south side to the sea, taking the children and their mother in a hammock, and twenty schoolgirls for a holiday. It was a long four miles; getting hotter as we came lower; but every bit of the road was beautiful, with high cliffs on each side, with the vacca maron pandanus clinging like spiders to their very tops, and five species of palm packed in quantities in the narrow gorge between. Great obelisks of creeping ipomceas and long snaky *VaniUa phalcenopsis* crept over all the boulders and branches, with their lovely white flowers and hanging beans.

When we got down to the sandy shore, all the schoolgirls rushed into the water, and stayed in it for hours, scratching up and collecting the pretty pink bivalve shellfish to make into soup; and Mr. W. did the same, with his trousers well tucked up above his knees. The children collected wonderful treasures for me to take to England. Meanwhile I strolled on under the cocoa-nuts and found a grand old barringtonia tree covered with creepers and parasites, many of its white lilac-tipped tassels on the ground below, and two more rivers running down to the sea. Water abounds everywhere in Mahe. Each of our girls had a large cake of manioc and jam, a salt fish, and a pine-apple and a half for her breakfast. They worried the pines like monkeys, beating them with stones till the rind broke and they could tear them to bits with their fingers, enjoying it all so much that the W.s said they would stay as late as possible, and I went on, enjoying the quiet stroll home alone. I like to be able to concentrate my attention on fine scenery without straining my ears to hear voices, or to have to talk in return of other less interesting subjects.

Mr. C., the Messagerie agent, thought he might get me off by the next mail; so I walked over the mountains to his house, to talk it over with him. He lived on the very top of the watershed on another shoulder of the mountains, and could look into the sea both north and south from his portico. It must have been fearfully windy there sometimes, though only 1500 feet above the sea. The house was raised on two terraces faced with stone, which had already given way. All the stone was procured by burning fires to crack the granite rock: at night the effect was fine. There was a small railway to move the pieces. It was nice to be at home with Mrs. E. again; but I had all the uncertainty of whether the mail would take me, and

when I got to the ship's side it would not. There had been thirteen deaths from smallpox in January, so I agreed to go into quarantine on Long Island with the C.s, who also wanted to go home. Another man joined them, and for ten days all was peace.

I painted continually, and looked at the lovely views, and the marvellous colours of the sea. One afternoon I heard a rustle close to where I was sitting under the trees, and saw a small hawk, no bigger than a thrush, pick up a green lizard, look defiantly at me for a moment, then fly away with its body. The tail fell to the ground, and began waltzing round and round. I took out my watch and timed how long it continued to move: it was quite half an hour, the last movement being just at the tip of the tail, and by that time it was quite covered with small black ants, which carried it off bit by bit, not only into their principal hole, but into little back doors which they had in a long crack of the dry ground. The next morning there was none of the tail to be found.

The first ten days on that quarantine island passed peacefully; after that some of the inmates took to playing tricks on me, and I thought they would rob and even murder me. God knows the truth. Doctors say my nerves broke down from insufficient food and overwork in such a climate. There being no banker, Coutts had sent me £200 in notes, which were stitched into my clothes; and for two days and nights I tied up my door, barricaded my window, and was in fear of my life, hearing things said behind the low divisions, which they tell me never had been said. The ship came at last, and we got home; but the same troubles followed me till I reached England, when I was again among my friends, and able to enjoy finishing and arranging my paintings in the new room at Kew, trying to forget all that dreadful time.

Her health was breaking down, her nerves partly destroyed, but the old spirit was still there; and till she had finished the last bit of the task she had set herself, and painted on the spot the strange forest-growth of Western South

America, she would not allow herself to rest. Just before she started on this last long journey, a great pleasure came to her in the following letter:

Osbokne, *28th August* 1884.

Madam—The Queen has been informed of your generous conduct in presenting to the nation, at Kew, your valuable collection of botanical paintings, in a gallery erected by yourself for the purpose of containing them.

The Queen regrets to learn from her Ministers that Her Majesty's Government have no power of recommending to the Queen any mode of publicly recognising your liberality. Her Majesty is desirous of marking in a personal manner her sense of your generosity, and in commanding me to convey the Queen's thanks to you, I am to ask your acceptance of the accompanying photograph of Her Majesty, to which the Queen has appended her signature.—I have the honour to be, Madam, your obedient Servant, Henry F. Ponsonbt.

Miss Marianne North. CHAPTER XVI CHILI

About the middle of November 1884, I started on my last journey.

All the biggest trees of the world were represented "*at Home* " in my gallery, except the *Araucaria imhricata,* and I could find no description of this tree in any new books of Chilian travel; so, with the kind help of Sir T. F., a cabin was secured all to myself all the way to Valparaiso, and till we reached Bordeaux all was enjoyment. Then my nerves gave way again (if they were nerves!), and the torture has continued more or less ever since. The ship was constantly in quarantine, and we were kept at anchor twenty-eight hours before we were allowed to land at Rio; but it was little penance to me in that lovely bay, and a drive on shore was very refreshing. At Monte Video there were more than a thousand poor people packed into a small quarantine station, with scarcely enough bread and water to live on, for a whole week. An Italian emigrant ship was sent right away, and but for the kindness of the Brazilian Government the poor people would have starved.

It became fearfully cold as we entered the Straits, and through the foggy morning we saw the wreck of a French steamer; but there were no distress signals, and after some observations we went on, and soon overtook its boat, with the captain and men. The former gave up his papers to be taken to Sandy Point, but would tell nothing of his story, only of the wreck of the *Cordillera,* the companion-ship to our own, in which I had nearly started, but fortunately could not get a good cabin. It was near sunset when we reached Sandy Point, and some of the distant snow mountains rose out of the sea like icebergs, pink and glittering behind it. All the lower summits near us were topped with snow, though the forests extended to a considerable height above the convict settlement. Many of the passengers from the *Cordillera* came on with us, and told different stories of the wreck. These were so different that it was difficult to find the truth; but at daylight we saw the poor ship resting on the black reef of rocks, under the cold snow mountains, and our captain went to see the poor old captain and his men. They were camping near the shore to watch the cargo, which was under water and out of reach of saving, but still had to be watched till a ship was sent to relieve them. Our captain had known the old wrecked captain long, and left him some guns; for the inhabitants were not an amiable race of savages, and might find him out, with his stock of provisions.

It was snowing hard as we passed, and the cold must have been intense in that tent. Later in the day it cleared, and we saw many grand glaciers winding down close to the edge of the sea, with clear green and blue crevasses in them; it was like a long lake of Como, without its buildings, only rocks, ice, and snow, with dark scrub near the edge of the water: very grand, but coldly monotonous. On the other side of the Straits of Magellan we came to rough sea and wind, till we entered the landlocked harbour of Lota, where we spent some hours in the gardens of Madame C., the owner of the coal mines, and one of the richest

women in the world. Her garden was full of jimcrackeries and bad taste; but the collection of plants from Japan, New Zealand, Africa, and Mexico, as well as those we see in gardens at home, was most interesting. Chili was the country least represented there, but we found great tangles of lapageria over the tree-stems and branches, though, alas, the season was over, and we found only one flower on it. After much searching, I saw for the first time great masses of the *Puya* chUensis, the flowers of a light yellow green, with intensely orange stamens, growing in bunches which were arranged spirally round the head of an aloe-like stem, eight or nine feet high, forming nearly a yard of thick head, as big as that of the agave. The bunch of leaves at the base of the huge flower was like that of the pine-apple, its relation. The group looked grand as I first saw them, standing out from the cliff with the deep-blue sea and sky for a background. That species of puya always grows near the sea. All the weeds seemed English there. Great bushes of gorse and docks were luxuriating close to daturas, pawlonias, etc. We had tea with a good English miner, who had been eleven years there without going home; he said the climate was perfect and the pay good. The next morning we stopped at Concepcion, and landed a good American woman with her husband, who was going to be a missionary, and to preach in Spanish, when he had learnt it!

One night at the Valparaiso inn was enough for any one, though the place itself was full of life and work, its quays, iron landing-place, and docks, neat and efficient. Large ships could anchor close to the town, in the calm landlocked harbour. Its suburbs extended along the coast for some miles, Salto being the most attractive of them, as there was a valley full of the native palm *(Jukm spectabilis)* which used to cover the country forty years ago; now, scarcely a hundred remain. They are strange, misshapen things, but seem quite in character with the rocky valley they grow in. The rail made a steep ascent to Quillota, where we came to the

richest meadows and gardens, bordered by enormous hedges of the common blackberry, quite like the brambles of England, only gigantic; and rows of tall poplars. Huge bouquets and baskets of fruit were to be bought in quantities. The former generally had a large white datura or magnolia in the centre, surrounded by dahlias, roses, heliotrope, marigolds, etc., all jumbled up without thought or taste. The cherimoyers were famous there, and strawberries abounded, but they were all white or pale pink, none were red.

After leaving Quillota we had a still steeper ascent, among rocky hill-tops, with a sprinkling of cacti, puyas, and other purely native vegetation, till we arrived at the summit, then descended to the great wall of Santiago, with the city in the midst of it, and the snows of the Cordilleras beyond. The highest point, Tupungato, 20,264 feet in height, was much talked of, but never seen, unless on some supernaturally clear day, from many miles out at sea. The letter my friend at home had written to our ambassador and his wife had been wrecked in the *Cordillera,* and, brought on by us, it reached them a couple of hours before I got to Santiago. Just as I was settling myself to dress and unpack comfortably in the hotel, there came a knock at my door, and I (thinking it was a jug of hot water) opened it in my dressing-gown, and let in Mr. Drummond Hay, our good consul, who had been sent to hunt till he found me; so I had to pack up again, and go off to Mr. and Mrs. Pakenham, the most hospitable of people, and they kept my room always ready for me, all the time I was in Chili, to return to at a moment's notice, and never put any one else in it. My hostess had a dull life in Santiago, seldom going out of the house, or associating with any but the small collection of diplomats who were also condemned to live there. But they were a very sociable set, and used to assemble for lawn-tennis in the garden at least three times a week. Sometimes some native grandee would come and look on, and declare he liked the "creekit," as he would call it, and meant to begin one in his garden.

It was not the thing for a woman to walk alone in the streets, unless she were wrapped up in a manta, or black Cash mere shawl, which is arranged like a nun's head-dress, so as to cover forehead and mouth. I used to go to market, hidden in my manta, with the cook sometimes, to get flowers and other curiosities to paint. I also made friends with Dr. Philippi, who lent me birds and wonderful nests from the museum. One little wren, "omnicolor," made an exquisitely finished nest, shaped like a small funnel; and I found another specimen of the same nest, with a loose, untidy dwelling on the top of it, built by a dowdy little brown bird, which had used the other as its pedestal. The *Acacia cavenia,* with terrible thorns pointing every way, was used to defend a curious nest by a delicate little bird called *Izwllaxis sordida.* It was entirely formed of these thorns, woven in and out, and the bird was very rightly called "the worker" by the natives. I tore my hands to pieces trying to get one of these nests, and had to give up the attempt; yet the tiny bird sat comfortably on a soft lining of hair and the sweet dry flowers of the tree, and seemed none the worse for weaving these terrible spines. Of course the first thing I tried to get was the great blue puya. I was told they were all out of flower; indeed, some people declared they did not exist, because they had not seen them. At last an energetic English lady bribed a man to bring me one from the mountain. It was a very bad specimen, but I screamed with delight at it, and worked hard to get it done before it was quite faded, for it was past its prime. Then I drove out to Apoquindo, over a flat ten miles of uninteresting, cultivated country, with high mud banks or walls on each side of the road, which prevented one's seeing anything; but English weeds seemed to abound, and to grow with far greater luxuriance than they did at home. Apoquindo is a large bathing establishment, much frequented by the people of Santiago, but then out of season. I had a choice of some fifty rooms, and every sort of kind care from the people there. It was quite perfect quarters for my pur-pose of flower-hunting. The hot springs bubbled out in abundance close to the house, and a clear cool stream came down to it from the steep hills behind the house, edged and shaded by many bushes: escal-lonia, berberis, etc., with wreaths of ecremocarpus and *TropcBolum tricolorum* over them, the fallen flowers of the former quite colouring the ground below. The exquisite loasa was everywhere, and soon taught me its nature (far more vicious than any British stinging-nettle), but it repaid one for the pain of examining its mechanism, which is as fine as that of the kalmia: the slightest touch sends the ripe stamens flying towards the pistil, and jerking out the pollen. Œnotheras, calceolarias, and lobelias were there in quantities, as well as verbenas, oxalis, and many pretty bulbous plants, *Placea ornata,* leucocoryne, and phycella.

My great object now was to find the blue puya, so I got a guide and a horse and started up to the mountains. We tied up the horses when it became too steep, and proceeded on foot right into the clouds; they were so thick that at one time I could not see a yard before me, but I would not give up, and was rewarded at last by the mists clearing, and behold, just over my head, a great group of the noble flowers, standing out like ghosts at first, then gradually coming out with their full beauty of colour and form in every stage of growth; while beyond them glittered a snow-peak far away, and I reached a new world of wonders, with blue sky overhead, and a mass of clouds like sheets of cotton-wool below me, hiding the valley I had left. Some of the groups had twenty-five flower-stalks rising from the mass of curling silvery leaves; about sixty branchlets were arranged spirally round the central stem, each a foot long, and covered with buds wrapped in flesh-coloured bracts; these open in successive circles, beginning at the base. The three flower-petals are at first of the purest turquoise blue, then they become darker, a mixture of arsenic green and prussian blue, the third day a grayer green, after which they curl themselves up into three carmine shavings, and a fresh circle of flowers takes their place outside, so that the longer the plant has been in bloom, the larger its head becomes; and as the ends of the spikes or branchlets bloom the last, it gradually loses its perfection of form, and looks ragged and disreputable. Its orange stamens shine out like gold upon the blue green of its petals.

A very large and beautiful moth, having all the colours of the puya on its wings (in one light they looked bronze, in another peacock blue), lays its eggs in the pith of the great flower-stalks when decayed, and the caterpillar lives on them, eating out a cavern or nest for himself and his future chrysalis there. The gum of the plant is valuable as a medicine, and much resembles gum-arabic. A third variety of puya is much smaller, with dark-blue flowers and pink stalks. Near these tall plants the quisquis or cactus generally grew: often fifteen or sixteen feet high, crowned with long white trumpetflowers and buds, and ornamented with a parasite whose white and scarlet berries were eaten. It was strange, but I found that the flowers of the two plants never faced the same way. The flowers of the cactus faced south. They were as large as German beer-glasses, and their foot-stalks full of sweet juice, most refreshing to suck on the dry hillside, and less stupefying than the usual contents of such glasses. Both the cactus and the parasite were leafless.

I spent more than a fortnight working in comfort at Apoquindo, now and then mounting an old horse and riding into the mountains alone, tying the horse to some tree while I scrambled about after flowers. One day my friend Mrs. Proctor (the only other English lady besides Mrs. Pakenham in Santiago) drove over, bringing Don Benjamen Vicuna di Mackenna, a very distinguished writer and patriot, to see me and my work, which impressed him so much that he wrote a long flourish in the newspaper about me, saying, among other things, that "I went about into sunny countries, painting blue sky and light, and brought it home to the poor people of London, who never saw it, and did not know what it was like!" He also invited me to come to his country house, and after my return to Santiago he fetched Mrs. Proctor and myself one morning, and took us, partly by rail and partly in a carriage over bad roads and bleak grazing country, to a pretty garden with a wooden one-storeyed house and verandah round it, farm-buildings, yards, and stables at the back of it. In front the garden was terminated by a clear river, broken up by sandy, stony islands, which joined the sea about six miles further. One side of the house was prettily furnished, and the Lady Victoria (as I called her, for she was of very high rank, though not recognised in the republic) and her family used to pass their summers there: now, only a few of the spare rooms were open. The whole place was under the care of a manager. There were also two rich young men whom Don Benjamen had persuaded to invest their money in cattle, while he supplied the land and food and divided the profits with them. They enjoyed the work, as it entailed much riding about, and every Chilian considers that the chief employment of life. They wore spurs as big as saucers, which rendered walking impossible.

The mode of living was of the coarsest. We had a clean tablecloth the first day, over which the son and heir spilt a whole bottle of red wine, and that cloth remained as it was until I left eight days after. The Don and my friend only stayed two nights, then returned to Santiago, leaving me to paint the yellow puya in peace (a grand specimen being cut and tied to a pillar of the verandah for me), and the manager sent for his pretty little wife and fat mother-in-law to "accompagnar" me. Near the house the country was ugly. The creeping large-flowered cenothera, whose flowers come out white the first night and pink the next, was the most conspicuous plant on the dry ground, with an exquisite scent. Near it grew the Chilian forget-me-not, a kind of everlasting *(TriptUian)*. I wonder it is not cultivated on English rockeries. Farther on we came to a forest of small bushes twelve or fifteen feet high, with tall grass and weedy flowers under them; it reminded one of

the old "shrubberies" of some neglected country-house in Europe. Beyond them again came the sea-sands and river-mouth, with *Argemone mexicana,* a yellow or white poppy with thistle-like leaves; also many kinds of fleshy-leaved plants.

But the great sight, my entertainers thought, was a " rodeo" which was to be held in the hills about five miles off, and to which we all rode one morning. The ladies' saddles are made rather like a pie-dish, with a two-inch rim round three sides of them. The rider is mounted in a peculiar way, putting her hands on the cavalier's shoulders as he grasps her waist with both hands, after which the lady keeps perfectly rigid till she reaches her seat, when she twists herself round into her right position. They rode very well, and we galloped nearly all the way, till we reached the sort of amphitheatre in the hills, where about 300 horsemen were collected, in flaming ponchos and hats as big as targets, one old man sitting perfectly still on his old horse, to direct each pair in turn to start, and what beast to hunt. When the two horsemen he had named started, they never lost sight of that particular beast, out of nearly 2000, till it was driven into the proper pen. The horses stood like statues, and the men too, till the word was given, then they rode like wild things, hooting and shouting, then suddenly pulling up their poor horses on their hind quarters. The dust and the sunshine and the general excitement were marvellous and most picturesque, surrounded as it all was by green trees and mountain-tops. My good little horse was perfectly broken in, and stood so still in the midst of the crowd that I might have sketched on his back, though he was ready to gallop at the slightest touch of my heel. There were dancing-sheds near, made of green branches, where we watched quaint and solemn dances like old minuets and jigs going on, to the music of some oldfashioned harps and singing. One deaf and dumb man was the model dancer of the party. After all this, a huge jug of beer was handed round, and every one had to take a sip from it, or pretend to do

so. We women went home early after our luncheon, with the manager to take charge of us. He said the manners of the company would not improve towards the end of the day.

But my chief object in coming to Chili was to paint the old *Araucaria* imbricata, known in England as the puzzlemonkey tree, rather unreasonably, as there are no monkeys in Chili to puzzle. Probably they crossed the Cordilleras in disgust at the general prickliness of all the plants there, especially the araucarias, and never came back again: there are plenty on the other side. It was not easy to make out how to reach those forests. People talked of difficulties, and even dangers. They said I must sleep out, be eaten by pumas, or carried off by Indians, a noble race which had never yet been conquered by the white man. Others declared the trees no longer existed, having been all sawn up into sleepers for railways; but as usual I found when I got nearer the spot that all difficulties vanished.

After two days of railway through the long wide valley or plain of Santiago, with the snowy Cordilleras on one side and the high hills which go down to the sea on the other, I was received at the country-house of a half-English lady, whose husband was then going through all the troubles of canvassing the district, to be again elected a member of the Lower House. He was a Liberal, and all the clerical party opposed him, as well as the Government, who were afraid of them. It was a happy home-party, with one charming little girl who had quite a genius for taming all sorts of wild creatures. She used to clap her hands softly, and give a kind of low whistle, when the locusts would fly to her and settle on her, and birds used to answer her when she imitated their notes. Mrs. J. had been anxious to improve the people round her, and started a school close to the house; but the schoolmaster disappeared one fine day, and carried off all the books and slates with him. She meant well, but was before her time. I saw many snow-capped volcanoes from her house, all alike, but diminishing in height southward, till, at the Straits of Magellan, Sarmiento is only 7000 feet above the sea.

Angol was the end of the railway there. The American Head of the Works kindly met me and allowed me to sleep in his house. I then found that the forests I was in search of belonged to two Irish gentlemen, one of whom came to fetch me the next morning at daybreak, and rode with me up a most picturesque and well-made road for some four or five hours, to the comfortable farmhouse where his sister and her family were living. From thence I could actually see the famous trees on the hill-tops, looking like pins loosely stuck into pincushions, as they stood out black against the sunset sky. Nothing could exceed the kind hospitality of my hostess, and no one could have wished for a more comfortable home. The house was very roomy, built as usual of one storey, with a verandah all round it, on a bare little knoll rising from green meadows and surrounded by hills, which were covered with trees resembling oak and beech. They grew separately, or in groups, so that the sun could peep through and sweeten the grass under them. This gave the best of food to some 2000 cattle which were straying over the property, and to about 100 cows, which at that time were giving quantities of milk and cream: the butter had already become famous. In the winter the cows were divided and given over in charge to the different cottages on the estate; their owners took care of them, and made cheeses, giving back half the profits, and keeping half for their trouble. The house might have been more picturesquely situated, but it was built at a time when the Indians were troublesome, and it was necessary to keep a good look-out, and to have no bushes for them to hide in near at hand.

VOL. II Y

The ride up from dusty Angol had been very delightful. After mounting the first rocky ascent of 2000 feet, sprinkled over with puyas, cactuses, and other prickly plants, we left a glorious view of snowy volcanoes behind us, and entered on mixed forest and pasture scenery, passing stream after stream of clear running water, and more lovely flowers than I had seen in all the three months I had passed in other parts of Chili. The embothrium or burning bush was in full beauty, growing in long sprays of six to eight feet high, quite covered with its vermilion flowers, which are formed like honeysuckles; but I saw no large trees of it, such as the one in my cousin's garden in Cornwall. Perhaps it enjoyed a new climate and soil, and throve in England as our common weeds flourish in Chili, where, on the Santiago plain, they had nearly driven all the natives out. The country showed instead an almost unbroken sheet of wild camomile, turnip, fennel, and different cornflowers, far stronger than any we see in Europe.

In the cracks near the streams were great masses of gunnera leaves (whose stalks are eaten like rhubarb), lovely ferns with pink stalks and young furry leaves, and among them, on the very edge of the streams, the *Ourisia coccinea* hanging its graceful stalks and scarlet bells over the water. Small bamboos and other graceful plants waved above these things; and overhead a most lovely loranthus hung from the branches of the "oaks," with bright green leaves and pale green buds, changing as they opened to yellow, then turning first orange and lastly red, before they fell to the ground. The flowers were often half smothered with gray lichen, commonly called "old man's beard," which waved in every wind, and grew in masses on all the so-called oaks.1 The beech also had its own pet parasite, a tiny mistletoe forming perfect balls of every shade of green and gold, and over the bushes climbed many species of pea, with lapageria, and the lovely pink star-flowers of the mutisia, which hooked themselves up by long tendrils 1 There are no true oaks in Chili.

at the ends of their leaves, while some yellow stars seemed to have no leaves, only tendrils. Tall fuchsia trees were there too, and buddleia with its golden balls, sweet as honey, whose leaves, when toasted and pounded, form the popular remedy for all sores or wounds both of man and beast. Another bush, called the "pincho," which looked like a lilac and white heath, was said to cure all diseases. The grass was in flower, quite red or lilac, and was sprinkled over with exquisite scarlet amaryllis, alstrcemerias of many tints, salpiglossis, and four species of ground-orchids, exceedingly lovely with exquisitely fringed petals, which it would pay one of our great gardeners to import and cultivate.

The first araucarias we reached were in a boggy valley, but they also grew to the very tops of the rocky hills, and seemed to drive all other trees away, covering many miles of hill and valley; but few specimens were to be found outside that forest. The ground underneath was gay with purple and pink everlasting peas, and some blue and white ones I had never seen in gardens, gorgeous orange orchids, and many tiny flowers, whose names I did not know, which died as soon as they were picked, and could not be kept to paint. I saw none of the trees over one hundred feet in height or twenty in circumference, and, strange to say, they seemed all to be very old or very young. I saw none of the noble specimens of middle-age we have in English parks, with their lower branches resting on the ground. They did not become quite flat at the top, like those of Brazil, but were slightly domed like those in Queensland, and their shiny leaves glittered in the sunshine, while their trunks and branches were hung with white lichen, and the latter weighed down with cones as big as one's head. The smaller cones of the male-trees were shaking off clouds of golden pollen, and were full of small grubs; these attracted flights of bronzy green parrakeets, which were very busy over them. Those birds are said to be so clever that they can find a soft place in the great shell of the cone when ripe, into which they get the point of their sharp beak, and fidget with it until the whole cone cracks and the nuts fall to the ground. It is a food they delight in. Men eat the nuts too, when properly cooked, like chestnuts. The most remarkable thing about the tree is its bark, which is a perfect child's puzzle of slabs of different sizes, with five or six distinct sides to each, all fitted together with the neatness of a honeycomb. I tried in vain to find some system on which it was arranged.

We had the good fortune to see a group of guanacos feeding quietly under the old trees. They looked strange enough to be in character with them, having the body of a sheep and the head of a camel; and they let us come quite near. On the other side of the mountains they are used as a beast of burden, though so weak that ten of them could not carry the load of an average donkey. After wandering about the lower lands, we climbed through the bogs and granite boulders to the top of one of the hills, and came suddenly to a most wonderful view, with seven snowy cones of the Cordillera piercing their way through the long line of mist which hid the nearer connecting mountains from sight, and glittering against the greenish-blue sky. Each one looked perfectly separate and gigantic, though the highest was only 10,000 feet above the sea. Under the mist were hills of beech forest, and nearer still the araucaria domes, while the foreground consisted of noble old specimens of the same tree grouped round a huge gray boulder covered with moss and enriched with sprays of embothrium of the brightest scarlet. No subject could have been finer, if I could only have painted it, but that "if" has been plaguing me for years, and every year seems to take me further from a satisfactory result.

The authorities at Angol had given me three dragoons as guards: a perfectly unnecessary escort, except as against their own comrades,who, since the war, have had little to do, and occasionally desert to find food for themselves. All my soldiers did was to hunt a small fox, flourishing their long swords over their heads and galloping furiously; but though they were said to have distinguished themselves in Peru, they could not (like the Frenchman in Punch) catch the fox! The Government of Chili had been most generous to me, and (as in Australia and Africa) had given me a free pass on all the railways, which en-

abled me to travel with far greater ease, as it made the guards good to me also; they always gave me a carriage to myself, or rather a small velvet-lined box inside the ordinary American carriage, in which I felt safe, and could shut myself in, and be less perplexed by the noise of the polyglot tongues around me. I returned between each expedition to my kind friends in Santiago, to finish my paintings, and leave the fresh ones to dry, instead of dragging them about with me as I have so often been obliged to do, to their great damage.

The baths of Cauquenas have often been described by travellers, but the one thing I was anxious to see there—the swinging-bridge—was gone. Some of the servants of the new manager of the baths had gone across and got drunk on the other side, so the bridge was pulled down, and people now had nine miles to go before they could cross the torrent! But it was a glorious situation, and many kinds of cactus and other prickly things were to be found in perfection, as well as alstrcemerias. The mountain views were grand, too, but there were more idle visitors than suited me, and I did not stay more than a week.

A visit to a good English family at Quilpue, nearer the coast, pleased me far better. They took me expeditions in a bullock-waggon, which was covered with a Union Jack (very gay, but trying to the eyes under a Chilian sun). A mattress and pillows were put in to sit on, as well as provision-baskets and many children, with their mother and her father, a wonderfully young man of eighty-seven (I believe), who was interested in everything, and read the *Nineteenth Century* regularly. The father and two elder girls were condemned to live at Toropilla, a place which was absolutely treeless and plantless, earthless and waterless; every drop had to be sent by sea or distilled from the salt ocean. Nitre was the temptation, and by it large fortunes have been made. The washing was done at home at Quilpue, and sent backwards and forwards every week in a steamer, and my friends said they would soon have to give up their pretty home and go to settle in that dreary

desert too. Our expeditions from Quilpu6 were generally made to some crack or narrow valley worn by a stream through the dry rocky land above, in which we found many evergreen trees and some few flowers: the litre, which has the same bad reputation as the upas tree, owing, I believe, to an almost invisible insect or blight which infests it, causing great irritation to the skin when it falls on any one under it; the soapbush *(Quillaja saponaria),* the bark of which is used for washing linen; and the boldo, which gives the most solid shade, and is sweet as our bay-tree. All these trees had curious nests in them, and children are the best companions for finding nests. A bush called *Lobelia salkifolia,* with bunches of orange-red flowers, was the favourite resort of the large Chilian humming-bird. Another curious habitation was made by a kind of miniature lobster, which bored down till it reached water in the flat lands, sending up the earth in small martello towers a foot high, and no doubt in time raising the earth's surface, after the manner of the less conspicuous but now historic earthworms.

I saw thousands of those towers, and have also eaten the builders. They turn red when boiled, and have a strong flavour of the mud they live in. Those clever burrowing creatures keep mostly to the great valley of Santiago, which is some 2000 feet above the sea, and is crossed by many large rivers. These flood their banks when the snows melt, bringing down and renewing the rich soil, making all the crops (more particularly the weeds) most luxuriant, and delighting the hearts of these land-lobsters by its general muddiness. The last place I stayed at in Chili was Las Salinas, a delightful house, hidden in a rich garden, ten minutes' walk from the sea-coast. Mr. and Mrs. J. were quite worthy of such a place. He was one of the best naturalists in the country. He had also made two fortunes in the nitre country. After the first, he went a long journey collecting, across Bolivia, and when he came back found his house and everything he possessed swept clean away by a "great wave" into the sea: nothing but smooth sand where it had been! He recovered nothing but an old watch, which was washed back again one day and found among the pebbles on the shore; so he started afresh, and I trust can now give himself up entirely to his love of natural history without more necessity for money-making.

Under my window was a thick hedge of heliotrope more than a yard high. All the sweetest roses, with carnations and jasmine, grew there, as well as a huge *Magnolia grandiflora,* which shaded a large extent of ground and scented the air; but the wild walks along the shore were my delight. There were a good many fishermen's huts, and all the people seemed to employ themselves in collecting seaweed, of which a sort of isinglass is made and eaten. The cliffs were wreathed with mesembryanthemums, calandrinias, cacti, puyas, fuchsias, oxalis, *Ephedra andina,* whose fruit is eaten and very sweet, and many fleshy plants whose names I did not know, reminding me of Africa. On the hills above was much wild scrub, low woods, and acres of wild artichokes and cardoon *(Cynara cardunculus),* whose silvery leaves and stems and deep-blue flowers were most striking. A scarlet mutisia and *Proustia pyrifolia* were climbing to the tops of the trees, the latter growing so fast that Chilians call it "Pie a dia" (foot a day).

I spent Christmas at Santiago, where Mrs. P. tried her best to make it look like home. She had a party of the "Polyglots," and taught the fat German baron to dance a Scotch reel, which he did with all the energy possible, as well as Sir Roger de Coverley; and on the 1st of January we went to an evening concert in the Quinta, almost in the open air, to hear sixty students of Salamanca playing guitars, all dressed in black velvet cloaks and ruffs. They were going round the world, and gave one concert only at each capital they visited, to pay their way: it was a funny waste of cleverness! They played overtures, valses, and many other kinds of music, and were all supernaturally grave. The place was crowded both inside and out, while the gardens were very pretty in the

moonlight. There was a collection of birds and beasts as well as of plants in it. I spent another night at the Salinas, and then steamed away in the *Mendoza,* touching at the nitre cities as we passed them, and landing on their miserable stony shores. We had a perfect market on board, and the poor half-starved, thirsty people crowded on board at each place, giving enormous prices for cabbages, oranges, water-melons, as well as for meat and fowls. What wise men call my "nerves" were following me always, and the noise of that ship was so distracting that I resolved to stay for a week at Lima, and consult an old German doctor whom the captain thought very clever. He gave me the usual "bromide," which had as much effect as toast and water, and said I must not attempt any expedition, but rest entirely quiet in the hotel.

I had a party of bull-fighters on each side of "the quietest room," which he chose himself for me. They gambled half the night, and strolled about gossiping on the verandah on which my one window looked all day, and below was the noisy salon: truly it was a "quiet" place! And I was glad to start again for Panama, where I felt too ill and wretched to attempt my proposed journey to Mexico, and took my berth home to England instead. The journey across the isthmus did not strike me as much as I expected, but then its beauty was all cut up and spoilt by the works of the canal. A kind pair of German fellow-passengers befriended me, and saw me through all the noise and crowd safely on board the beautiful English ship.

At Jamaica I landed early and drove out to see my old friend Mrs. C., who was then a widow, living three miles from Kingston, near her husband's grave. She screamed with delight at seeing me, and persuaded me to stay a month with her and have a real rest, as she was going up to a country-house on the hills for a change herself. I was easily persuaded, and she settled it all for me, and made me see her doctor, who gave me more bromide, which had as much effect as the last; but quiet and much good feeding did me real good.

Raymond Hall was one of the highest houses on the south side of the island, and the views were exquisite all round it; but one thing had altered for the worse since I was last there: the grass-ticks had crossed the mountains— they were never known on that side thirteen years before. It was generally supposed that the mongoose, which had been introduced from India by Sir J. P. Grant, to eat the rats in the sugar-cane, had preferred chickens, and found there were more on the Government side, so came over and brought the little vicious ticks with it. These put a stop to all walking in the forest or grass, while the mongeese were so bold that they used to run into the houses and cany away any food that was on the table. But I thought the island was even more lovely than before. The *Phajiis Tankervillice* and the white hedychium, though both really natives of Asia, were growing wild in great luxuriance, and some wonderful wild bromeliads were flowering on the trees near.

The old wooden church at Craigton had been blown down and a new stone one had taken its place, much larger and much emptier, as the popular archdeacon had preferred a comfortable English living after seventeen years of semibanishment there. His successor was slightly coloured, and therefore avoided. I left some sweet flowers on the grave of my two friends, the brother and sister who had died in the same hour of yellow fever there, and then rode up for a couple of nights to another very high house to get a sketch of the Blue Mountain I had promised to make for a friend at home. I passed tangles of the sweet waxy bells of the *bettandia* creeper on my way up. It was then in its fullest beauty: another of the plants which I wonder is not more cultivated in hot-houses.

1885.—Afterwards I returned straight to England, where it took me another year to finish and rearrange the gallery at Kew. Every painting had to be renumbered, so as to keep the countries as much together as possible, the geographical distribution of the plants being the chief object I had in view in the collection.

After that was finished, I tried to find a perfect home in the country with a ready-made old house and a garden to make after my own fashion, "far from the madding crowd" of callers and lawn-tennis.

1886.—I have found the exact place I wished for, and already my garden is becoming famous among those who love plants; and I hope it may serve to keep my enemies, the so-called "nerves," quiet for the few years which are left me to live. The recollections of my happy life will also be a help to my old age. No life is so charming as a country one in England, and no flowers are sweeter or more lovely than the primroses, cowslips, bluebells, and violets which grow in abundance all round me here.

Here her record ends. The long hard journeys were over, and, alas, with them was gone the greater portion of that indomitable strength which had seemed never to flag, which had carried her triumphantly through poisonous climates, never breaking down under incessant work, fatigue, bad food, and all those hardships which few women, travelling absolutely alone, would have dared to face. I have often thought how much her natural stately presence, and simple yet dignified manner, helped her in facing all sorts and conditions of men in those long distant journeys. Just the qualities she admired in her friend Miss Gordon Cumming were hers in an eminent degree. She inspired respect wherever she appeared, and good men everywhere were ready and eager to help her. Her work was always her first point: for that she travelled, not to pass the time, as so many mere globe-trotters do, in this age of easy locomotion. Her gallery at Kew is a monumental work: to finish it she fought bravely against increasing weakness; when it was done her strength was also gone, and the restful life she had dreamed of in her pretty Gloucestershire garden was not to be.

Yet one more year of hard work of a different kind remained to her. In the summer of 1886 she rented from General Hale, at Alderley in Gloucestershire,

a charming old-fashioned gray stone house, with fields, orchards, and a garden, neglected hitherto, but exquisitely placed on the steep slope of one of those secluded valleys which lie hidden away in the folds of the Cotswold Hills: an old-world region which took her fancy, and in which she determined to make for herself a paradise. That sleepy corner of West-Country England was soon astonished by her energy. Out of the dead level of the lawn-tennis ground she planned a terraced garden, sloping steeply to a pond and rockery which were to be stocked with rare plants from all corners of the globe. A little walled yard full of currant bushes she turned into a lovely rose-garden, sheltered by the old gray stable with its lichen-covered stone roof. The whole place had the rare charm for an artist of having been let alone for many years. Both trees and buildings were old, and all the trees had grown luxuriantly in that kindly WestCountry air. A few fine old Scotch firs gave picturesqueness and shelter to her immediate surroundings; beyond were orchards and a clear stream, which, after turning many mills, gradually led down to the wider landscape of the great Severn valley. When I came for the first time to stay with her in the Jubilee summer of 1887, I thought I had never seen so lovely a bit of English country as this which a chance had led her to.

Her landlord, General Hale, lived in a big house just across the road: tall box-trees from both gardens overarched the steeply-winding lane—his trees met hers overhead, and a noisy colony of rooks lived in both. Beyond were the church and the tiny village, with its trim cottage gardens and gray stone roofs: just such a village as Miss Austen has described a hundred times, and as our American cousins love to dream of. It had been larger and more populous once, when cloth-mills worked by water-power were still a profitable industry among the Cotswold valleys. Nowhere among the so-called "Home Counties," within fifty miles of smoky London, could such a bit of unspoiled homely village life be found: so prim-

itive, yet so eminently "respectable." The neighbours were few, but all were kind.

Alderley, with its old bowery gardens, was especially a paradise for birds. The squire was fond of them, and passed kindly despotic laws for their preservation. Big towns were far off, and even cats were scarce; so they throve and multiplied exceedingly. That handsome bird, the English redstart, always conspicuous by the bright streak on his black head, had chosen her arbour to build in that summer, and was continually darting up and down the gravel-path after his prey. The small gray flycatcher sat all day long on one of the spikes of the old iron railings outside the dining-room windows, whence he made sudden perpendicular flights into the air after an invisible fly, and down again. A pair of big wood-pigeons, so shy generally of human neighbourhood, had their nest in one of the Scotch firs at the bottom of the garden, and took their daily bath, with much fuss and noise, in the pond beneath the Alpine rockery. And in the kitchen-garden a riotous crowd of blackbirds and thrushes set nets at defiance, and held festival among the currants and raspberries: when the gardener grumbled, she said she liked the birds better than red-currant jelly, and there was enough for both! And so there was.

But the patriarch of Alderley birds was the great white owl who lived in the big pollard elm just at the church gate. He or his immediate ancestors had lived in that tree ever since the squire was a boy, and it was a joy to stroll out on a starlight night and listen to his luxurious snores. So human was this snore that the local policeman going his nightly rounds was once surprised beneath the tree, where he was busy lighting matches and bits of paper, and trying to peer up into the thick branches, convinced that a burglar lay concealed there! There was a tame jackdaw, too, which had belonged to our girls; when they went away he gave his affections to the cowman, and regularly at milking-time might be seen at the tail of the procession from the cowhouse to the orchard, hopping along the road after the man, the little Jersey cow, and Sambo the black retriever. What a happy, peaceful life it all seemed. If only it could have lasted! I think what I liked best of all were the white tumbler-pigeons who lived in the dovecote under the eaves of the old gray stable, and were always sitting about on the red brick walls or taking their baths on the lawn. They were so fearless that they would fly in at her bedroom window and feed from her hand.

The garden grew apace. Kew sent her all sorts of foreign rarities, a fine collection of cistus, and splendid todeas for the fernhouse. Her nieces at Davos collected Alpines for the rockery. All her florist-friends—Mr. Wilson, Canon Ellacombe, Miss Jekyll, and many others—sent generous contributions from their famous gardens: all were interested in her success. And how she worked! Every tiny plant, every bulb, was put in with her own hand or under her own eye, every label written by her, and entered in a book as the plants were fitted each into the nook which suited it best. All was order. In the mornings, long before six, before her men were out of bed, she was out upon the lawn with the garden-hose, patiently watering her fragile treasures; for that Jubilee summer was a terribly dry one, and very trying for those hundreds of young plants so recently imported into new surroundings. Every day fresh treasures came, in hampers and boxes of all shapes and sizes, from every quarter of the globe. Surely no garden on so small a scale ever had so much thought and loving care put into it. The good taste of her artist's mind helped her to utilise the things she found ready to her hand; instead of cutting down, she adapted what was there before, making a half-dead holly tree the prop for a luxuriant tangle of honeysuckle and tea-roses, while more fragile clematises were coaxed into flinging their flowery wreaths over the stout mass of American brambles. An old sundial she had the luck to find in a neighbouring garden was set up on the lawn, a monument to the last survivor of the three little opossum-mice

she had brought from Tasmania, whose virtues and voyages were recorded on a brass plate by J. A. Symonds, "Sir Henry" being buried underneath.

Her head was full of quaint happy schemes and fancies for the adornment of her new home; only the time to carry them out was wanting. Many old friends came to stay with her that first summer and the next: the spare rooms were seldom empty. Professor Asa Gray and Mrs. Gray from Boston came with Sir Joseph Hooker, the Forrests from Western Australia, Mrs. Ross from Florence. But even then illness was creeping on her; she was never quite free from physical discomfort. The "enemy" of her last two voyages—those weary, constant noises—never ceased. In the quiet of her country garden, as in noisy London, the overtired brain still translated these into human voices, whose words were often taunts. Her deafness was of course responsible for this, and her brave common-sense recognised that the voices were delusions; still she suffered more than she owned, and dreaded being alone with those invisible but mocking foes.

In the autumn of 1888 a deep-seated disease of the liver, brought on originally, no doubt, by long exposure to all sorts of bad climatic influences, declared itself, and for many weeks she was as ill as it was possible to be. Her niece, Miss Kay Shuttleworth, was with her through all that winter. At Christmas we thought her dying; but her great natural strength, aided by medical skill and most careful nursing, enabled her to rally for a time, though her life had become one of constant suffering. The next summer she was better, and could even walk painfully about her garden and watch its progress. Her favourite nephew came down with his lawbooks in vacation time, and always cheered her. Strange to say, with the approach of active local disease, the unkind voices fled, and the relief of this was immense. But mortal illness was only arrested, not cured, and with her long habits of strength and self-reliance the life of invalidism and dependence on others became terribly trying. Her last letter to

me is dated the 11th of June 1890. In it she writes: "We women are in great triumph over Mr. Fawcett's only child having got above the Senior Wrangler; it would have pleased her father so much...." She also mentions an active-minded friend who had just left her "to sit on a Board somewhere, a process which makes my old bones ache to think of."..." My peonies are a grand sight, and the iris and poppies and tree-lupins, rhododendrons and gaillardias; the great pink and white eremurus from the Himalaya have flowered for the first time in the rose-garden, but I only managed to get there twice. Bleeding comes on if I walk much, and I fear I do not get stronger, in spite of turtle soup." The next day a telegram from her faithful maid Emily told me she was "very ill." I went home at once, and from that time never left her for more than a few days, until the end came. She died on Saturday, August 30th, 1890, and was buried in the quiet green churchyard at Alderley.

Her life there had only lasted five years, and of that period more than half had been shadowed by painful illness. But into the fifteen years immediately after her father's death had been compressed work sufficient for the lives of four ordinary women; and I have often wondered whether, if her strength had lasted another ten years, she could really have been content to sit down and wait for old age in the lovely green nest she had prepared for herself. Who shall say? She was a noble and courageous woman, whose like none of us shall ever look upon again.

The one strong and passionate feeling of her life had been her love for her father. When he was taken away she threw her whole heart into painting, and this gradually led her into those long toilsome journeys. They no doubt shortened her life; but length of days had never been expected or desired by her, and I think she was glad, when her self-appointed task was done, to follow him whom she had so faithfully loved. Her deafness, which had increased in the last years, really separated her painfully from the pleasure of daily intercourse with those around her. There is no sadder solitude than deafness.

But she was full of kind thoughts for her own people, and kept more men employed upon her pretty garden than were really needful for its work, even after it had ceased to be an active pleasure to herself; because, as she said, giving them work was the best way in which she could help those poor people whose own lives were so hard. And that principle of unostentatious kindness to those immediately belonging to her had been her rule through life, making her often seem indifferent to other people's wider schemes and charities.

I think she was intolerant of "Rules " in all things (except, perhaps, in music), exceedingly and scornfully sceptical as to rules in art: for instance, the limitations and laws of composition in painting. She painted as a clever child would, everything she thought beautiful in nature, and had scarcely ever any artistic teaching. In music it was different, and there, I think, her real genius lay. While her beautiful thrilling contralto voice, so absolutely true, lasted, she patiently submitted through long years to the drudgery of steady musical training under her mistress and great friend Madame Sainton Dolby. But that beautiful voice deserted her just when its cultivation had reached the highest point; and then painting, less cared for hitherto, was taken up to fill the void. She could never be idle.

When she once began to study plant-life, she read much and constantly about the trees and flowers she drew and cultivated, always with special regard to their out-door habits and characteristics. Her name has been given to five; four of which were first figured and introduced by her to European notice, viz.—

Northea Seychellana
Nepenthes Northiana
Crinum Northianum
Areca Northiana
Kniphofia Northiana

This last is a Cape plant and a near relation of the familiar "red-hot poker" of our gardens. The nepenthes, the large pitcher-plant of Borneo, has been engraved on the cover of this book.

J. C. S.